The Miserable Marriage Handbook
for
Women

How to Survive and Grow While Trapped
In a Miserable Marriage

Kathleen Keith

S & G Publishing
Los Angeles, CA

Ten percent of sales of books published by
S & G Publishing is donated to Childhelp®
www.Childhelp.org

Do you have a story to inspire others?
To publish your story of growth and survival
contact S & G Publishing
SurviveAndGrowBooks@gmail.com

Library of Congress Control Number 2020900091

ISBN: 978-0-578-64002-0
eBook ISBN: 978-1-7923-2954-8

This publication is intended to provide accurate and informative information regarding the subject matter covered. It is sold with the understanding that the author and publisher are not engaged in providing legal, accounting, or other professional advice. If legal advice or other expert assistance is required, the services of a competent professional should be sought.

To My Daughter and Her Family
The Love of My Life

CONTENTS

CONTENTS

She will rise up on wings like eagles,
She will run and not grow weary; she will walk and not faint.
Isaiah 40-31

We are only meant to come half way, or go only so far—when any person,
situation, or idea requires we sacrifice our inner nature, or compromise
our inner dignity, that is going too far. – Book of Runes

Marriage should be a gift, not a life sentence.

If you want to transform your life change your behavior,
and also change how you think.

Survival requires strategy and goals, not denial.

Dignified feminine strength is formidable.

Be careful about what you put into your mind.

Be careful about what you put into your mouth.

Be careful about what comes out of your mouth.

Be careful about whom you let into your life

Handbook
A book that contains instructions or advice about how
to do something or the most important and useful information
about a subject — Cambridge English Dictionary

Author's Note

This book shares details of the Survive and Grow Steps© which I developed (stumbled upon might be the more accurate term) when I was trapped in a miserable marriage and became desperate to save my sanity and my life.

I wrote this book because women are hurting today just as much as they have hurt in the past. We all desperately need validation of our experience and intuition. We also need compassion for, and understanding of, our situation.

And we need help.

The goal of this book is to help you discover your potential to create a life for yourself that is emotionally, mentally, physically and spiritually healing and healthy—to become empowered.

The Survive and Grow steps are practical, clear and concise but require determination, the same determination that has kept women going since the beginning of time.

It has been said that from great pain can sometimes come a gift. I sincerely hope that this book will be a gift for millions of women who are struggling to survive while trapped in a miserable marriage.

God bless you.

Kathleen Keith

This book covers everything that took ten years of therapy for me to figure out. – Nicole C., Los Angeles, CA

Finally, an easy to understand discussion of difficult relationships, and a practical way to survive the nightmare. – Martha Emms, Author of "Portrait of Our Marriage"

1

No one believes me. Everyone thinks he is a great guy.
Only I know what he is really like.

You Are Not Alone

The appalling way that millions of women are treated by their husbands or partners in the privacy of their homes, is the biggest secret in our culture.

Countless women unknowingly form a secret sisterhood, unaware there are other members. This club never meets or holds a convention because its members dare not speak of that with which they live. Younger members are exhausted from trying to cope and older members are emotionally depleted. And whether they live in a ten-bedroom mansion or a one-bedroom apartment, the fundamental issue is the same for every woman trapped in a miserable marriage—we know that the 'really nice guy' we are married to, isn't.

He is a man the world outside our home would be surprised to see, but they never do.

We participate in the cover-up and protect our secret from outside view because we desperately want our relationship to work, to last, to fulfill our dreams and be as good in private as it appears to be in public. We are afraid and ashamed of what we judge as our ineptitude because we can never please our man. We're never good enough.

And no one will believe us if we tell the truth about our private life with him.

Embarrassed that our marriage and family aren't perfect, because we assume most other families and homes are better than ours, we protect our secret. We don't want anyone to know because we berate ourselves as failures. We assume we are inadequate because we cannot live up to our husband's standards or keep him happy. And he tells us that everything is our fault, that we misunderstand his words, actions, and motives.

He assures us that he is well-intentioned and only wants to help us be a better wife.

We participate in the cover-up, the disguise that hides from the outside world the truth that our really great guy isn't so great. He is a cold, indifferent, cunning, often calculating and unpredictable, master of disguise who destroys the spirits of his wife and children.

The Great Lie

But if *we* could be better life would be happy. That's what he's told us and we believe that lie until we hit the bottom of our endurance and become committed to searching for answers and finding solutions for our miserable life, which is what this book is about.

My heart aches for women whose spirits are broken by the men who vowed to love them, who perhaps still say, "I love you," to the women they destroy emotionally and sometimes physically. Countless women suffer from the words, and at the hands of, men.

I am a survivor of that life.

I have walked in your shoes and I share your life experience. A life consumed by sadness, despair, anger, fear, exhaustion and confusion. A life of: What's he going to do next? How do I get through today, tomorrow, and the next day? Why won't he stop hurting me? Why does he do this?

Anguish and confusion dominate a relationship with a man whose behavior kills you emotionally and spiritually, and damages your psychological and physical health. Life is consumed by tension, fear, and devoting yourself to placating an impossible-to-please man.

No one understands life trapped in a miserable marriage, trying to make it work day after day, unless they have experienced it.

No one.

Only those of us who are or were trapped understand the overwhelming pain of betrayal, the destructive subtleties of sarcasm, the injustice of secrecy, the frustration of dishonesty and denials, the fear and hopelessness of financial games, the suffocation of control and manipulation, and the unending tension in always coping with his mind games and trying to avoid his unpredictable rage.

No one can learn this from books, interviews or compiled data. You have to live it.

4

The Survive and Grow Steps©

This gentle, yet challenging and empowering book, reaches out to women who are hurting and searching for answers, understanding, compassion and practical help. It challenges us to replace wishful thinking with willpower and courage. And to face some ugly truths about the man to whom we are married, some potentially ugly truths about ourselves, how we got to where we are, our role in our marriage, and to finally take steps to save our sanity, heal, find wellness, acquire personal dignity and achieve peacefulness. Ultimately, it is a journey of emotional and spiritual healing because it is from our essence that we survive, grow and triumph.

We cannot achieve peacefulness in our life until we discover peacefulness in ourselves. And we must also develop standards for our behavior that require a mutually nurturing, kind, respectful, and genuinely loving relationship, and the courage to accept nothing less of ourselves and others in our life. But it is unrealistic to expect us to become women with these qualities when we live in an environment of derision and hatefulness. We must have tools to help us, to lean on, in order to survive and grow and ultimately triumph over our current entrapment.

Where Do We Begin?

How do we make changes? It is overwhelming. I felt overwhelmed, until I discovered the steps detailed in this book. Along the way, I realized my journey required that I engage simultaneously with my intelligence, my emotions and my spiritual nature. I craved wellness, wholeness, dignity and peace.

There are some harsh realities in this book, some perhaps startling conclusions, and I came to believe that God, the Life Source, the Universe (whatever you prefer) did not put us women on this earth to merely be pawns in our homes, but to be pillars. But we don't know how because we were never taught, or this is the only type of marriage we've seen, or we were never exposed to a broader world and do not know that cunning, intentionally hurtful men exist, and we fell into the trap.

To survive and grow becomes a journey of healing and

transformation that engages our intellect, our emotions, and the spiritual essence of what it means to be a woman.

Interestingly, I have been asked why I don't use the word 'thrive' instead of 'survive.' The answer is, because it is virtually impossible to truly thrive while in an environment of derision, and our most immediate need is to survive with dignity, grace, courage and self-respect, which is the goal of this book.

Two Important Parts

The Survive and Grow Steps powerfully guide you through two stages of a wellness journey. Part I gives you the tools necessary to establish the foundation on which you can build a better life. It guides you to face and accept the realities of your current life, and offers specific actions you can take to help you recognize and respect yourself as a valuable human being, a valuable woman.

When you live in a miserable marriage filled with derision, scorn and neglect, you lose a sense of your value as a woman. But your self-respect can be reclaimed and your life can dramatically change. Steps one through four guide you to accomplish this.

Step two is the most important step because it is the foundation for growth, and is detailed in Chapter 9. When you learn and practice step two, and then incorporate the remaining steps, you can be on your way to a transformed life.

With a foundation in place from Part I, Part II guides you to create a better life for yourself. You no longer will be defined by what others say you are, must be, or must do. Each step builds on the step before it and doing each step in its order is important. You cannot build a new house until you first lay the foundation and then build from the ground up.

Part I – Becoming a Valuable Woman

Step One:	Facing and Accepting Reality
Step Two:	Climbing Back Inside Your Body
Step Three:	Learning Who You Are Now
Step Four:	Choosing Who You Will Be

Part II – Living from Your Core Values

This Book is for Us, Not About Him

This book is for us, for all women who are or have been trapped in destructive marriages. This is not a book about repairing him, about why the man in your life is the way he is. This book is about coping with him and reclaiming your human dignity, your female dignity.

There are many books about the character traits and destructive behaviors of difficult men: Verbal abuse, psychological abuse, passive-aggressiveness, narcissism, addictions (drugs, alcohol, pornography, anger, gambling, online gaming, etc.). We can become so involved in trying to understand our man, and searching for the all-revealing reason for his destructive behavior, that we miss our own life in the process.

Important Notes About This Book

The Survive and Grow Steps also apply to unmarried relationships. Women who are in any miserable relationship will benefit from this book. The legalities of the marriage contract do, however, complicate the dynamics of being trapped, as any woman who has been the target of legal maneuvering in a divorce action will attest.

Women Only?

Am I implying that only women can be miserable in a marriage? No, of course not. But statistics speak for themselves. The number one reason for injury to women is battering at the hands of a spouse or boyfriend. And this statistic does not include women whose emotional, psychological and spiritual health are destroyed even though their bodies are not. Those of us who are, or have been, in a miserable marriage know that battering can happen without him ever physically striking you. Mental battering is violence too.

7

And yes, there are many women who are the perpetrators of mistreatment of their husbands/partners. Everything in this book applies equally to men who are the targets of abuse in any form from the woman in their life. In several ways, a marriage that involves an abusive woman is uniquely difficult because society is even more skeptical of a woman being abusive. A man attempting to explain or describe an abusive woman faces derision as a weakling.

This book is aimed at women because they significantly outnumber men in these situations and my experience, which this book details, is obviously that of a woman (although I have seen first-hand the emotional and psychological abuse of a man by a woman). About twenty percent of married women—around 13 million—live in an abusive environment (all forms of abuse) in the United States.[1]

How to Read This Book

This handbook provides a guide to survive and grow and can be re-read in sections numerous times as your life expands and transforms. It cannot, of course, guarantee success in changing your life but it does provide recommendations that you may consider following. Only you can decide the extent to which you decide to implement the Survive and Grow Steps. This book is not intended to encourage wishful thinking and foolish decisions when you are involved with a difficult, or potentially physically dangerous, man. It is intended to provide you with information that can be useful to you as you navigate through the difficult aspects of surviving in your miserable marriage and/or getting out of one.

Counselors, Therapists, Clergy

This book is not intended to replace personal counseling which can be helpful if the counselor is mature and experienced. The complexities and falsehoods in miserable marriages elude inexperienced counselors so careful evaluation of a potential counselor is advisable. Pastoral counselors have limited relationship training and are not equipped to deal with the

---

[1] Domestic Violence Statistics; domesticviolencestatistics.org; 2019

complex dynamics and well-disguised character defects portrayed in this book. When only one partner in a marriage insists that both partners go to counseling, the results are almost always unproductive regardless of the type of counselor involved.

Counselors can do great harm and cause tremendous pain to women in these marriages because many therapists do not grasp the extent to which difficult men can project a false image. Therapists are as susceptible to the charming public persona of a difficult man as all other members of a man's 'public.' Therapists are usually trained to evaluate a situation from a fifty-fifty perspective and frequently under-estimate, or fail to recognize the imbalance of power and seriousness of mind games taking place in a miserable marriage. The results of meeting with a therapist can be deadly if the husband uses the therapy sessions as a weapon to further the destruction of his wife's emotional and mental health. This is the reason why couples counseling should not be attempted if either spouse is NPD (narcissistic personality disordered) or has any other untreated personality disorder.

A mature, experienced, compassionate therapist can, however, provide comfort and support to a woman struggling in a miserable marriage. But ultimately each woman must do the practical and hard work to transform her life.

Self-Medicating

If you are medicating yourself to numb the pain of your situation by using alcohol, drugs (prescription, legal pot, or illegal substances) abuse of your children, compulsive spending, promiscuity, or affairs, this book does not directly address those issues. Chapter 12 examines your behavior which may be helpful to you, but if you have any of the above compulsions it is strongly recommended that you locate a highly-trained expert to assist you to overcome your dependencies.

If You or Your Children are Physically Battered GET OUT NOW!

Psychological mistreatment damages us, and while the unseen

injuries may be gradual, they do permanent damage. But if you or your children are being physically beaten up, get out! Get out now! This rule also applies to sadistic masochistic sexual physical abuse—sex accompanied by physical harm is abuse.

There are shelters to help you. This book does not suggest or encourage you to stay in a situation that is or may become physically harmful or life-threatening. Look online for shelters in your area or call a medical doctor or the police for a referral and take action! Do it now! Your children need you. Please, don't let him kill you! **The National Domestic Violence Hotline number is 1-800-799-7233.** Trained assistants are available 24/7 every day of the year to take your call. Add this number to the contacts in your phone and call immediately when he starts to hit you or your children. Embarrassment, humiliation and shame are irrelevant when faced with saving your life or a child's life!

Is It Miserable or Abusive?

Which leads to the questions I am often asked: Why do you call it miserable marriage? Why don't you refer to it as abusive marriage?

Because no woman ever wants to admit to herself, or anyone else, that she is abused and married to, or partnered with an abuser. And no woman readily accepts the fact that his treatment of her constitutes abuse.

Women arrive at emergency rooms with black eyes and broken bones and they'll make excuses for the man who did those things to them. "He's been drinking," or "He's having a terrible time at work," or "He had a terrible childhood," or "He loves me but he just gets so mad at me sometimes." And of course, the ultimate, "I love him."

Women make these same excuses for their men even if he never lays a hand on them but instead psychologically abuses them in ways that leave them mentally and emotionally scarred for life.

No woman ever looks across her sandwich at lunchtime and says, "My husband abused me this past weekend." But she will say, "My husband was an asshole this past weekend." To which most women at the table will nod their heads in understanding and at least one will say, "My husband was an asshole this past weekend too." And that will be that. For never let it be said that it was abuse. Abuse is for other people. Abuse belongs to 'those types.' Or does it?

Based on my personal experience, my definition of abuse and thoughts about men who mistreat women are: Abuse is any behavior that treats a woman as a non-human, a creature who is owned and used, whose emotional or material needs are ignored, and who serves as a prop to a man's controlling behavior—behavior that provides him with satisfaction, triumph and pleasure from the control he exerts over the 'creature' he owns. Physical harm is not required to qualify as abuse. Most abusive relationships are solely emotionally and psychologically abusive, but nevertheless destructive. Abuse can be occasional or on-going, but regardless of frequency, it is abuse.

Abusers are killers of the human spirit, if not the body. They are relentless and they derive silent and secret pleasure in seeing their targets bend, comply, hurt and diminish over time. Many men, if not most, want their personal lives to be effortless, for the women and children in their lives to acquiesce to whatever demands, desires or proclivities they have. Abusers leave no room for any variation in this equation and they constantly move the goal posts in order to make it perpetually impossible to meet their demands.

Abusers are unfeeling, uncaring and have no empathy for the pain they cause. They are also cunning, clever and masters of disguise. In their world, women and children exist to serve them and nothing should be expected from the abuser in return. Cold, unrelenting, dangerous and often deadly, it is a miserable world in which to be trapped.

And what is the answer to the question: Why are abusers abusive?

Abusing gives abusers great satisfaction, even pleasure. A book-long analysis is not required, just the truth: Abusers abuse because winning is pleasant, to always get their way, to control other humans. Regardless of theories about childhood roots, the answer is basic. Abusers like to abuse, they feel no remorse for their behavior because, in their minds, their behavior is always logical and justified. And if forced to apologize they do

11

so only for expedience. A sincere apology is impossible for an abuser because they never admit their behavior should be defined as abuse. In their minds they 'had to' do what they did or said. This is the essence of the injustice that permeates a miserable marriage.

It never occurs to an abuser that anyone would refuse to indefinitely endure their destructive behavior. Once you are assigned your role as the target of an abuser you will hold that position forever in the mind of the abuser. They are shocked and enraged if a woman says, 'Enough' and escapes from their web. Increasing and intensifying the abuse is an abuser's automatic response to what they perceive as betrayal. This applies to both physical and non-physical abuse. Revenge abuse via legal maneuverings in family court can be intentionally vicious and destructive.

How do you 'deal with' abuse? There is only one way: To not tolerate it. To completely reject it intellectually, emotionally, and ideally by distancing yourself geographically. Unfortunately, many women claim, "I don't tolerate it! I give back what he gives out!" They fail to recognize that screaming, arguing, and all the other angst, only serves to copy and perpetuate the abuse. Like a stone thrown into a pond, abuse patterns travel outward for generations.

The Vital Question

But the vital question remains: How do you survive when your life circumstance traps you with someone like the men mentioned in this book?

In Chapter 4 you will meet Kelly, a woman like you and me. Perhaps you will see aspects of your life in hers. Some readers may say, "Her life is easy compared to mine!" But look closely because the universal elements of being trapped and looking for ways to cope are embedded in her story. Kelly's journey of survival, growth, transformation and triumph echoes mine, and may be yours if you choose.

2

No one understands what I live with.

Who Are We?

No two versions of misery are exactly the same, but those of us who experience this hell recognize the universal components of a miserable marriage:

Turmoil

Anger

Deceit

Denial

Isolation

Loneliness

We also realize that no one sympathizes with 'trapped' because they do not comprehend a relationship from which a woman cannot escape. Those who dismiss us with, "Just leave!" don't have the personal experience that you and I share. They make it sound so simple and easy but that isn't our reality.

Loneliness and emotional complexities suffocate your life when you are trapped in a miserable marriage. Similar to riding a roller coaster with a blindfold over your eyes, you never know if your husband's moods will be up or down, if a day will be a good one or a bad one, if he will ignore you or rage and blame you for every inconvenience and discomfort in his life. Or if he will retreat into his impenetrable silent fortress which you are never allowed to enter.

You live with injustice because secrecy binds you. No one witnesses the private mind games and verbal cruelty and describing those torturous maneuvers and manipulations to someone else is nearly impossible. When you do try, you sound like a moron or a maniac. How do you describe being silenced by a hateful look, paralyzed by a whispered threat, or made desperate and terrified by your financial helplessness because of his control of money or his irresponsibility or addictions?

Who We Are

We cannot find logic in the unprovoked attacks that occur without warning—his instantaneous rage that ruins a day and shatters family events.

We are ignored and receive the silent treatment.

We are lonely because he is emotionally unavailable, cut off, boarded up behind an impenetrable wall, checked out from our day-to-day life and living in his separate world.

If we complain, we may be bombarded by foul language, accusations, ridicule, sarcasm, threats and demands, and receive vile messages, ugly photos and more, via texts, emails, and social media.

Everything must be done his way in order to keep the peace. We dread unexpected changes or inconveniences that are beyond our control because he will blame us. He tells us we should have known in advance and the problems would have been avoided.

We are interrupted, shouted down, and forbidden to explain or discuss our needs. If we persist, he will walk out of the room, shout to shut us up, tell us we don't know what we are talking about, and that we are ignorant and worthless.

We yell back, we lose any dignity we might have had, we repeat old patterns, we fight for our position, we shout for recognition, we scream for his attention, we demand that he listen to us. But he ignores our pleas, or insults us with brief and sarcastic feigned attention.

We apologize whether it was our fault or not because we want some peace and the pain to stop.

We are told that what we say happened didn't really happen, that we made it up even if it took place only an hour before. And that we're crazy, that we need help.

We are laughed at and made the target of jokes and sarcasm. We are called names.

Our opinions, hard work, and accomplishments are waved away and ignored.

Regardless of how much we support and encourage his career our help is considered immaterial and never acknowledged. 'Thank you' are words we never hear.

We are told what we will wear, drive, and think.

We may receive expensive gifts one day, and called bitch or whore the next day.

We are humiliated by his infidelity, angered by his lack of loyalty, and enraged by his denials, lies, and diversion of funds for other women.

We are told that we exaggerate and have an over-active imagination.

Our access to money is closely monitored or controlled, even if we earn it, and the financial insecurity we feel from the secrecy and control he maintains, frightens us.

Recreational time with anyone not pre-approved is restricted and our family and friends are never good enough. Isolation in one form or another narrows our world.

We are told we overreact and don't know how good we have it, and no one else would want us, and that if we dare try to leave, he will take our children away from us.

We think we will die from the pain and sometimes we wish we would, except for the damage it would cause to our children.

We are overworked because his expectations are so high and we wake up so weary we wonder how we will get through another day.

We come home from work and attend to our children, their homework, the laundry, the house, the meals, and juggle food shopping, medical appointments, music lessons, sports practice, and holiday entertaining of family, while he opens a cold beer and relaxes to watch his favorite sports teams on TV or immerse himself in electronic games.

We earn a living, give birth, care for infants, raise children, attempt to maintain a clean and orderly home for our families, and are expected to never allow those responsibilities to interfere with our appearance, our patience or our desire for sex.

We tolerate his sexual clumsiness, impotence, or premature ejaculation, and may also cope with his demands for sexual exploits that disgust us and are fueled by his involvement with pornography. Some of us discover we are a false front to conceal his homosexuality.

We try to go the extra mile. We try to understand, we try to reason, we try to discuss, we try to learn. We suggest compromise. We try counseling. We try being silent.

Some of us are chosen for our looks, to be his unquestioning and dutiful arm-candy, to ride in a beautiful car, wear beautiful clothes, to be seen and not heard, and to encourage others to think he adores us and is the perfect husband.

We support his dreams. We struggle to pay the bills and patiently wait for the big payoff he promises. But if the payoff happens our support is considered immaterial to his success.

We sacrifice our dignity by begging him for kindness, consideration and caring. We are told we shouldn't feel the way we do.

We become so frustrated at the injustice in our lives that we 'lose it' and rage and scream and are told we have an anger problem.

We are burned out. We are drained. We are empty.

Some of us go to church and are told that to be a good wife we must be submissive. And we wonder if this means our duty is to die inside.

We cling to the time-worn adage that we should always put others first because we have been promised that if we do, we will eventually be rewarded with love in this world or the next.

We are damaged, broken, wounded and hurting much of the time, and our husbands are indifferent to, dismissive of, and even mocking of, our pain.

If we run for our lives, figuratively or literally, we discover that the torture continues via the legal process for which we are unprepared emotionally and financially.

Our children are our joy, and our broken hearts hurt even more when we see them learning to be withdrawn in order to hide from the chaos. Or worse, copying their father's behavior.

Many of us are threatened with fists, bashed-in walls, broken mirrors and torn-off doors, and are slapped, shoved, punched, strangled, beaten and raped. And afterwards, he may tell us he loves us.

We have a tendency to always look for the good and put a smile on our face. We deny what is happening to us and we adjust, we adapt, and we minimize how the mistreatment gets worse as the years go by.

If he threatens to leave us, we beg for him to stay because we are terrified of being alone, of being abandoned, of losing him to someone else. We hate ourselves for being so dependent on him, for wanting him regardless of how he treats us. We are confused and condemn ourselves for our weakness.

We may receive a note, a text, an email or a voicemail, telling us he is leaving or filing for divorce and in our paralyzed shock we realize he planned this long before he tells us.

We blame ourselves for having fallen for him in the first place. How could we have been so stupid, so naïve, so weak? Why didn't we recognize his hidden side? Why didn't we see the red flags that are obvious to us now?

We criticize ourselves for continually listening to him, giving in to his ensnaring charm and convincing arguments. We are brutal to ourselves with our self-condemnation.

We fail to see what this life does to us mentally, emotionally, physically, and spiritually, and we fail to see what it does to our children who are captive witnesses with no choice.

We are told that we don't know how to raise our children, how to choose items for our home, or how to handle money.

And we are always too fat, too thin, too old, or not intellectual or spiritual enough.

It never ends.

Confusion

But then it does end.

It stops when your parents are in town (he's your Dad's best pal and flatters your mother). When you have dinner with his business associates, when you meet with your child's teacher, when you meet with a marriage counselor. Or when he is in a good mood and wants sex.

An audience, a witness, provides a reprieve and you feel his arm around your shoulders and a gentle pat on your arm to remind you of how lucky you are to be married to the great guy everybody likes. There may be gifts, a surprise vacation, good sex. Maybe he's changed?

It's all so confusing because life isn't bad all the time. He's accommodating and charming with other people. What is wrong with you and the children? What is truly him? Who is this guy? What can you believe? Your life is a hall of mirrors.

And you forgive. Again. And you push aside how discouraged you felt and you vow to try harder, to be better. And you think he might be trying to be better too. For a brief moment, a week, a month, you allow yourself to feel loved and to hope. Maybe it could be this way all the time?

You may notice a pattern. Your life is like a roller coaster car climbing up the incline of his brooding anger. At the top he explodes or sentences you to the silent treatment, and you plunge into the depths of terror and depression. But he cools off and life is pleasant, even fun, and the sex may be good. But the roller-coaster car goes up the incline again.

You wonder: Why can't he be nice all the time? Why can't you be better or smarter and figure him out so that he will treat you kindly? Why isn't he as patient and considerate with you as he is with friends or complete strangers?

Why? The never-ending question, 'Why?' plays its loop inside your head and you search self-help books that theorize about why he is the way

18

he is. If only you could understand him better.

You keep it together for your kids, for your financial security, for your image, for your role in your extended family, your community, your neighborhood, your employer, your church, your friends, but the 'keep it together' is a lie. You're not keeping it together inside yourself. Inside you're tired of trying to make it work, tired of begging, pleading, explaining, looking for the right words, waiting for the right time, endlessly hoping for understanding, validation and appreciation from the man you pledged your life to, and with whom you've perhaps made babies. The underlying complication is, you love this man and your children, but he is destroying you.

Validation

Confusion tortures you and you crave validation. You long for someone to tell you that what you feel is valid, understandable and justified. That you aren't crazy. That what happened did happen, and how your husband treats you isn't right, isn't solely because of you, and you don't deserve to be treated this way. And not all marriages are like yours. And yes, someone to validate what your instinct is screaming; that what he did or said to hurt you was intentional.

But who can you ask? Who can you tell? Who will believe you? Who will validate what your instinct is telling you? A counselor is neutral when you describe your anguish, your hopelessness, or his impossible-to-describe behavior that is destroying you.

The confusion is maddening. If the way he treats you is right and justified, as he says it is, because he says his behavior is because of what *you* do or say, then why can't you fix your behavior so that he will never get upset? Why can't your counselor or self-help books tell you what to do?

You long for understanding, compassion, and straight-forward answers. You want to fix your marriage. But regardless of what you try, how many recommendations in self-help books you follow, nothing changes for very long, if at all.

What is the truth?

Those of us who have lived this life, the secret and silent sisterhood, can tell you the truth. We should offer compassion for each other and validate our shared experience.

- You're not crazy, not even a little bit crazy. You are being used, although you can't really see it or recognize it for what it is.

- You deserve respect, kindness and caring because you are a human being, and perhaps the mother of children.

- Your emotions are correct and your sense of injustice is accurate.
- What you experience with him is real and not your imagination. It did happen even if he tells you it didn't, whether an hour ago, a year ago, ten years ago or more.

- Yes, he is clever. And yes, he lies. And he knows he is lying.

- What your instinct tells you about his motivation is correct. And yes, your intuition is wiser than the sales pitch he gives you. Yes, he does do it intentionally and with purpose, and often because he enjoys upsetting you. It gives him a sense of power, control, satisfaction and self-righteousness.

- Your intelligence and good sense are correct. But you don't trust them because you've been told you are stupid.

- You aren't stupid. You're smart. Your interpretation of events is correct.

- Your feeling of shrinking as a human, of being invisible to him, are murderous to your self-worth.

- Your melancholy and depression are serious and should not be ignored.

- You don't know that you are valuable because your husband treats you as though you have no value as a human being or as a woman.

- Your pain is real and justified and is not a product of your imagination or a misinterpretation of his behavior.

When we are attacked in the battle zone of a miserable marriage, even if it is a silent attack, we are damaged, we are diminished, and we can be destroyed (God forbid, even physically). We may feel as though we are dying because in fact we are, bit by bit.

Our instinct for self-preservation screams at us, attempting to warn us that his behavior is destructive. But we don't know how to listen to or trust our instinct because we accept his verdict that we are at fault, unworthy and unlovable. The complexities, the lies, the twists and turns are mind-bending and impossible to describe to others. And no one wants to listen to anything negative about the 'nice guy' they know. Helpful support when you are trapped in a miserable marriage is very hard to find.

Those of us who have lived it can validate that being trapped in a miserable marriage is a torturous, emotionally deadening, spirit-destroying experience. It will damage your physical health even if you are never slapped, kicked, punched or hospitalized with broken bones or a concussion. And it distorts your thinking, your ability to know what is right and what is wrong because you learn to live in his world, a dishonest world with a false front, a world of lies.

We are most often trapped by our complex emotional entanglement with him, as well as issues of money, children, religious beliefs, community position, long-established family behavior patterns, and by our terror of what he might do to us or our children if we defy him. We are afraid of being alone, of becoming like the elderly lady in the check-out line with her disheveled wig, talking to a miniature dog hidden in her oversize handbag. 'Oh no, anything but that!' So, we settle for our particular brand of miserable marriage because the thought of being alone paralyzes us.

But a miserable marriage should never be casually dismissed as, 'That's just the way men are.' A miserable marriage is a very complex dynamic and it is ultimately a psychologically and physically deadly one, because it eats away our spirit, our essence, our soul, and eventually damages our physical health.

21

Transformation Action Plan

1. Carefully re-read the list of characteristics under the section 'Who we are' and highlight all of the phrases that apply to you and your marriage. Do this several times, as you may discover more descriptions apply to you than you at first realized. You may have additional items to add also.

2. Create a list of your husband's behaviors in private compared to his public behaviors. Note them side-by-side so that the contrast between what he says and does in private, versus in public, are clear to you. Develop this list over the course of days or a week as you remember specific incidents.

3. Create a list of all the ways you are trapped in your marriage. Do this over a period of days. Be thorough. Next to each item, note what you think you could do to escape each entrapment. Don't be afraid to note 'nothing,' if you believe there is nothing you can presently do. Keep this list in a safe place for future reference. (It is also a good idea to protect your privacy when reading this book.)

4. **Say this Affirmation**

   I deserve to be treated with kindness and respect
   …you are God's temple and God's spirit dwells in you
   1 Corinthians 3:16 ESV

   An affirmation is a strong, positive statement that is transformative—affirmations can alter your life. You do not have to believe an affirmation when you say it because its goal is to plant a positive and strong belief in your mind. Often an affirmation is the opposite of a negative message you've absorbed about yourself. Whether a good day or a bad day, say this affirmation frequently aloud or to yourself. Say it many times, emphasizing a different word each time – **I** deserve to be treated with kindness and respect. I **deserve** to be treated with

22

kindness and respect. I deserve to be **treated** with kindness and respect. Continue in this manner for the remaining words in the affirmation.

NOTE: You will find affirmations throughout this book. It is a good idea to create a complete list of them for reference.

5. **Respect and Reward Yourself**

   Respect, rewards, compliments, and encouragement are rare in our lives when we are trapped in a miserable marriage. It is important to respect and reward yourself for any accomplishment. If you have read this far, selected the characteristics in the list above that apply to you, created a comparison list of your husband's public and private behaviors, created a list of the ways in which you are trapped in your marriage, and said the affirmation, respect yourself for doing so. Reward yourself—give yourself a hug, buy yourself a bouquet of flowers, treat yourself to a few minutes of solitude with a cup of tea or a quiet walk. Take any action that rewards you for you have just accomplished something important. If food is a negative issue for you, please do not reward yourself with food. Consider a small jewelry item to wear as a symbol of how far you have already come.

6. **Create a List of Rewards**

   Over the next few days, think about ways that you can reward yourself for your accomplishments and create a personal Rewards List. Because we are accustomed to denigration, we overlook the many ways in which we accomplish tasks and goals and for which we can reward ourselves. Be creative, because rewards can take many forms. One woman included on her Rewards List permission to do nothing. She relished giving herself time to just simply be present enjoying solitude. Keep your Rewards List where you can refer to it as you proceed on your wellness journey.

3

Take my hand and show me how to save my life.

The Components of Surviving and Growing

The pain of having your spiritual lifeblood, the essence of who you are, drained from you by someone you love, and who vowed to love you, defies description. Wondering who that empty person is staring back at you from the mirror, and knowing you no longer resemble the alive person you once were, is so debilitatingly depressing that only those of us who have experienced it can grasp the despair.

A miserable marriage drains your enthusiasm for life, robs your energy, vitality, self-worth and self-image, and causes you to question your sanity. It unsettles your decision-making capabilities, undermines your mothering skills, puts fear in your heart and damages your emotional and physical health. Living in a miserable marriage can literally kill you bit by bit, day after day, because life-sustaining loving is absent from a miserable marriage. Love, like our body, requires nourishment to stay alive.

And sadly, if you seek help from family, friends, and even therapists, you discover that kindness, understanding, and useful, practical assistance is very hard to find. Everyone may give you their opinion but no one wants to really help. The world outside your marriage seems as cold, unresponsive, judgmental and uncaring as life inside your marriage.

But there is hope and a way to survive and grow, to be transformed and triumph while trapped. Determination and courage are necessary, but self-respect, dignity, poise, graciousness, kindness, courtesy, strength, discernment, wisdom and peace can be resurrected in your life. I found all of these and I began my wellness journey from a place of complete despair and hopelessness.

Step-by-Step

The Survive and Grow Steps detailed in this book are the steps I took to change my life while trapped with a man consumed by anger, who constantly criticized me, attempted to control every aspect of my life, worked me nearly to death, derided me with sarcasm and hatefulness, threatened to kill me and vowed to take my child away from me if I defied him. The Survive and Grow Steps rescued me from that torturous marriage and forever transformed my life.

The essential components of growth, survival, transformation and triumph are:

Truth

Acceptance

Self-Respect

New Behaviors

Personal Core Values

These fundamental foundation blocks don't just happen. You need tools and must practice them to move through the transformation process. This is the strategy this book provides. If you truly want to change your life, you need an action plan to do so, which is the opposite of passively hoping and wishing life could be better, or endlessly wishing your husband might change.

Goal of the Survive and Grow Steps

This book can be considered a goal-oriented training program. Coping with an impossible husband is equivalent to a mental and emotional boxing match between a heavy-weight champion and an amateur featherweight. And just as for an athlete faced with such a challenge, a training program requires commitment, dedication, determination, goals, and allowing enough time for all the hard work to pay off with stronger muscles; in our case, a stronger, focused, accurately-thinking mind and new behaviors. Not following through, of course, is similar to reading a diet book while eating a bag of chips; the knowledge is interesting but doesn't result in change. Commitment to transforming your life is the key ingredient for a better life.

In this book you will learn:

- To face and accept the truth about your marriage, your husband and yourself, and to grow from that knowledge.
- To reclaim your value as a human being, as a woman, and to appreciate and honor the wonder of your uniqueness.
- To learn new behaviors and grow strong because changing your behavior leads to a change in your thinking, which ultimately transforms your life.
- To develop a personal code of standards to live by, your Core Values and Guiding Principle, that you maintain without hesitation or apology to anyone.
- To develop a formidable feminine strength and become empowered in your humanness and womanhood.

Transformation Action Plan and Affirmations

This book provides an action plan, a strategy, goals and a suggested timeframe to help you transform your life. Throughout this book each of the Survive and Grow Steps is explained, as well as why regularly practicing each step is vitally important.

Many chapters include affirmations, strong statements that help you navigate through each step. Affirmations are important because they teach us to believe good and strong things about ourselves, regardless of how we feel in the moment. Affirmations plant new, positive thoughts in our minds and repeatedly saying them strengthens us and encourages us to grow.

Affirmations are vital to our transformation because they directly confront the negativity in which a miserable marriage submerges us. Phrases such as, 'No, you can't, you shouldn't, you must not, you can't have, you can't say, you can't do,' become air we breathe in a miserable marriage. Strong, positive statements—affirmations—become our shield that gives us strength.

Included in this book are my observations, insights and wisdom which I experienced as I journeyed through the Steps. These are solely mine. Whether or not you agree with them, if you embark on this wellness journey, I believe you will experience your own insights too. As you grow, you will become aware of your instinct/intuition and learn to listen to it as a source of truth and wisdom. You will learn to respect your inner wisdom, for wisdom is always portrayed as a woman.

Not a Quick Fix

The Survive and Grow Steps are not a quick fix because no simple solution exists for the complex situation you are in. The circumstances of your life evolved over time, so growth into healing and wellness must evolve too. The Survive and Grow Steps require determination, patience, practice and a willingness to keep going. But you probably already know how to keep going in spite of everything because that is how you have been living. For many of us, our love for our children, our extended family, even our pets, is our only motivation to get out of bed and keep trying.

Desperate for Change

As a young wife and mother, my marriage deteriorated into such a crazy-making wilderness that I became desperate. I began to question every aspect of my life. I reached out to friends who assured me that, "All men are like that," or "You're so lucky because [Joe] is such a terrific guy," or "Maybe you're depressed and need some meds." My mother lectured me to count my blessings because, "He's so nice-looking any woman would be glad to be married to him." I concluded that *my* short-comings were the reason for my unhappy marriage and the problems lay exclusively with me. And that I deserved nothing better in my life.

I berated myself because I assumed all marriages were like mine and since other women apparently coped so well, I obviously was unskilled and inadequate. But I wanted answers, because the confusion, the anger, the tirades, the financial insecurities and the derision were wearing me down and tearing me apart. I recognized that I could not endure much more.

I met with a counselor who listened patiently while I described the put-downs, the sarcasm, the endless criticism, the money problems and

27

more. She asked me how I felt, kept one eye on the clock and told me she'd see me next week. Not once did she give me a practical suggestion of how I could actually handle my horrible situation.

I much later realized that neither my friends nor the counselor had a clue as to what my life was really like.

Impossible Goals Without an Action Plan

Broken and lonely, I read self-help books. They told me I should improve my self-esteem and set boundaries. The majority of them explained that the clue to my husband's behavior lay buried in his childhood and I needed to be empathic and understand him. They also described my personality deficiencies that caused me to be married to him in the first place. The message seemed to be that I had a responsibility to understand him but it never seemed to be his responsibility to learn about himself. And just knowing more about him didn't improve my life. It all felt like telling someone to swim the English Channel when they didn't know how to swim.

If only words could fix marriages. The countless words written by experts, and the countless words spoken by women trying to convince their husbands to stop behaviors that destroy relationships and families, would be successful if the all-holy word 'communication' is truly the key. But words aren't sufficient.

I tried. I went to counseling and for a while my husband and I went to counseling together. Week after week I struggled to describe the craziness of my daily life. I listened to my husband explain why his actions were logical, reasonable and justified. In his opinion, our life simply consisted of cause and effect: "If she didn't, then I wouldn't have to…" After a while he quit going but I soldiered on. Many hours and dollars later nothing had changed in my marriage.

As I struggled, I discovered that well-meaning counselors and self-help books told me in general terms what I should do to improve my life but none gave me specific guidance on how to survive in my terrible marriage.

How do you 'improve communication' with a husband who won't

28

talk to you?

Countless times, I read or heard platitudes such as, 'start loving yourself.' But they failed to consider that when you are broken and constantly demeaned you don't have the strength or knowledge to love yourself.

You have to do preliminary work to reach the point where you can start 'loving yourself' or 'improve your self-esteem.' You have to begin stretching some muscles before you can swim the English Channel.

Searching for a Solution

As I searched for answers, I collected information that resonated with me. Inspiring words from one source, insight from another, sometimes suggestions that were aimed at something far afield from what I struggled with. I slowly began to do things differently. I began to examine my life from a new perspective.

Without realizing the subtle process taking place, gradually, step by step, I began to build a new way of living and my life began to change. What evolved for me became the Survive and Grow Steps that are the subject of this book.

The Wellness Journey to a Better Life

This book describes a wellness journey, a journey to emotional, spiritual, and physical health, because living in a miserable marriage is not healthy—it is destructive.

The goal of this book is to help you discover your potential to create a life for yourself that is emotionally, mentally, physically and spiritually healing and healthy; to become empowered.

'Empowered' means to become stronger and self-confident in taking control over your own life. It does not mean waiting to be given permission by someone else for you to have control over your life, but to learn, step-by-step, how to gain control over the precious life that is yours. As over-used as the term is, to become empowered is possible even while trapped in a miserable marriage. I know because I did it. This book evolved from the wellness journey I traveled to transform my life.

If you are trying to cope with a miserable marriage, are struggling emotionally through the difficulties involved in disentangling from it, or are plagued by painful memories of a miserable marriage now ended, you will find this book of value.

Many turning points and significant insights happened in my journey, sometimes painfully and at other times quickly and peacefully. But eventually in the end with startling results.

It is difficult to describe a transformative personal life experience, which is why, beginning in Chapter 4, I share the story of Kelly, a woman who embarked on the journey of the Survive and Grow Steps and whose story includes my own. The journey was arduous and required courage and commitment, but we both survived, grew and transformed our lives.

Similar to any seemingly hopeless task, we took one day at a time, one step at a time, and doggedly rebuilt our lives. Never again would we live as we lived in the past. When life becomes good and filled with hope and new dreams, you never look back. Regardless of how difficult, it is a journey worth taking.

But I know we each have our own timing in life and not every woman will commit to undertake the challenges detailed in this book. I suggest you read it anyway, and when you are ready to move forward and transform your life, it will be available to you as a resource for strength and encouragement. And perhaps just knowing there are so many of us doing our best to cope will be meaningful to you. Hope, peace and a better life are possible.

Courage is Within You

Only those of us who have walked this path can fully appreciate your courage if you undertake the challenge to create a better life for yourself. I believe all women should strive harder to help each other. Our lives and the lives of our children are too precious to waste. And be gentle with yourself. While the journey is difficult, life can be better. A profound sense of peace awaits when you arrive at a complete understanding of who you are, the standards of behavior you require of yourself and others, and when you accept the choices that others make as *their* choices for which *they* are responsible, even when they break our hearts.

Transformation Action Plan

1. Begin now to maintain a daily or weekly journal. Whether electronic or written by hand, record your thoughts. Be cautious and make sure your journal cannot be accessed by anyone.

2. To create a starting point, describe the turmoil in your marriage and life.

3. Describe the anger in your marriage and life.

4. Describe the deceit in your marriage and life.

5. Describe the denial in your marriage and life.

6. Describe how you feel—sad, despairing, hopeless, worn down, exhausted, etc.

7. Make a list of all the ways you would like to see your life transformed.

8. **Say this Affirmation**

   I am open to a new direction in my life
   We ourselves must walk the path – Gautama Buddha

   Whether a good day or a bad day, say this affirmation frequently aloud or to yourself. Emphasize a different word each time: **I** am open to a new direction in my life, I **am** open to a new direction in my life, I am **open** to a new direction in my life. Continue in this manner for the remaining words in the affirmation.

9. **Respect and Reward Yourself**
   If you have read this far, started your journal, described the turmoil, anger, deceit, and denial in your marriage, created a list of how you would like to transform your life, and said the affirmation, respect yourself for doing so. Choose an item from

31

the Rewards List you created in Chapter 2 and reward yourself, for you have just accomplished something important.

4

Everywoman

It may be necessary to encounter defeats so you can know who you are
and what you can rise from. – Maya Angelou

Kelly's Story Begins

Kelly tugged the blanket up to her chin, stared at the ceiling she
could not see in her dark, pre-dawn bedroom and thought the same
thoughts her mind had tormented her with in a continuous loop since she
fell into bed at midnight: I don't know what to do. Something is very wrong
but I'm not sure what it is or how to explain it to anyone, even to myself. I
can't figure out what is going on. I don't know how I can continue to live
this way.

Her body hurt with a pain of total fatigue. Over and over, the same
questions nagged her. She rested her hand on her chest, over her heart, and
wondered if the pounding she felt meant she might have a heart attack. Her
head throbbed and her mind felt numb with an unbearable sadness,
frustration, anger, fear and hopelessness. They weighed her down like bags
of wet sand and she pictured herself going through life with cement blocks
attached to both her ankles. Her despair hurt beyond belief.

But at the same time there was something different about how she
thought about her situation. She could tell. This time her total exhaustion
was too deep to ignore. It felt deadly, like death hovered over her.

She had been through this before, more times than she could count.
But in the early morning darkness she realized a corner had been turned.
Something had shifted inside her, and she asked herself questions for which
she knew she needed answers. Why does he act the way he does? Why does
he treat me so horribly? What have I done or said to him that causes him to
have hate on his face and in his eyes and want to upset me, fill our home
with negative energy, anger, arguments and raw hatred? I can't live like
this!

Kelly lay on her back and listened to Dan's soft steady snore beside

33

her. She touched her eyelids and felt how swollen they were from lack of sleep and crying. Her body screamed exhaustion and she wanted to go to sleep and never wake up. But she couldn't because her mind would not stop those nagging questions. How had life turned out this way? Why had life turned out this way? She tried to be a good person but everything seemed to go wrong. Why couldn't she be a better wife? What was wrong with Dan?

Waves of despair, hopelessness and anger flowed through her.

She was angry that Dan enjoyed a deep restful sleep while she tossed and turned in turmoil, reliving the past two days. The weekend had been a disaster. A raw fury made her want to hit Dan's back, wake him up, and scream at him that he was an unreasonable bastard who made her life nothing but hard work, disappointment and anger.

She'd tried to reason with him before and wanted answers from him, tried to get him to respond, to explain. "It doesn't have to be this way and it doesn't *need* to be this way," she'd said to him. "Why do you want to live in a home where you are never happy, never satisfied, angry all the time, won't talk to your wife, and nag her with standards she never can meet?"

It didn't make sense to her and she wanted him to explain to her why he behaves the way he does, and give her reasons, tell her what he wants her to do to fix their relationship. She wants to learn, to try and figure things out, to find a way to work with him to make their home peaceful and happy.

But she knew from past experience that waking up Dan to have a discussion, or a screaming fight, never turned out well. The noise frightened the kids and the quarrels never accomplished anything except to make her even more angry when Dan told her she was crazy, or worse. "I can replace you in a week," he once told her with his trademark snarl and snapped his fingers in her face. She reeled back and felt as though he had slapped her in her face. Shock and fear swept through her. She felt sick to her stomach from hopelessness that anything could ever be different or that she could do anything to change the situation. The future looked like a wasteland of ups and downs, fights, hard work and unhappiness, or just little glimmers of happiness sandwiched in between Dan's temper tantrums.

She had lived with this craziness long enough to know how the approaching morning would unfold when the clock finally pointed to 6:00 a.m. on this Monday morning. Exhausted, she would get up to start another week, and apply enough makeup so that no one at the office asked her if she felt all right because she looked so tired. She would get the kids ready for school, pack their lunches, make sure the daily load of laundry was started in the washer, and manage to get everyone out the door on time.

She and Dan would be polite with each other, saying little. Dan would ignore her tired face and swollen eyes, and act as though nothing was unusual. Kelly would swallow her emotions to keep the peace and get the day underway with as much calm as she could muster. Nicholas, her oldest child, might tilt his head, frown, look at her face and ask, "Are you sad, Mommy?" She would lie and say, "No, honey."

As Kelly lay in bed and thought about the Monday morning routine ahead of her, she realized that yes, for Dan nothing out of the ordinary did exist. For him it was life as usual. But for her it meant pick herself up, regroup, recover, and rebuild her emotional equilibrium from the horrible weekend because it had definitely been a horrible weekend.

For the thousandth time she relived the past couple of days and the same questions started to loop again in her brain. What went wrong? Why did Dan have to ruin the weekend? Why couldn't he see that she needed some down time, some pleasant time free from arguments and tension? What did he want from her? How much more could she do? Were all men like Dan? How did other women handle their husbands? Did all husbands treat their wives this way? What was it about her that made Dan so angry? Why couldn't they discuss things in a quiet tone of voice? Why couldn't they work together? Why couldn't she express her concerns and fears without Dan blowing up at her or ignoring her?

Frustration started to overwhelm Kelly and she fought back tears. Her eyes were swollen enough.

As a midlevel manager at a company that manufactured millions of vehicle parts, Kelly shouldered a lot of responsibility. It wasn't a career she ever imagined for herself. As an English major she dreamed about teaching creative writing at a small college. But she met Dan, they married right after graduation, and when Dan went to graduate school, she needed a job to support them so she took the first one offered to her.

She discovered her talent for managing people and solving production problems. Fortunately, the men she worked with respected her and she received steady promotions. Most importantly, her job paid well because they definitely needed the money.

Dan was fired from the first two jobs he took after grad school, so he decided to start his own business which hadn't paid off in the way they had hoped. When he announced he wanted to start a business, Kelly silently decided that she couldn't go through the trauma of him losing jobs so maybe he could do better on his own. She shouldered the burden of supporting them until he succeeded.

She now regretted her decision, just as she wished she could undo other decisions she made when she was too young to be making them, such as deciding to marry Dan. But she believed in marriage and wanted to do everything she could to make it work, and she thought Dan also wanted their marriage to succeed.

But if he does, why does he treat me this way? The loop started to play in her head again.

On the previous Friday, Kelly picked her kids up from day care and they laughed and enjoyed time together before Kelly began to prepare dinner. Kelly loved being a mom and she derived happiness and sustenance from Nicholas and Tracy's laughter. She sometimes felt they gave her an opportunity to be a kid again herself because her childhood had not been a particularly good one. Kelly enjoyed cooking a nice meal for her family, so she settled the kids at the table with colors and paints and engrossed herself in washing veggies, chopping and sautéing.

A year earlier, she and Dan acquired a second mortgage and remodeled the kitchen. It wasn't fancy with high-end appliances but it was attractive and pleasant to Kelly. As she chopped and stirred, she tried not to think about how Dan assured her that he would make the payments on the second mortgage. Kelly now knew he meant that if he conveniently forgot about his commitment the payment could come from her stretched-thin salary.

She criticized her foolishness when she remembered how she blithely signed the second-mortgage documents while believing that Dan planned to make the payments. When they paid the bills each month and she had to come up with money for everything, she sometimes reminded him about his promise to make the payments for the kitchen remodel. But he always had an excuse.

He paid no attention to how Kelly scrimped to pay for everything. If she complained, Dan tuned her out or exploded in rage. He always had a detailed and lengthy explanation about her faulty perspective and his correct one, and he would not allow Kelly to interrupt his discourse or ask any questions that might second-guess his opinion. He held up his hand in front of her face like a traffic cop and forbade her to speak. She hated him when he did that.

While Kelly cooked dinner, she kept an eye on her kids and commented encouragingly about their artwork. Regardless of how tired she was, watching her kids play always warmed her heart and made her smile. Nicholas, age six, and Tracy, age four, were adorable in her opinion. They were full of life and being with them gave Kelly the joy that she thrived on. She loved the feel of their warm little bodies when she held them close to her and she took every opportunity to hug them or gently touch their hair or cheeks. Sometimes her heart ached that she couldn't be at home with them full time, or at least part-time, but that dream drowned in financial reality.

Dan's small business never produced enough money to make any significant contribution to the family expenses. Whenever Kelly brought up the subject that perhaps the business should be abandoned if it couldn't produce income for their family, Dan went ballistic. He told her, "It would all just go for taxes anyway," and, "You don't know jack shit about business and taxes, do you?"

He also liked to remind her, "You're the one who wanted kids, not me. And you're the one who slipped up and got pregnant the second time." She once told him angrily that Tracy could not be considered a virgin birth but he just ignored her. She suggested he get a vasectomy after Nicholas' birth but Dan laughed at her and said, "Aren't you feminists always yammering that the baby thing is a woman's body issue? So, you should take care of it." Several times the thought occurred to her that Dan's laziness in producing income was a punishment of her for having these two cute little kids. But she pushed that thought out of her mind. And she never really considered the idea of describing herself as a feminist. She just wanted to take care of her family.

Whenever Kelly pressed Dan about contributing to the family income, he pointed out that he bought his personal clothing with money from his business, a comment that infuriated her. She wondered what kind of thinking led a man to believe it impressed his wife if he bought clothing for himself rather than taking care of his family? Whenever Dan defended himself with the comment about his clothes-buying largesse, Kelly felt nothing but disgust for him.

And she also felt used. Dan seemed to have a scale of human value operating in his head and she ranked lower than him, much lower. In his world, she owed him his privilege and his freedom to make decisions independently from her. At least that is what her mind nagged at her. Dan regularly intoned, "Next year it will really pay off. We'll have more money than we'll know what to do with." The next year blended into the next year and the next, the payoff indefinitely postponed or unwise from a tax perspective. That tax argument made no sense to Kelly but she knew it was pointless to try and actually discuss the issue. Dan's idea of discussing anything meant he ignored her, walked out of the room, or shouted at her that she didn't know anything about anything.

If Kelly pointed out that she was exhausted from trying to cover all the bases and she needed some help from him, Dan looked at her with what she silently referred to as his trademark snarl and total indifference, and then he would walk away or turn back to his computer screen or iPhone that he was always looking at. It was pointless to even try to discuss with him anything that mattered to her. He simply dismissed it as her being emotional. "Are you PMS?" he insultingly asked her. Sometimes the thought crossed her mind that he considered her to be very stupid to let him get away with his manipulation of her. She pushed that idea away.

On this past Friday, Kelly was looking forward to the weekend. After a tough week at work, the weekend held the promise that she could enjoy doing things with Dan and the kids and find time to do a little gardening, which she loved, or maybe do a couple of things around the house that she seldom found time for. She thought perhaps they could go out for dinner one night or maybe go to the beach. No, not the beach, because Dan hated the hot sun and got upset if too much sand got in the car. Maybe go to the park for a long walk and take time for the kids to swing in the play area? Those were her ideas anyway. Dan rarely suggested doing anything just for the fun of doing it. Sometimes Kelly got tired of being the social director, of being the one who tried to inject some fun and lightness into their lives. She wished Dan would once in a while act like he wanted to be with her and suggest a nice dinner out just for the two of them. But that never happened and when she urged a date night on him, he spent the evening looking at his iPhone or blandly answering her questions when she tried to make conversation.

On Friday evening when Dan walked in the door, Kelly saw his face frozen in his all-too-familiar rage look and she knew that none of her imagined plans for the weekend were going to be possible. A well-known knot of fear and tension formed in her stomach and she felt the weight of disappointment and apprehension descend on her. Now what? Maybe he saw the crumbs in the car from the kids' snack and is going to rag on me for not taking better care of my car.

Kelly never knew what Dan was mad about, but there always seemed to be something. Dan looked at her as though she were week-old, foul-smelling roadkill. His unpredictable moods or verbal attacks always unnerved Kelly, caught her off-guard, and triggered a self-defense mindset before she had any idea of what was going on with Dan. Usually she never did find out and he slammed things, yelled, accused her of something bizarre or sulked in a scowling and forbidding silence that she could never penetrate.

Kelly did what she always did and pretended not to see what she recognized as his seething anger. She had no idea why he was mad at her this time but knew that if she asked him the situation would quickly escalate into a shouting match, the last thing she wanted or needed after a demanding week at work. She wanted complete down time, not a confrontation with Dan.

Dan ignored Kelly's feigned cheery, "Hi, how'd your day go?" but responded to the kids' hugs and then he retreated down the hall. Kelly turned back to the sink, deflated and unenthusiastic about any of the plans she had so hopefully embraced just moments earlier. Dan could do that to her, wipe out in an instant the glass-is-always-half-full attitude she tended to have toward life.

Sometimes it took all her strength to keep going, even peeling this lousy potato! She knew she'd have to be very careful to keep Dan from going off on her. She felt the closing in and withdrawal of her enthusiasm. She had a physical reaction as well as a mental one and her body felt heavy, like a thick, suffocating blanket had been thrown over her. She'd been through this drill many times and she felt tired thinking about it. She hoped she didn't get a migraine. Sometimes a tension-filled weekend caused her arthritis to flare up. She'd have to keep an eye on that and do her stretching exercises and take a migraine tablet when she went to bed.

Dan ignored Kelly's existence during dinner and the kids silently ate their food. Kelly tried to lighten the mood by encouraging Nicholas and Tracy to, "Tell Daddy about your day," but Dan only responded to their lively chatter with a smile and didn't ask them any questions or encourage them. As soon as they could, they asked to be excused and ran off to the family room. Kelly asked Dan how his day had been and he looked at her with the snarl Kelly hated and haughtily said, "What does it matter to you?" They finished their meal without saying anything except, "Pass the salt."

Kelly did the dishes and got the children ready for bed, read stories to them and tucked them in. As she bent over each child and gave them a kiss, her heart swelled with love and she silently thanked God for the gift of her children. She brushed their hair off their foreheads and relished the feel of their soft skin. They looked up at her with tired eyes that completely trusted her. Kelly wanted to cry. She so often felt a tremendous burden of responsibility for these two innocent lives and wondered if she could do more to provide for them. She worked hard at her job so that she could give them the material things they needed but she wanted to give them a happy home life too. She sometimes wondered why Dan didn't enjoy them as much as she did. She knew he didn't seem to value her, but why didn't he treasure his children? He wasn't mean to them. He just didn't seem to derive any pleasure from them or seeing the joy that emanated from their cute faces. It was a mystery to Kelly and made her sad.

Kelly finished picking up toys and wet towels from the kids' baths and got ready for bed herself. As she climbed into bed beside Dan, she made another attempt to break the ice by asking him the subject of the magazine he was reading. He responded in a neutral tone and told her it was an article about something scientific. She felt relief and a slight lifting of her tense apprehension, because he didn't completely ignore her question or snarl at her. She considered this to be a good sign. Maybe Dan felt better and was no longer mad at her.

On Saturday morning, with the sun shining in the window on a glorious Spring day, Kelly activated her life-is-beautiful mindset and got out of bed with an upbeat attitude, leaving Dan asleep. She hugged her kids and together they headed to the kitchen to make a special Saturday breakfast. Over pancakes and sticky syrup, they decided to spend most of the day outdoors. Kelly told Nicholas and Tracy she thought they should go to the garden center and buy some really special seeds to grow flowers, "All the way up to here," and she put her hand up above her head. Life felt good again. She was happy in her home with her family and they could have fun together.

Eventually Kelly heard Dan showering. She wondered why he didn't come to the kitchen first to say good morning to his family, but over the years she had accepted the fact that Dan did things the way he wanted. He could be sociable to strangers but he just didn't engage spontaneously with his wife and children. Kelly often felt lonely, even when she and Dan were in the same room. She wished they were a happy family that included the Daddy, but Dan couldn't consider doing anything as flexible as delaying his morning shower for something as mundane as hugging her and the kids. Kelly knew from experience that if she suggested to him that he consider loosening up a bit he would look at her with annoyance because she didn't appreciate that things were fine just the way they were.

After he showered and dressed, and after all the laughter and fun in the kitchen were finished, Dan appeared and rather formally said, "Good morning." Kelly puzzled over the aloofness Dan maintained in their home because it vanished when other people were around. She assumed Dan thought other people were better than her. "Maybe he's right," she often thought.

With the sun shining, a happy breakfast with her kids concluded, and a cheery outlook on life, Kelly made a mistake. With enthusiasm she told Dan that she and the kids were talking about getting some sunflower seeds and planting them and suggested, "We can go to the nursery to choose the seeds."

In an instant Dan's face changed. He looked at her with hatred and snarled, "Don't you ever think that maybe I have things to do?"

Deflated and instantly on guard, Kelly quickly said, "Oh, you don't have to come along. I need to go grocery shopping so the kids and I can get the seeds. I was just letting you know our thoughts, and of course we would love to have you come along but I wasn't inferring that you had to."

But the damage was done. Dan did not intend to see the bright side. That wasn't his way. He turned and slammed the cup of coffee he was holding onto the counter, the handle broke, the cup slipped to the floor and hot coffee went everywhere, including onto Dan's bare legs because he was wearing running shorts.

"God dammit! Why the hell can't you do anything right? Can't you adjust the control on that cheap piece of shit coffee machine you bought so that it doesn't boil the coffee?" Dan's face was red and twisted into rage. He clenched his fists and Kelly instinctively drew back. Dan had never struck her but when he clenched his fists or raised his hand to her face she wondered if the day would come when he would actually knock her down. She reached for a kitchen towel and started to dab at Dan's legs. He batted her hand away, hard, and then held up his hands in a traffic cop manner and screamed through clenched teeth, "Just. Leave. Me. Alone!"

Kelly grabbed some paper towels and bent down to wipe up the coffee from the floor and the cabinets where it had splashed. The kids, still sitting at the table when Dan started to shout, quickly left the room. Tracy started to cry and Nicholas put his arm around her shoulders as they headed for their rooms upstairs.

"Please don't track your shoes through the mess," Kelly shouted at Dan.

Dan looked at her with his snarl and walked to the refrigerator to get milk, leaving footprints of coffee.

With disgust and anger, Kelly threw down the paper towel and followed Nicholas and Tracy. They were in Nicholas' room sitting on his bed and Kelly went to them, sat down between them and hugged them both to her. Tracy cried harder and Nicholas looked down.

"It's OK," Kelly said, "I'm here and I love you both very much and we're going to have a nice day. Let's get our shoes and hats and we'll go to the grocery and get what we need and then we'll get our sunflower seeds and come home and plant them."

"Is Daddy going to come along?" Nicholas asked.

Kelly thought her heart would break when she heard Nicholas' sad little voice. "No, honey," she said quietly, "he has a lot of work to do so he can't come."

Kelly wondered if Nicholas asked from disappointment or relief that Dan wouldn't come along and spoil their fun with his sour attitude. She sighed and wanted to cry but didn't because she believed her kids needed her to be strong. Now that Dan was entrenched in one of his moods, she needed to try hard to make the weekend as pleasant as possible

43

for Nicholas, Tracy and herself.

She felt so weary of this situation. Nothing she did or said ever stopped Dan's foul moods. His unpredictable anger caused her and the kids to continuously walk on egg shells, always trying to guess what might set him off and doing everything to avoid his rages. And his anger was so destructive and illogical. Once he pushed Nicholas off of his new two-wheeled bicycle because Nicholas didn't know how to balance and wasn't peddling fast enough to please Dan.

Now the weekend was barely underway and Kelly already felt emotionally drained. She could tell from the children's body language that they were sad too. Oh well, keep on keeping on.

Kelly returned to the kitchen and Dan was nowhere in sight. Probably on his computer looking at his spreadsheets or porn. Or emailing strange women. She knew he did that, too.

She fought back tears and when Nicholas and Tracy came into the kitchen with their shoes on and hats in hand, she put a big smile on her face, finished wiping up the coffee mess and said, "OK team, let's go."

On the way to the car, Kelly texted her hair salon. She'd scheduled a quick trim later in the day but now she'd have to cancel since she couldn't count on Dan to watch Nicholas and Tracy, and she wouldn't consider asking him to do so, since she already knew the response she would get.

As Kelly and the kids cruised up and down the grocery aisles, Nicholas and Tracy played a familiar game of asking for everything they knew Kelly disapproved of. One or the other of them begged, "Pleeese Mommy?" and Kelly pretended to be annoyed and said, "No, no, no, no," and they laughed because they knew they were going to get a few of the items they considered to be treats, like fruit popsicles, and a lengthy debate took place over which flavor to choose.

When they went through the checkout line Kelly felt happier. Time with her kids did that for her.

Until her debit card was rejected.

Maybe she incorrectly entered her PIN number. She asked the clerk to go through the routine again.

No. Still rejected.

Cold panic froze Kelly. She knew her direct-deposit paycheck went into the account yesterday. She knew there should be money in the account. She felt violated, like a thief had broken into her home. And then she thought of Dan.

But rather than hold up the checkout line she pulled out her credit card, the one she had worked so hard to reduce to virtually no debt by diligently making payments for months and not using the card to make purchases. She swiped it and they were free to take the groceries to the car.

Kelly's happy frame of mind vanished in that checkout line. Something was wrong. Very wrong. She felt numb. And old and tired out, like the weight of the world had crashed down on her in the past half hour.

"Is something wrong, Mommy?" Nicholas asked as she fastened the kids into their car seats.

He's so perceptive for a small child but he's been living with Dan's moods for his entire life so what can I expect? Kelly felt bitterness and choking tears in her throat because her children were sad and wary due to the situation they were in, through no fault of theirs.

"No honey," Kelly lied. Yes, a great deal is wrong but I don't know what to do about it. Her stomach knotted with fear. No money in her account! She suspected Dan as the culprit of the missing funds. What did that man expect from her? How much more could she take?

"Let's go get our seeds," she announced with false cheerfulness. Nicholas and Tracy clapped.

"And then we'll have a treat." Anything to delay going home.

Kelly's frustration and anger lifted a bit as Nicholas and Tracy looked at the colorful seed packets in the display rack, pulling them out and putting them back again as Kelly guided them towards the giant sunflower seeds. Thank heavens she had a little cash in her wallet because she had planned to get some extra money when she checked out at the grocery.

Kelly felt more anger building inside her. In her mind, a normal daddy might want to accompany them, and even pay for something, she thought bitterly. Damn him. Why did he have to spoil everything? Why

45

couldn't he just go away and leave them alone if he disliked her and the children so much? Why did he have to constantly introduce anger and commotion into their lives? Why couldn't she even enjoy just buying some seeds for the garden without him taking all the fun and joy out of it? Her impulses made her want to drive straight home and scream at him. She felt pure rage and hate.

"Let's go get some lunch," Kelly said to the kids and like a chorus they both sang out, "Happy Meals!"

Drive-through food was a special treat because Kelly prided herself on being nutrition conscious. To hell with it. If Dan is at home I don't want to go there until I absolutely have to. She remembered the popsicles getting soft in the grocery bag and really didn't care if they melted all over the trunk of the car.

They ate their lunch in a nearby park and then Kelly pushed the kids on the swings. Every bit of her look-on-the-bright-side attitude had disappeared. She felt sick. Was it too much to ask to want a quiet peaceful life with her family? She worked hard and did her best to keep her part of the wedding vows she'd made. Didn't she deserve a little kindness and consideration? She started again to feel anger and hate toward Dan and she did her best to push those emotions down.

When she could postpone the inevitable no longer, they headed home and Kelly breathed a sigh of relief when Dan's car wasn't in the driveway. She assumed he'd gone to his office. Or God knows where or with whom.

Kelly unloaded the groceries and put them away in the kitchen while every few minutes Nicholas asked, "Can we plant the seeds now?"

"Yes, now," Kelly said with all the enthusiasm she could muster. They went to the garage for a rake and shovel and the toy-sized garden tools that belonged to the kids. Together they dug and hacked at a patch of ground next to the house where a couple of Kelly's prized roses grew. After the sunflower seeds were planted, the kids ran and played on their playset while Kelly pulled weeds and dug in the moist spring soil.

Gardening and cooking helped Kelly keep her sanity. Much as she longed to have another adult to share her love of the dirt and seeing things grow, she welcomed any time that she could find to lose herself digging, planting, and letting her mind wander.

Unfortunately, all too often her mind whirled with painful thoughts about her marriage. Dan never complimented her on her gardening, or anything else actually, but he seemed to take superior pleasure in pointing out the amount of their water bill or how much she spent on a garden hose or fertilizer. She knew it was his underhanded way to criticize her.

Dan monitors the money like he's the one who actually earns it, Kelly thought ruefully. Describing Dan as fundamentally lazy and just along for the ride was too painful—that a man merely wanted to use her. But the nagging thought did return, that Dan considered her a fool for letting him manipulate her.

By the time Kelly and the kids went inside, Kelly's spirits had lifted. Being outside with her kids always did that. She began to prepare dinner and put the kids into the bath tub to splash around, wondering if Dan would show up in time for a meal with her and the children. She knew to never question him about why he sometimes arrived home at irregular times because he always yelled at her that she wasn't his mother and he could damn well arrive home at his house when he chose.

She was drying the kids from their bath when Dan arrived, and he acted as though nothing was out of the ordinary. Kelly made a conscious decision to not give him the cold shoulder because she didn't want to spoil dinnertime. Dan seemed more normal and although he ignored Kelly he at least smiled at the kids. The children's bedtime arrived and all was quiet.

Kelly dreaded trying to discuss the rejected debit card with Dan, but she went into the spare bedroom that served as his home office. He stared at his computer monitor and quickly closed out of the screen but not before Kelly caught a glimpse of a well-rounded female bare behind.

"Dan, we need to talk."

"What about?" Dan didn't look at her and continued to focus on the monitor which now displayed a spreadsheet filled with numbers.

"When I tried to pay for the groceries today my debit card was rejected. My paycheck went into the account yesterday so there should be money in there. Do you know anything about it?"

"What do you mean?" Dan nonchalantly asked, and continued to look at the computer monitor.

"I want to know if you withdrew money from the checking account and if you did, how much and what for. If you didn't withdraw the money then someone has been in our account."

There was a long pause and then without looking at her Dan said, "Yes, I did need some money. I have expenses too you know."

"How much and what for, Dan? It's a joint account and we need to coordinate expenses so that we have enough to cover necessities. If there wasn't enough to pay for a week's worth of groceries, you must have withdrawn a lot of money."

Dan slowly turned toward her, as if he reluctantly took time from important duties to give an underling his attention. "Are you saying that I'm not to touch our joint account?" He slowly snarled at her and emphasized the word 'joint.'

"That's not the point." Kelly could feel her anger triggered but she held it back. She'd tried having conversations many times with Dan about money or other important topics, and it always went this way. Dan immediately began to accuse her of something, when she only wanted to discuss what she thought should be important to both of them. His accusations threw her off and made her doubt herself and her point of view. She sometimes couldn't think straight when he started telling her how she was wrong.

She backed away from her anger and switched to a cooperative tone.

"Look, since we're sitting in front of the computer let's bring up the bank account and see what we have in there."

It seemed like a sensible request. Looking together at the account's transactions would give Dan an opportunity to explain the withdrawals he'd made and they could decide what to do to cover this month's household bills.

"You don't trust me," Dan said very quietly, sounding deeply wounded. "You really don't trust me." He paused for a minute and then whispered, "And I don't appreciate you ordering me around."

Kelly immediately felt her body and mind become tense and on-guard. His quiet responses were always a warning that an explosion was building up steam.

"It's not a matter of trust," Kelly said. She could feel her frustration starting to rise. "And I'm not ordering you to do anything. It's a matter of planning. If we can work together to plan our expenses then we can both feel more secure." How many times had she made that statement over the years? Kelly had lost count.

"So, you're saying that I don't know what I'm doing?" Dan asked in his unnerving quiet tone.

Here we go again. Kelly was so disgusted with this endless cat and mouse game Dan played whenever she brought up money or other important topics. She wanted to scream at him but she held back. Instead, she said, "Dan, we have to start working together more, particularly on our finances. I only earn so much. If we can figure out what we need then we can go forward carefully."

"Now we're getting to the heart of the matter," Dan said, looking at her with hatred in his eyes. "It's the same thing as always. Dan doesn't do enough. Dan doesn't work hard enough. Dan is a failure."

"You are not a failure," Kelly lied. "But we need to decide how we are going to approach our future. If the business isn't earning any money to contribute to our livelihood after years of hard work, then maybe it's time to evaluate it. The bottom line is that we need more money as a family and we each need to communicate what we're doing with our money. I don't earn enough to supplement the business and cover our family's needs. I just want to discuss our financial situation calmly and rationally with you."

"So now you're the great financial wizard," Dan snarled back in a mocking tone. "The great one who earns all the money and should control how every penny is spent. Dan shouldn't use any money unless he checks with Mommy," he said this in a child-like voice.

Then he switched to what Kelly called his pompous-arrogant-ass tone, with his chin raised like a superior being looking down on an unworthy peasant. "Besides, I'm not going to discuss anything with you when you are in one of your moods and whine and attack me. Are you on your period? Do you have any of that anti-depressant your doctor prescribed for you a year or so ago? Go take some!"

Kelly lost her patience. "Dan, you have a responsibility to our family too. I'm tired and I'm already doing everything I can to earn a good salary but we need an income from you too. It's time to bite the bullet about the business and either start taking some money out for personal expenses or close it up and you can get a job."

Dan leaned towards her and through clinched teeth shouted in her face. "It's easy for you to say, 'Go get a job, Dan.' I've been out of the job market for over five years working on the business. No one is going to hire me!"

"That isn't true!" Kelly was fed up with him claiming he was unemployable except for dabbling with his small business that he admitted (or was he lying?) didn't make any money. "I'm trying to have a discussion with you about our finances so that we can decide together what to do!"

Dan switched to his quiet tone and said with mocking admiration and a Cheshire Cat-like smile as though complimenting her, "You know, you can be a real bitch when you want to, can't you?" Then he dramatically and loudly sighed, and added, "You're so much like your mother."

Dan knew Kelly loathed her abusive mother and never wanted to be anything like her. He might as well have stabbed her in the heart.

"It's time for you to grow up and start helping with our family!" Kelly had reached her limit and she knew the grow-up comment would ignite his anger. But she went on, "I'm tired, Dan. Really tired. I need your help."

"Now we get the Kelly is a martyr routine." Dan smirked. "Well, let me tell you, I'm tired too. Tired of having a wife who is always complaining but can't even make a decent cup of coffee!" Dan was shouting now and she didn't want the kids to hear and wake up.

"Dan, I'm telling you that something has to change. Your wife, *me*, couldn't pay for the groceries today! That is humiliating! It is also puzzling because my paycheck went into the account yesterday. Yesterday, Dan! Not a week or month ago. Yesterday. Where is the money, Dan? What did you spend it on without telling me?"

"Listen, you stupid bitch! I work my ass off trying to build a business while you waltz off to a cushy job at a big perfect company with all the benefits and perks you could want. I'm not the one leaving my kids at home while I travel around the country to attend cocktail parties."

"Cocktail parties? Are you crazy? I sometimes have to travel because of problems that are difficult to unravel and solve. Do you think I want to be away from the kids? I hate having to be out of town and alone in a hotel room. I do it because I have to, Dan, because I'm the one who is keeping a roof over our heads!"

Kelly's frustration burned and she wanted to pick something up and throw it. Instead she started to cry. She knew, since the morning episode with the broken coffee cup, that a blow-up would eventually erupt.

And Dan knew the buttons to push that shoved her emotionally over the edge. Implying anything negative about her mothering of Nicholas and Tracy tapped into the ultimate rage button.

She felt at the end of her rope trying to deal with this man. Trapped in a marriage. Completely and thoroughly trapped because she had two little kids, a jerk for a husband and no money to buy groceries even though she earned a good income.

As Kelly's tears of sadness, frustration, and hopelessness flowed, Dan looked at her with contempt and detachment. He'd been through this scene before. Kelly knew from countless replays that Dan assumed, "She'll get over it. Women are so emotional. She's incapable of taking the long-range view or understanding anything."

Kelly felt defeated and worthless. Her husband apparently thought of her as a plow horse, as having no limits of endurance. How were they going to pay the bills this month? She gave up and went to take a bath to try

51

and relax and sort out her thoughts. Kelly referred to it as drowning her sorrows.

She settled back in the tub with her Kindle and started to read one of the many self-help books she'd downloaded over the past several years, all of them dealing with problem marriages and men with character flaws.

Sometimes she wondered if Dan was a narcissist or suffered from borderline personality disorder. She'd studied the information in her collection of books looking for answers, searching for the key, the vital clue that would give her the help she needed. They all had various suggestions but they were so general with their advice. One said that she should confront her spouse with the marriage problems. Well, she'd just tried to confront Dan, as she had many times before, and anyone could see how well that went.

Another book told her to improve her self-esteem (yeah right, while I'm being told I'm stupid!). And still another said that she should make her needs and wants known. Kelly almost laughed at that one. How do you make your needs and wants known when your husband completely ignores you or always turns a problem back on you?

The only helpful sections were diagnostic concepts that might describe Dan's possible personality disorder. But they emphasized how she should try and be understanding of his problems, his difficult childhood, his need to have his own space—his man cave—and on and on.

What about me? What about what happens to me from trying to live with this guy?

Kelly went to bed on Saturday and tossed and turned while Dan slept like a baby. She'd noticed that about Dan in the past. When he was in one of his moods, he pushed her until she broke, until she finally became so angry that she shouted at him. It felt like a stick being poked through a cage at a small animal until it became frantic. And when Kelly started to cry, that seemed to be the prize Dan wanted to win. He appeared to derive a sense of calm from seeing her lose control. Never did he ever express concern or care that his wife was upset and in distress, but rather his facial expression and body language appeared triumphant from seeing her 'lose it.'

52

Once, a thought occurred to Kelly that Dan might be playing a sick psychological game with her but she pushed the thought aside. After all, he was her husband and sometimes he brought her flowers and he told her he loved her. But she just couldn't understand how someone who said they loved a person could be so demeaning to them. There had to be a specific reason that was the key to the mess of her marriage. What's wrong with him? What is it about me that makes him dislike me?

On Sunday morning, after the Saturday night argument with Dan, they went to church as they usually did each weekend. The kids loved Sunday school and Dan relished being a saintly member of the men's group, the go-to guy if they needed an extra usher or wanted someone to serve on a committee. Dan never failed to be charming to people when they were in public, the happy-go-lucky, never-upset great guy who said yes to any request and whom everyone liked. And although he largely ignored Kelly when they were in public, he sometimes put his arm around her shoulders, almost like an actor playing a part. Dan never missed his Thursday morning men's Bible study group. He could quote lots of scripture to her, pointing out that her behavior wasn't Biblical and she should be submissive to her husband.

I wish I could go to a morning women's Bible study group but I have to work. Kelly felt some bitterness and didn't like it. That's not how she wanted to be.

Once or twice she pointed out to Dan that his behavior in public was completely different from how he behaved towards her and the kids in private. She even went so far as to say to him that he was a Dr. Jekyll and Mr. Hyde. He told her it was her imagination working overtime, that she was crazy, and she needed to get some psychiatric help. When she lost her patience with him and became beside herself with frustration, he told her she had an anger problem and then recited scripture that said she should never show anger. It made her so mad she wanted to strangle him. But she didn't know how to deal with any of Dan's maneuvers and manipulations of her.

A couple of years ago they met with a pastoral counselor at their church but that became a complete waste of time and worse, it made her feel more inadequate than she already felt about herself. Dan charmed the counselor and they almost became buddies. When Kelly tried to describe Dan's behavior in their home, both men looked at her as a pathetic whining child. They only met with the counselor a few times and Dan said that, clearly, he didn't need help but maybe she did.

As Kelly lay in bed now, on this Monday morning with the early dawn beginning to light the window, she thought about her life and her entire body felt heavy. She felt defeated, with a sense of death, a slow dying inside her, the enthusiastic spark she always maintained towards life, drained out of her.

She realized she didn't like being around Dan most of the time because he made her so tense. No, to be honest, she feared being around Dan because of how he twisted her up in her words and in her mind. Dan could be nice, fun, and even make her laugh at times, but just as with his quick temper, the good times were unpredictable and sporadic. And they often signaled he wanted sex. It was so confusing. Did he love her or didn't he? She wanted to believe that he did. Maybe she just wasn't lovable. And yet, something she could not explain tied her to him and endlessly made her want to connect with him, to convince him to care about her.

How can I face years and years of this? Nicholas and Tracy are so little. At the very least I have decades of this ahead of me. I married for life and I can't get a divorce. I don't have any money for an attorney and I don't want my babies in a joint custody situation where Dan might bring home God knows what woman to be around them. I feel like I've been sentenced to prison, to solitary confinement. Kelly started to silently weep and tears flowed down her cheeks and onto her pillow. What's wrong with me? Why do other women handle their marriages better than I do? Dan is right. I do need some help. I need some help in how to cope with living with him!

Kelly vowed to herself that when she arrived at her office that morning, she would call her family physician and ask for a referral to someone who could help her. Her telephone call was the first step in what became her journey out of the dark.

54

Part I

Becoming a Valuable Woman

5

Survive and Grow Step One

We see and hear what we want to see and hear—not the truth.

Facing and Accepting Reality

Kelly called me for an appointment and over the course of several weeks I became acquainted with this attractive, intelligent, neat and tidy woman who listens intently, asks careful questions, and genuinely wants to unravel the mysteries of her marriage. She told me about her life with Dan, tears streaming as she shared her sadness and pain. She clenched her fists, described her frustration and rage in trying to cope with Dan's manipulations, and then she slumped in the chair, her shoulders folded in hopelessness.

Kelly loves her husband and children and wants to fix her marriage. She longs for Dan to be kind and loving and cooperate with her so they can have a calm and happy life, enjoy their children and plan a future together. She believes Dan wants the same things and she assumes he just doesn't comprehend how his behavior undermines their marriage.

She's tried to discuss their relationship with him, begging, pleading, applying logic, quoting self-help books, asking him to go to counseling, loudly arguing, and crying about the pain he causes her, thinking that if she can make him recognize and understand the problems then he will want to correct his behavior.

She's followed several suggestions from her self-help books that address the difficulty of dealing with what Dan perceives as her criticism of him—what he refers to as her attacking him. She doesn't want to just criticize Dan; she wants to convince him to discuss what she considers to be problems in their relationship and work to find mutually satisfactory solutions.

None of her efforts changed anything.

After a miserable weekend, Kelly constantly thinks about what happened, what she and Dan did and said, reviewing all the details, trying to figure out what went wrong and searching for clues to what she could do differently. On Monday, emotionally drained and with little energy for her job, she focuses on her work so she doesn't think so much about Dan. When Kelly has a free minute, she calls her best friend and describes the weekend. Her friend offers sympathy and then launches into her speech titled, "If you think that's bad, let me tell you what the jerk I'm married to did last weekend." Unless something changes, Kelly and her friend will have this same conversation for the next twenty years.

Kelly arrives for today's appointment with me and she looks nice and seems happy. She tells me Dan brought flowers to her when he came home from a quick trip to the grocery.

"Did he apologize for his bad behavior last weekend?"

"No," Kelly says slowly, "but we did have sex and he wasn't as rough as he can be sometimes. It was good."

Kelly exists on the emotional crumbs Dan occasionally tosses to her—flowers purchased from the display conveniently located at the grocery store entrance. Why not spend the extra fifteen bucks? After all, it's amazing what a bouquet will do with a woman, right? When he's in a good mood, Dan enjoys being with Kelly and oh, by the way, he got some sex, didn't he? Once again, the pattern of Kelly's life repeated and her marriage returned to 'normal,' which meant she figured out how to pay the bills and Dan never told Kelly what he did with the money. Kelly's upsetting weekend was just another bump in their roller coaster marriage.

Kelly survives on hope and enticement; hope that things will get better, hope that Dan will change, hope that she can unlock the code to his behavior, and the enticement to keep things the way they are because Dan can be nice sometimes, bring her flowers and provide good sex. Kelly is like a fish on the line of a skilled fisherman, reeled in with false hope and jerked hard if she tries to fight back.

Survive and Grow Step One

After Kelly settles herself in a comfortable chair and we finish our chat about the flowers, I hand Kelly a hard-boiled egg.

58

She looks puzzled.

I ask her to hold the boiled egg and examine it carefully. And then I tell Kelly that her task is to unboil the egg.

The look on her face tells me she thinks maybe she's made a big mistake in meeting with me. But I ask her to be patient because this exercise is important.

"I want you to look at the egg and talk to it, and persuade it to unboil itself."

Now Kelly is convinced I'm crazy.

"You'll learn something," I say to her.

"Pretend the boiled egg is Dan and repeat everything you've ever said, begged, pleaded, argued and shouted at Dan to convince him to stop behaving the way he does, to stop hurting you. Use all your persuasive powers.

"Your task is to use words to unboil the egg, the words you use with Dan when you try to discuss your relationship and his behavior. Include every logical and emotional argument you've ever used; how you could have a good life if he would stop being angry all the time, how you are hurting, how you could both be happier if Dan, the boiled egg, would unboil itself and become understanding, kind and no longer cruel. Take as much time as you need and don't leave anything out."

Kelly is very uncomfortable and self-conscious, but she begins to embrace the exercise. Gradually, she unburdens herself and tells the boiled egg everything she's said to Dan over the years, how she feels, how she is tense and tired and doesn't know what to do. She tells the boiled egg that she loves it [Dan] and she doesn't understand why he treats her the way he does, that she adores her kids and wants the best for them, and she's concerned their fights frighten the children. She starts to cry and says she feels trapped because she is trying her best but nothing seems to work and she's miserably unhappy in her marriage.

I allow Kelly plenty of time, and when she becomes quiet, I gently ask her, "Did you persuade the egg to unboil itself?"

Kelly looks up at me and quietly says, "No, of course not. You've

59

just taught me about Dan and my marriage, haven't you?" Kelly pauses and then says sadly, "I guess the lesson is that I have to accept things the way they are."

"No, the lesson is that you cannot convince someone to change if they choose not to. It is one of the hardest lessons in life to learn. Talking, arguing and obsessing about someone else's behavior changes nothing. Waiting and hoping for someone to change can go on forever. It's a very harsh but important reality, a truth, to face."

Facing Reality Brings Fantasy to a Close

While a bit theatrical, the boiled egg exercise is the first step to help Kelly recognize the role she plays in her marriage and to impress on her that nothing she says will convince Dan to change his behavior. She will also eventually recognize that begging, pleading, screaming, crying, and endlessly arguing with a boiled egg—Dan—demeans her. And that is precisely the point. How ridiculous is it, to try and reason with, or argue with, a boiled egg? There is no dignity or self-respect in trying to communicate with a boiled egg, and yet that is what we do, often for years. Or we accept our fate and allow a boiled egg to control every aspect of our life and our children's lives.

Facing reality about our life is a process we prefer to avoid. But when our life is eating away our soul, we desire change. Change from what, we aren't exactly sure, but change nevertheless. And what is it we need to change? Looking at the realities in our life is not an exercise for the faint of heart. It requires courage.

Another Lie

We are often entrenched in a deep-seated belief, a lie really, that no one *wants* to hurt other people, that their behavior is a mistake because they simply don't know or understand how they hurt us. This false assumption keeps us trapped.

Lots of people don't care about how they hurt others, and many *do* enjoy damaging other people, even take pleasure in doing so. But this reality is so far beyond what we want to believe that only an agonizing

60

acceptance of the truth can overcome it.

We don't want to face the possibility that we may be married to someone who doesn't care, or worse, intentionally hurts us. Instead, we think that if we can adequately explain to them how they hurt us, then they will be ashamed, even horrified, about how they harm others, and they will naturally want to change their behavior. This logic never works in a miserable marriage. It's the equivalent of shouting English to someone who doesn't speak the language.

In Kelly's marriage, Dan is comfortable with the way things are. If he wasn't, he would have called me and made an appointment rather than Kelly. Or he would willingly and open-mindedly accompany her.

When you identify and face uncomfortable realities, painful truths, then you have a difficult choice: To choose the pain of acceptance, or the dishonest comfort of denial. If we choose acceptance, then we have an additional choice to consider: To cling to the familiarity of our current behavior patterns or to make changes in ourselves. This is the dilemma Kelly faces.

Heartbreak, confusion, and disappointment descend on Kelly because accepting the truth about Dan is a bitter pill and Kelly feels desperately alone. She has two small children and she is married to a man who emotionally and financially abuses her. Sometimes she hates Dan, but the thought of breaking up their marriage and family is unacceptable because she loves him and wants her children to have a daddy. She does not believe in divorce and has limited financial resources, so she is trapped for the foreseeable future.

Accepting Reality is the First Step

Facing the devastating reality that your husband will not stop hurting you is a kind of death that needs to be taken seriously and mourned like any loss that wounds us deeply. Kelly realizes she must let go of, release and surrender, the hope that Dan will change his behavior. Because so much of her life has centered on that hope, she now must reclaim herself as a separate valuable human being, and then release her fantasies. Survive and Grow Step Two, in Chapter 9, will guide her to accomplish this.

When I ask Kelly if she wants to give the Survive and Grow Steps a try, she looks at me and says, "What do I have to lose? I can't go on this way."

I give Kelly an assignment: Once each day she is to hold an imaginary (or real) boiled egg and attempt to convince it to unboil itself. She is to repeat all the pleading, explaining, and screaming she has previously directed at Dan. I emphasize that it is important to repeat the exercise at least ten times. Only through this repeated experience will Kelly fully grasp the futility of trying to convince a boiled egg to change, and the demeaning behavior she engages in when she repeatedly tries to accomplish the impossible.

Transformation Action Plan

1. Yes, you may feel foolish, but do the boiled-egg exercise because you will discover how meaningful it is. Do not substitute a rock or other object. The egg is important because it had a different consistency before it was boiled, so maybe we can talk it into changing?

2. You may want to draw a smiley face on one side of your boiled egg, and a frowning face on the opposite side, so that you can talk to Happy Husband and Angry Husband and spin it around to simulate how fast your husband can become angry. Or you may wish to draw a suit and tie on one side and a devil costume on the other side to symbolize your husband's public and private personae.

3. When you speak to your boiled egg, be sure you include all the arguments, begging, pleading, screaming, reasoning, logic and so on that you have said to your husband to try and persuade him to change his behavior. Don't leave anything out and become emotional if you wish.

4. And yes, at the end of the exercise you can stomp the egg into a smushed mess if that helps you with your anger, another reason to use an egg and not a rock.

5. **Say this Affirmation**

   I can accept the truth and not be destroyed by it
   Let no one deceive himself. – 1 Corinthians 3:18 ESV

   Whether a good day or a bad day, say this affirmation. Say it many times, emphasizing a different word each time – **I** can accept the truth and not be destroyed by it. I **can** accept the truth and not be destroyed by it. I can **accept** the truth and not be destroyed by it.

7. **Respect and Reward Yourself**
   If you have read this far, poured your heart out to a boiled egg—whether real or imaginary—and have said the affirmation, respect and reward yourself. Choose an item from the Rewards List you created in Chapter 2 and reward yourself, for you have just accomplished something important.

8. **Insight to Ponder**
   We often see qualities in a person we love, or a person with whom we are trying to have a relationship, that simply aren't there. Sometimes we project our qualities of empathy, kindness, caring, responsibility and love onto them when in reality they simply do not possess them.

9. **Watch for Your Personal Milestone of Growth**
   My Personal Milestone
   In the middle of one of our typical arguments, I attempted to explain to my husband how he hurt me with his sarcasm and put-downs. I suddenly stopped mid-sentence, looked at him and realized my words meant nothing to him—absolutely nothing. I saw a hard-boiled egg, impossible to unboil, and I profoundly realized he was never going to change. A few weeks

later, when I had incorporated Step Two (Chapter 9) into my life, I formed the first **Rule** of survival with my husband: **Never expect anything from him.** This was the first signal that my life began to change. My attitude toward my husband changed when I profoundly faced and accepted the reality of who he was.

Rule Number One: Never expect anything from him

NOTE: Before you say, "But this is terrible. This is nonsense. Of course, we should expect things from our husband," let me remind you that we are dealing with reality not how things should be. We already know what we can and cannot expect to receive from difficult men so endlessly wishing for him to be supportive of us is the perpetuation of an unchanged life. But this does not mean giving up and giving in. It merely is the first step in learning that he is separate from us and his life compass is different from ours. The journey that lays ahead for us is to let him be who he is while we carve out a better life for ourselves. Survive and Grow Step Two in Chapter 9 fully addresses this.

6

The truth will set you free. But facing it can break your heart.

The Perspective of Reality

When you believe someone loves you, and you assume they want the same relationship that you want. When you finally see and face the ugly truth that you are mistaken, it hurts. It is a loss that needs to be recognized, honored and mourned. But without any mechanism for discarding the fantasy that Dan wants what she wants, Kelly can spend the rest of her life trying to unboil the egg and forever repeating her efforts to convince Dan to stop mentally torturing her.

It is extremely difficult to fully accept that the person to whom we have pledged our life simply has zero concern about what causes us pain, or what we want and need.

Perhaps subconsciously when we marry, we assume that our husband will add us to his list of life priorities, even place us and our relationship at the top of his list. When we recognize that we're at the bottom of his list, we suffer. Have we been duped? Are we really that worthless? Do we truly have no value?

Like many, if not most women, Kelly envisions marriage as conjoined twins who think and act in constant agreement. Many wedding ceremonies include the words, 'two shall become one' and women are surprised to discover the 'one' in reality often turns out to be 'him.' Marriage ceremonies also often include words such as, 'to comfort, love, hold and cherish' but those qualities lack reciprocity in a miserable marriage where only one partner gives and the other takes.

The unspoken expectations women have when we marry often turn out to be largely fantasy. Kelly entered her marriage expecting a partnership of equals. Dan entered the marriage expecting to be the unquestioned Captain of his ship on which Kelly would be the lower-ranked first mate.

Further, it never remotely occurred to him that with the arrival of children in the marriage, Kelly would of necessity turn a large percentage of her attention to them. The arrival of children is frequently the turning point in a marriage because the wife's focus is no longer exclusively on her husband. Whether a shift in direction, or an elongated death blow, children change the dynamic between a wife and her husband, usually dramatically.

It is not an exaggeration to state that women marry for what they can get and give. Men usually marry for what they can get. Kelly now spends every waking moment trying to juggle all of her responsibilities and at the same time please Dan. She's trying to resurrect her marriage dreams and vows and has stopped being a separate and well-defined individual. She is enmeshed in trying to get inside Dan's head, while he lives rent-free inside her head.

Giving up and letting go of the expectation that Dan will one day recognize how his behavior hurts her and their marriage, or that he even cares (more about this issue in Chapter 16) and releasing the hope that he will eventually want to change, needs to be grieved as the serious loss it is. Countless times Kelly grasps onto the good times, thinking they might be the longed-for turning point. That 'this time' Dan will decide to be nice all the time, that he will stop the verbal violence—verbal and emotional abuse are violence—that he will want to have a peaceful life, a mutually beneficial life as she envisions marriage. Surely, he can see how much better their life is when he isn't angry? But the good times are always short-lived.

Kelly feels as though a lifeline is being removed from her because she has been clinging to the hope that Dan will eventually change, that somehow, she'll figure out how to solve their relationship problems. Her hope keeps her going. Steeped in the tradition that patiently waiting and doing good is her duty regardless of the cost to herself, Kelly emotionally drowns under the burdens she's allowed to be placed on her. Life is one disappointment after another.

Kelly is symptomatic of an enormous problem in our culture today that is largely ignored—women like Kelly are exhausted. We women are trained to believe we can do anything, which is true, but we have deduced that we should do everything. And there is a secret hidden in this belief. Men have silently said, "Yes! Let her do it!" I recall my husband said, "I love the women's movement! I don't have to do everything!" I had no idea at the time how prophetic his words were. Women are expected to unquestioningly fulfill both the male and female roles in a family and that is a lot of hard work for one person, man or woman.

Now, Kelly is facing me, feeling hopeless and trapped in her misery. Tears stream down her face when she looks at me and asks, "What am I going to do?"

Changing our Response Behaviors

Quietly and slowly, so that she can ponder my words, I say to Kelly, "You can make changes that will give you a better life if you learn to stop thinking that everything depends on Dan changing his behavior.

"You have a choice. Continue to devote yourself to trying to keep Dan from becoming angry, and trying to convince him to be more loving towards you, or you can do the hard work to learn new ways to react and respond to Dan—to react and respond as a dignified, self-respecting, self-valuing woman, not his door mat or convenient punching bag.

You are Not the Reason for His Behavior

"This does not in any way mean that you are the reason for Dan's manipulations and hateful behavior. And changing your reaction and response behaviors does not mean that you capitulate to him, give in to his expectations or demands or ignore his destructive behavior.

"But when you fully accept that you cannot change Dan, then you can focus on learning how to become a valuable woman who does not automatically react to him or respond to him in anything less than a well-thought-out manner. You can learn to make decisions and choices about you, not decisions and choices based on what a boiled egg wants. But, like any new skill, it requires time and practice and a commitment to learn new ways of looking at your life and learning new habits and new behaviors."

"But why should I change? I'm not the one who won't communicate, who won't earn a living for my family, who is always angry. Why doesn't Dan have to change? All I do is try and make things OK for him. Isn't it time for him to take some responsibility and change how he treats me and the kids?"

I look at Kelly and attempt to answer this question that every woman asks me: Why should she, the woman who is suffering, who is worn out from trying to please a man who hurts her, take on the task of changing her way of living? She is the innocent party to abuse so why does it fall to her to take on more?

I search for the words that will help Kelly understand, and learn to accept, that she alone can change her circumstance. Dan isn't going to meet her half-way. Dan isn't going to change his behavior, ever. Only she can save herself from the destruction that is inevitably the result of living with an emotional, psychological, and possibly eventually physical, abuser.

"Yes, of course, he has responsibilities. And yes, he should treat you with respect and kindness, just as you should treat him with respect and kindness. But he doesn't want to. He sees absolutely nothing wrong with his behavior so why would he want to change it? And there is nothing you can say or do to alter that reality."

This truth is so painful that we never want to believe it. Acceptance of a hurtful truth requires time and effort.

But if I Keep Trying

Kelly lives a form of logic that simply doesn't work. She subconsciously thinks she earns points with Dan by always being supportive of him, by always picking up the loose ends of their lives. That if she works hard, if she makes the effort, if she covers all the bases, if she tries to keep Dan happy then maybe he will wake up one day and appreciate her and want to emulate her efforts, even reward her with affection, tenderness and caring.

Sadly, this is not only a false assumption or hope, it is foolish and fruitless. Dan has what might be termed a 'good gig.' He has a wife whom he can depend on and it doesn't cost him much beyond the annoying occasional argument when Kelly 'loses it' or the few dollars he spends once in a while for flowers when he happens to stop at the grocery store.

Convincing Kelly, or any of us women, to move beyond our version of logic is very difficult. We are stuck on the idea that surely our man wants us to be happy, or has a concern that we are happy, or wants marriage to be like syrupy media portrayals, and so we avoid facing the realities in our miserable marriage because we believe we can convince him to stop hurting us. We deeply believe, we assume, that 'of course' he wants the marriage to be a fifty-fifty proposition where two people work together towards mutually agreed-upon goals.

The valuable information we fail to recognize is, men who yell, have hair-trigger tempers, throw fits without warning, are silent immovable objects, and more, consider their behavior to be completely logical and perfectly normal. Their version of logic is simple: 'If you are not doing what I want, if you are not agreeing with me, and if you dare to challenge me in any way, then I am justified in behaving the way I want. And because you cross me, I *have* to behave this way.' In almost every case, these men grew up with yelling, hitting, silent, unemotional men or women (fathers, mothers, caregivers) and there is nothing that will change this ingrained and learned pattern. Lack of conscience is a major factor too, as detailed in Chapter 21.

Making Changes or Staying the Same

Kelly is tired and worn down and I am suggesting that she take on a commitment to make changes in herself, while she is convinced that she already knows what is wrong in her marriage and it's Dan. And of course, she's right. Dan mistreats her and isn't doing his part. But perpetually focusing on trying to change Dan is like a needle stuck on an old-fashioned vinyl record. It isn't going anywhere and it certainly isn't making beautiful music.

I once again gently remind Kelly that she cannot convince Dan to change his behavior. Her complete acceptance of this fact will take time, but once she arrives at total acceptance, she will find some peace—and yes, sadness. Ultimately, her acceptance will strengthen her resolve to transform her life.

And Kelly can transform her life. She can learn new response behaviors and new thoughts about how she values herself, and ultimately how a dignified, self-respecting woman should react and respond to Dan.

"Think about the structure of your life," I say to her. "How much of your time is spent dealing with Dan, anticipating his moods, doing what you think he wants, arguing with him, altering your schedule, [remember Kelly's haircut appointment that she cancelled?] planning ahead to avoid unexpected problems that will set him off?"

Kelly stares at the floor as she thinks about what I've said. "A lot," she answers, then, "actually, all the time except when I'm at work. I'm thinking about what he wants, or will do next or defending myself about something. Sometimes I don't even know what he's angry about, but I have to cope with it."

"Every action you take, even the thoughts you think, are reactions to Dan's behavior. If you want your life to change then you must alter your reactions to Dan. And to accomplish that you first must become a woman who has self-respect."

"You mean I'm supposed to learn to not react to him at all, to just go along with him? To learn to put up with whatever he does or says?"

"No. Quite the contrary. You can learn new behaviors, the behaviors of a self-respecting, self-possessed woman, a woman who knows how to react and respond so that she is not controlled, devoured, destroyed—no longer a puppet with a puppet-master. These new behaviors are very different from how you currently react to Dan.

"If your goal is to transform your life then you must change how you are living the life you are in. Only you can decide if you wish to continue to live the way you are, or if you want to learn how to alter your situation. Fundamentally, to transform means to learn to respect and value yourself, to learn to view Dan and your marriage more clearly and accurately, and to learn new ways to react and respond to Dan.

"Learning to respect yourself comes first. It is the most important goal to achieve.

He Expects Your Predictable Reactions

"Here is the secret to the dynamic between you and Dan: He expects you to react and respond to him in the same way you always have. In fact, he depends on you to react to his crazy-making behavior in the way

70

that you do. He knows what buttons to push, how to upset you, and he likes the ability and control he has to cause you to predictably react.

"If you learn new response behaviors, new ways to react to Dan, that dynamic will change. This is not to say that he will suddenly see the light and change his behavior—that is not going to happen. You can learn new ways to react to Dan whether in person or via phone, texts or emails. When you change your reaction behavior you will discover strengths in yourself that you currently don't know you have."

The Reality of Letting Go

Kelly's dilemma is a very difficult one. How can she fully grasp that she has been subconsciously shaping her life around a hope and expectation that simply isn't going to happen?

I wish I had a dollar for every time I've read or heard someone say, "Let it go. Just let it go." I always want to respond, "OK, let go of your foot. Or your arm. Just let them go." Letting go of something as close to your heart, as attached to you as your foot or your arm, such as your entire life built around a marriage, is not something that you just drop with a shrug of your shoulders and a let-go attitude. Various 'letting-go rituals,' such as sorrows written on paper and tossed into a fire, petals torn from a flower and sent to drift out to sea, rocks tossed, and items buried, are symbolic acts that can be helpful but the letting-go continues after the paper, petals, and rocks have fallen from our hands. It's a slow process.

Alternate terms are, 'giving up, surrendering, and releasing.' Giving up or surrendering intrinsically means you've tried, given it your best effort, done everything you can think of to do and then you give up on the hoped-for outcome. You surrender it. We 'give up' something every day, so giving up is more a part of our lives than we realize. We give up the desire to reach home at the hour we planned because traffic is snarled and there isn't anything we can do about it; we give up trying to convince a friend to stop drinking; we give up trying to fit into jeans we wore when we were sixteen; we give up hoping the barking dog three doors down will be quiet. We 'give up' continually, so why do we hopelessly cling to some people?

How long should you love someone until you give up? Love can

71

change form. It can change from reaching out, straining, trying, hoping, to finally just sitting with it as a quiet, perhaps rather sad, 'knowing' that you love while letting the other person go on in the path they have chosen. But you no longer allow their choices to damage or destroy you.

And facing the idea that you may need to change yourself, giving up the idea that you are without faults, is very difficult. How do we release deeply embedded patterns, beliefs and behaviors? Releasing, much like giving up, means we stop holding on and release the grip we have on a person or an idea, or a false hope.

Releasing has a gentle sound; we figuratively slowly open our hands, unfold our fingers and release to the wind that to which we were clinging. Sometimes life forces us to release something, such as the physical capacity to undertake a task or compete in a sport because our body ages. Releasing our hold on an imagined relationship can be similar. We can mature beyond the false hope of waiting.

7

The Decision to Transform Your Life

It takes as much energy to wish as it does to plan – Eleanor Roosevelt

Acceptance

Accepting the harsh reality that he will never change can crush us with despair. This is it? This is the way my life will be forever? The answer is yes, but we never want to accept that as final. It's a crushing disappointment and too painful. We cling to the good times, numb ourselves to the bad and hope for the best.

Some may say, "One should never completely give up hope! People are always redeemable. People can change!" Yes, perhaps, but only if they want to change and make a commitment to do the hard work involved (ask any veteran of Alcoholics Anonymous and they will confirm this). As discussed in Chapters 12 and 16, this book deals with the reality that the men in miserable marriages are committed to *not* changing their behavior.

Most important, studies show that repeat batterers are *psychologically incapable* of *ever* changing their behavior. If he hits you or your children, get out and don't go back!

I Refuse to Really Believe It

Confusion, uncertainty and lack of self-confidence pervade our thinking. We are fragile and vulnerable because we have the capacity to be loving and we refuse to believe that he doesn't. We think maybe it's buried deep inside of him if we can only draw it out. We never stop mentally and emotionally dancing the same dance. We make unwise decisions until we finally turn our attention on ourselves and reclaim our value, our humanity, and allow ourselves to believe that our lives are valuable because of who we are, not because of to whom we are married.

He can berate us for years, stomp our self-respect into the ground, parade us as a trophy, isolate us from everyone but him, criticize everything we do, not speak to us for days or weeks, shout at us about everything, flaunt his adultery and possibly leave without warning to marry someone else, and still we emotionally and mentally don't want to detach. We have a mysterious attraction to this person who hurts us. And even if he leaves us, we may allow him to be a poisonous factor in our lives forever, whether via the connection we have through children, property, or just our history, we often cannot bring ourselves to face reality and emotionally sever the tie. Even if we go our separate ways, we delude ourselves into thinking the occasional text, email, phone call or family gathering doesn't matter, that it isn't really being tied to him.

Denial and hope keep us tied to relationships. Enough good times happen, or we deny the bad and focus solely on the good things we have. We hope that eventually things will be OK, that he'll be satisfied and calm down. That he'll want to have a life without fighting and maybe he'll open up and communicate. That he'll want to work together and not be so mean, cold, distant and entrenched behind his self-constructed barricade. We women are masters of spinning the endless ways we hope.

We assume we score points for hard work, patience and fortitude so that he will eventually appreciate us. We fail to recognize that our inner strengths of kindness and patience are judged to be weaknesses by bullies such as him. And if we're the hard-worker type, he'll look at us as willing fools for trying so hard to please him.

Living life from the ineffective perspective of false hope, we do the same things, say the same words, explain, argue, scream, and think the way we've always been thinking.

There are many stories of famous women who've overcome adversity and achieved great heights. But the bravest women in the world (millions of them) are those of us who get up day after day knowing we face a wall of anger from men we cannot please no matter how hard we try. Against the background of his destructive behavior we get out of bed, go to work, make sure the school backpacks are complete, pack lunches, fold the just-washed laundry and put a meal on the table when all we really feel like doing is crawling into bed and shutting out our lives. It is this level of determination and steadfastness against all odds that we can tap into for the

74

strength to transform our lives. We are the brave ones when we say, "Enough" to ourselves and look for answers and guidance, which is probably why you are reading this book.

Give yourself credit, a great amount of credit, for the strength of character you already have that keeps you going. The important point is, strength of character is still in you if you tap into it with your mind, heart, and a commitment to make changes in your life. But, as already stated earlier, you need a plan and some practical help, which is the subject of this book.

Looking at Ourselves

Introspection is very rare. A few people may occasionally take a look at themselves, grimace at what they see and quickly close the door on what would be a difficult, long, and harsh task—changing their beliefs, patterns of thinking and behavior.

Refusing to see what is in front of us is the heart of denial, while committing oneself to a lifelong practice of examining oneself is a very humbling experience. None of us wants to be humbled or humiliated more than we already are by our difficult marriage.

Making the commitment to look at ourselves is the first step in the long process of transformation. If we want our life to change then we need to take a thorough look at how we are living. Very few of us are brave enough to self-examine, to take a close look at ourselves.

Instead, we focus on how he should change, even though we intellectually know he isn't going to. We think his behavior is the key to our life happiness, but it isn't. The key is how we react to him; how we behave around him. We are *not* in any way the reason for his hateful behavior. But our behavior *is* the key for us to create a better life for ourselves, to save our sanity and find self-respect and dignity.

Most of us don't see any need for us to transform ourselves. We're pretty good as we are, we think. We're reasonable, patient, kind to a fault and put up with a lot more than we probably should. But life hurts. We need to look more closely, dig deeper and uncover the truth about

75

ourselves.

It's virtually impossible to raise ourselves above what we married into or were born into until we step back, look closely at our life and ask, "Is this what I'm willing to settle for?" In many cases the answer is yes, but this book is for those women who say, "No, I want to get beyond this." Whether the moving beyond entails one's marriage or an abusive birth family (I deal with how to move beyond an abusive birth family in the book, *Keep Walking and Don't Look Back©*).

But our lives *have* changed we say, changed to meet his needs, his wants, his demands. Why should we do more?

It seems to be an incredible injustice, to be told that the passport to a better life lies exclusively with us. Constantly we have to remind ourselves that yes, he does have a responsibility to change his behavior *but he won't* so we have only two choices: To live as we are or change how we are living in our marriage. It's a bitter and enraging reality to accept because he always seems to be let off the hook. He always seems to get a free pass. Yes, there is an enormous injustice involved but until we learn to completely accept that fact, we cannot grow beyond living as his pawn, his puppet, his go-to punching bag, his scapegoat.

Endlessly Waiting

Most of us live in a perpetual condition of waiting. Waiting for him to change. Waiting for the kids to grow up. Waiting for financial security. Waiting for 'things' to change. Or waiting for the final blow that will be the signal to us that we are through, that we are done with the torment. "If he ever...I'll..."

We wait for something outside ourselves to change, to give us the sign that we need to do something differently, that we need to take action. Waiting for permission from someone—waiting for someone to tell us, "You shouldn't put up with that." But hearing from someone else that we are in a destructive relationship rarely causes us to act. And the truth is, we don't really know exactly what or how we should change. No one seems to know or wants to tell us or won't tell us. We need help but help seems to be elusive, particularly when you are trapped and isolated.

Ironically, the person from whom we seem to be waiting for permission is him. Because our lives revolve around what he thinks and does and tells us to do, we endlessly wait for him to somehow understand and bless our desperate need for change. What could be a more quintessential entrapment? Years go by while we wait for the ultimate reason, the last straw, the blow we can no longer handle, before we take any steps to actually begin to transform our life, if we ever do.

And of course, we can wait and hope and the years go by and one day he announces that he has found someone new. He's found someone who wants him the way he is? Yes, because she's only seen his public persona. He isn't going to be different with her in private than he was with you. You've been waiting and hoping that he would make 'some changes' and now he has, but not the way you'd hoped and not with you in the picture. What life are you left with then? You've wasted years you will never get back.

8

Obstacles

Changing yourself is the loneliest task you will ever undertake.

Patterns

For those of us in miserable marriages we gradually learn, like a trained circus animal, to adapt to the demands of our husbands.

The patterns begin as small things. I remember an incident with my then future husband when he pointed out, with the seriousness of a physician diagnosing a fatal disease, a light switch I had left in the 'on' position. I'd transgressed because I failed to turn off a light, a breach of his rules. That seemingly insignificant event should have been a voice screaming in my head to, "Run!" But infatuation over-ruled. The light switch incident became the precursor that all things would be done his way. And I put up with the seemingly insignificant and subtle early-on demands because, "It's really a little thing. No big deal if it makes him happy…"

But when and if we can no longer completely ignore the effects of living in a miserable marriage, we may begin to ask ourselves, 'When will he do something that is the final straw? When will I tell him I can't take it anymore and actually mean it? When will I have had enough? When will something happen that causes me to actually do something about how I am living? How many times can I hit the bottom of depression? How many nights will I lay awake thinking about the last argument, the ongoing silent treatment, the financial problems, the isolation from family and friends, the effects on our children? When does it ever end?'

We think we will somehow know when he goes too far, when the ultimate bad thing happens and we will finally take action to protect ourselves. Unfortunately, we don't recognize how well we have been trained and conditioned to accept the misery. Like the proverbial frog cooked in a pot of water because the heat is gradually turned up, we adapt until there isn't much left of the person we once were, while we wait until the right time, the worst event, the recognition that we've reached our limit.

One day my husband put his face close to mine and without emotion quietly announced that he was going to kill me. He had never laid a hand on me but I knew he meant what he said. Because of his professional training I also knew he could kill me in a way that everyone would assume I suffered a heart attack.

Believe me, when someone says they are going to kill you, you can tell if they mean it or not. It is a chilling experience. My brain froze in an out-of-body-like experience. We lived in a big house in a prestigious neighborhood and were the 'nice' people. This couldn't be happening. This surreal, beyond belief experience didn't happen to people like us. Surely, he didn't mean it?

Yes, he did.

I called my therapist and told her what had happened and then I took my daughter to a hotel for the night. I felt like a walking corpse, frozen and without feeling. I later learned that my therapist called my husband and initiated a conversation with him by asking, "How are you doing?" He said, "Fine." She told him that she knew what happened. It didn't faze him one bit.

And I went back.

I did follow advice to notify the local police and they said they would make a note so that if I called them in the future, they would prioritize getting to our house quickly. I guess that meant that if I called them soon enough, they might get there before my body grew cold.

How can any woman become so adapted, so trained, so brainwashed that she would return to a man who meant what he said when he threatened to kill her?

The answer is, because we simply cannot believe that the person we married, who once treated us well, who even now may tell us he loves us, could turn into someone who makes life so impossible, even life-threatening.

How can a woman become so addicted to misery and steeped in denial that even a serious threat to her life and possibly the life of her child, is still not enough to make her change the dynamic or get out?

79

We just cannot believe it and we don't want anyone to know because it is so shameful and embarrassing.

What Could He Do That Would Cause Me To...?

One day after a typically miserable quarrel, I asked myself, "What could he do to me that would be the final straw? What could he do to me that would go beyond what I could endure? What could he do to me that would hurt me more than anything else and would finally make me say, 'I've had enough?'"

The answer stunned me because, as clear as a voice, I realized, "To witness my daughter married and treated by her husband the way my husband treats me."

It would break my heart.

My daughter, still a child, would not marry for years but that didn't matter. The reality of what could happen to her, no, what *would* happen to her, hit me like a hammer to my heart. I failed my daughter now because of my inaction. I demonstrated marriage to my daughter. These were her parents behaving this way, her mother reacting to her father's abuse. So, isn't this the way marriage is? How would she know otherwise? How could her parents be wrong? This would be her model.

I love my daughter more than anything else on this earth. The thought of one day seeing her mistreated in a marriage and subjected to the abuse she regularly witnessed, horrified me. I faced the ugly truth that my response to the abuse, and my behavior, guaranteed that she would end up in a marriage like mine. I realized I needed to stop kidding myself. She wouldn't beat the odds. Her fate would be sealed because this would be normal to her.

I finally came out of the haze of hope in which I lived. I needed to do something about my situation now, not in some vague future when my husband might finally feel remorse about his destructiveness.

But My Situation Is Different...

We women can rationalize anything: I'm doing OK. Sure, it's hard sometimes but I'm doing OK. My family has never had a separation or divorce. My mother would have a fit if I told anyone. My religion doesn't allow it. My Pastor said I should pray for him. I think he'll eventually realize how the kids are pulling away. I think things will be better when he retires. I don't know anyone with a happy marriage. Every marriage has a few problems. I really like the anti-depressant I'm taking now. I just keep busy. One day he'll realize how much he's missed out. I don't want anybody to know. I tell the kids to just ignore it.

Mistreatment Takes A Toll

If we think mistreatment doesn't take a toll on us, we are fooling ourselves. I once saw a movie about the French Resistance in World War II that brilliantly portrayed the effects of abuse.

In the movie a Nazi officer interrogates and tortures a prisoner. He tells the prisoner that eventually he will lose control and reveal his secrets. The Nazi officer then shares this story with the prisoner: As a boy, he observed a beautiful, perfectly symmetrical spider web outside his window. He tore the web down and the spider promptly rewove the web, as beautiful and symmetrical as before. He tore it down again, and again the spider rewove the web. But the Nazi officer tells the prisoner, eventually the spider did not weave a perfectly symmetrical web. Eventually, as the game wore on, the spider's efforts resulted in a less than perfect web. Even a spider has a limit of endurance; the spider still wove, but its skill had diminished.

In a miserable marriage the spark goes out of our life and eventually we barely recognize ourselves. We often deteriorate physically and our emotions evaporate because we learn that when we stop feeling, when we numb ourselves, we stop hurting. Tragically, when we stop feeling we lose our humanity and our essence as a human being, as a woman.

How serious is this? A ten-year study released in 2017 by researchers from four British universities, concluded that the stress of having 'relatives' who are "critical, unreliable, and annoying," causes people to more likely develop dementia. There is a direct correlation between living for an extended period of time with a 'difficult relative' and the eventual development of dementia in the person who is the target of abuse. Is this a risk worth taking? Is it wise to perpetuate a relationship that can ultimately be damaging to our mental health?

Addicted to Mistreatment

In many ways our lives are similar to an addiction. We become so accustomed to being mistreated, and we have nothing better to compare our situation to, so we accept what happens to us even as it increases in frequency and severity. Over time, the mistreatment must increase in frequency, volume and seriousness to have an effect on us and cause us to 'lose it.'

Or, as already mentioned, we may become numb. Or we become like him (our tormentor) in many ways, sometimes in an 'I can give as good as you can dole out' contest of wills. We all become what we live with, even if it's a gradual metamorphosis. It's permanent unless we decide to transform our life.

A few years ago, while checking into a hotel, I noticed a crowd of older couples dressed in colorful square dancer outfits. The ladies wore frilly skirts and the men sported fancy shirts and string ties color-coordinated to match their wives' bright outfits. They were laughing and apparently having a good time.

About an hour later, I heard voices through the wall from the room next to mine. I couldn't understand the words but the tone unmistakably indicated a heated argument, a his-and-hers, back-and-forth exchange with each volley becoming firmer and louder. Then, very loud and very clear, the man angrily shouted, "Do you want me to start shouting?" Then silence. He shut her up and ended the argument with his threat.

A few minutes later I heard their door open and her skirt rustled as they went past my door. I knew what would happen next: They would descend to the lobby in stony silence, the elevator doors would open, and with smiles they would greet their friends. Someone might say, "Have you met John and Martha? They're a great couple. They've been married for forty years!"

Did you know that John has shut Martha up for forty years by threatening to shout at her? What a life.

82

What Happened to Our Sense of Right and Wrong?

We adapt, we adjust, we comply and we mold ourselves into his world, his way of thinking and his moral code.

When I finally did the hard work to look at myself, I was shocked to discover the extent to which I had acquired my husband's emotionless, cold-blooded attitude toward life. Living with him eroded my enthusiasm for life, my positive outlook and spontaneity, and I lost much of my sense of right and wrong. His personality was taking mine away from me and I didn't realize it as it happened.

When you absorb the traits of someone you also absorb much of their character. You start to lose sight of your moral code and replace it with his because going along to get along is how you keep the peace. That is why women will take the heinous step to abandon their children if that is what their man demands as the price to be with him. And some women will ignore horrors, such as abuse of their children by their men, because they've incorporated into themselves his twisted logic. It is these unseen, unrecognized and gradual changes in us that can only be uncovered and corrected through a commitment to the hard work to find our true selves, and restore and rebuild our lives.

Deciding to make changes in our life by transforming ourselves is the loneliest thing we will ever do. No one supports us because our reality of living with him isn't seen by anyone else. Comments are made to us or behind our back, and they hurt us. "He's such a great guy. If there are problems it must be her fault. I can't imagine what she wants when she already has such a good man. Honestly, some women are never satisfied. Maybe she's in early menopause. You can see that he loves her so what is her problem? Why on earth is she spending all that money meeting with a shrink? He's more patient with her than I would be. I wouldn't allow her to spend money sitting around with someone complaining about me."

But It's Not Bad All the Time...

And other factors affect us too. There is a mysterious magnetism about wanting a man who mistreats us to love us. Perhaps some primordial desire to prove to someone that we are worthy of their love, kindness, and respect and to experience the sudden awakening of their conscience, compassion and tenderness. It is romanticized in stories such as *Beauty and the Beast* and it speaks to this strange desire that keeps us trapped.

There can be a titillation and addictive quality about living in a drama-filled, argument-filled life. Similar to a drug high, the adrenaline spike from a fight may come to be the only reliable spark.

One woman I met was so enmeshed in the drama of her marriage, and so obsessed with her husband's behavior, she became literally incapable of talking about anything other than her husband. You could mention the weather and she would turn it into a discussion about the injustices in her life she attributed to her husband.

And more than a few women have the experience of being horribly mistreated, psychologically and even physically, and then succumbing to the sexual seduction their spouse cleverly employs. A riveting dramatization of the extraordinary power of sexual seduction by a man who is an abusive cold-blooded killer is portrayed in the series *Tin Star*. It is truly amazing how we women can adapt to even the most horrific circumstances and lose our sense of right and wrong if a man tells us he loves us and is sexually seductive. We crave being wanted and desired, even by a man who is brutal.

Perhaps there are similarities to Stockholm Syndrome wherein hostages develop an alliance with their captives. Being trapped in marriage with a mean-spirited, cunning or brutal man certainly has a hostage aspect to it. Apropos is the fact that an FBI database of identified victims of Stockholm Syndrome attribute a very high percentage of these cases to domestic violence.

But My Family, His Family...

Family patterns are impossible to change. By that I mean, you cannot ever change the family as an organization. Some members of the family may make changes, but this is rare. If you decide to transform yourself and grow into a self-possessed and strong woman, be aware that you will probably be categorized as the strange one, the misfit, the individual no one understands, or even tries to understand. Being the outcast is not an easy path to follow but is often the only road to survival.

There is a social aspect to not changing anything in the family, to not upsetting the long-established behavior patterns. If you walk out or file for divorce before working on yourself, before becoming a self-valuing strong woman, you will almost always be cast in the role of the bad guy, in addition to facing the revenge and legal maneuvering for which women are never prepared emotionally or financially. (In addition, there is a phenomenon involved which I call 'bar stool psychology.' This is explored in detail in Chapter 23.)

Without first taking steps to grow, you are not equipped to handle the backlash. This is the reason women repeatedly return to a destructive marriage or attach again to the same type of man. It's the problem mentioned earlier: You can't swim the English Channel if you haven't learned to swim. Countless women have naively initiated the divorce process thinking, 'He would never do that'—crush her financially, take her children away from her, or worse, only to discover the court process is not about the truth. It is about winning, sometimes by destroying one of the parties. In the family court process, he or she with the most expensive attorneys usually wins.

That is why it is vitally important to grow first, one might say, grow up and wise up, before blindly stumbling into the wasteland of divorce. When you initiate the divorce process you are handing your life over to attorneys and to a judge, not entering into a reasonable, fact-based, calm and rational process. The plethora of lies that permeate divorce proceedings is beyond the imagination of anyone who has not gone through the excruciating process, not to mention the interminable length of time and expense involved.

The rule to follow is to transform yourself into a very strong woman before you embark on the divorce path. However, the more important rule applies: If you or your children are beaten up, get out now!

Living our Assigned Role in the Family

Often within the extended family there is the perennial 'poor Mary,' the one who seems to always have problems with her spouse. It's an entertaining private reality TV show. If you change the role you are assigned in the family and you alter the dynamic, they will not understand why you want to end the drama. Hard to believe perhaps, but other people's misery makes their lives seem better.

And sometimes the matriarchal or patriarchal individuals in a family do not want anyone to make alterations in the family structure that are not pre-sanctioned by them. Family power structures are hideously difficult to overcome, and moving against them often means becoming the scapegoat or outcast. Tremendous self-growth is necessary to withstand the onslaught of opposition from extended family.

Trying to Uncover His Problem

The decision to make changes in ourselves can also be indefinitely postponed if we become caught up in the idea that if we thoroughly understand our husband's behavior our lives will automatically improve. The concept we attach ourselves to is: To learn everything about him so that we can better empathize and apply the adage that the love of a good woman can overcome anything and everything, a popular theme in novels and movies. It is important and helpful to learn everything you can about your husband's difficult personality, but you can waste years playing detective on your husband's character while you stagnate and deteriorate.

Closely related to this quest for knowledge is committing yourself to undertake the goal to repair your husband. It can become a life-long project, a continual work-in-progress that massages your ego and encourages your self-righteousness. Your life will not improve but fixing your husband gives you purpose, until one day he unexpectedly leaves you.

And because we women love to talk when we have discovered something new, we tend to want to generously share with him the marvelous insights into his shortcomings that our research reveals. We assume he will be as enthusiastic as we are to learn what is wrong with him

86

and how he can fix his problems. Unfortunately, at best he will be uninterested and at worst he will be offended that you dare to suggest that he has anything wrong with him. And he will retaliate by increasing the bad behavior you detest.

Learning about your husband's behavior is helpful and there are many excellent resources available. Like so much in life, knowledge is power. But knowledge about your husband's traits, character problems and harmful behaviors serves you best when it is accompanied by a strategy and plan for you to transform your life.

It Must be God's Will

Many women are genuinely terrified they will be condemned to hell for all eternity if they don't patiently and meekly accept whatever their husband says or does to them. They endure psychological and physical mistreatment that would be frowned upon by clergy if applied to prisoners of war.

Tremendous confusion permeates their lives. The dictate to be submissive replaces a divine God with their husband. And if God is reputed to be kind and compassionate, then why is their husband-god so lacking in empathy? The destruction of a woman's spirit at the hands of her husband-god seems incongruous, but these women dutifully subjugate their emotional needs.

The confusion involved can be paralyzing; a purported duty to allow ourselves to be emotionally, if not physically, killed. Does the edict of 'Thou shalt not murder' take second place to a woman's required subjugation to a man because of the marriage contract?

Extraordinary mental and emotional courage is required by these women if they undertake personal growth and strive for change.

It's my Fault, I only Have Myself to Blame

How did I get myself into this mess? Why did I attract him to me? Why did I choose him? There must be something I'm supposed to learn from this. Self-blame can go on forever and we often hear the popular belief that we drew this to ourselves, another variation on the theme we live with, that it's always our fault.

No, the truth is, *he* chose *us*. Difficult men are clever and cunning and they have a sixth sense about women who are empathic, kind, caring, gentle and vulnerable. There is a great deal of truth in the metaphor of a wolf in a sheep's disguise. They 'love' us because they think they can push us around, and they are generally correct in that assumption. Until we grow up, or grow out of, the role he assigned to us.

Our choice is to grow or not to grow regardless of how we became entangled with him. Just because we naively took him at his word when we fell in love with him, we are not required to forever unquestioningly accept punishment for our innocent mistake.

The Years Go By—Motivation and Purpose

Whatever the circumstances, waiting for the ultimate reason to finally decide to transform your life can waste a lot of years and lead to a lot of regrets. But making the decision to undertake major changes in your life is very serious and requires commitment to do the personal work involved. Sometimes it's easier to medicate for the depression and other physical problems that inevitably happen in a miserable marriage, rather than commit to something that we know at the outset is going to be difficult. Tremendous courage is required by those of us who are willing to self-examine. But confronting the problems in our life can bring us wisdom, give meaning to our lives and cause us to grow mentally and spiritually.

Key Motivators

What motivates some women to walk away the very first time he hits or is psychologically abusive, or disrespects or steals? Usually these women have a foundation, a knowing, a self-respect that those of us stuck in miserable marriages lack.

But setting aside the reasons for our confusion and indecisiveness, we still can summon courage because we are courageous every day of our life, if we can only allow ourselves to acknowledge that fact and honor it. Lying within us, perhaps deeply buried, is an element of self-preservation that can motivate us to make major changes in our life, even if the first one-

88

hundred efforts are baby steps.

Each of us have Key Motivators that direct our lives, whether we are aware of them or not. Identifying our Key Motivators can help us survive. Another word that applies is 'purpose.' Most of us who have been in a miserable marriage for a long time lose any sense of motivation or purpose that we once may have had. Resurrecting our Key Motivators and purpose(s) in life can help us to survive and grow.

The worst place to remain is in a state of denial and paralysis as I did for years. I met with a therapist and yet my life did not improve because I didn't make the crucial decision to examine and change myself. Not making the commitment to work on myself was merely treading water while drowning.

I discovered that when I finally became willing to examine my role in my marriage and admit that I didn't always see things for what they really were, I stopped wasting money and time endlessly whining to a therapist and I began the hard work involved in learning new ways to behave, and subsequently a new way to live my life. That hard work resulted in the Survive and Grow Steps detailed in this book.

Tragedies That Could Be Avoided

Each year three types of horrible tragedies take place. Men kill their wives and girlfriends, women in miserable relationships commit suicide, and women kill their husbands or boyfriends.

In all three of these tragic scenarios, children are left without parents. Perhaps some of these could be prevented if we women can find the courage to transform our lives at an earlier point in the drama.

Transformation Action Plan

1. Create a list of all the things you are waiting and hoping for. If additional items occur to you in the next few days, add them to your list. It can be helpful to also use the words, 'I hope, I wish, and, If only.' Next to each item on your list note how long you have been waiting.

2. Create a list of all the ways in which you are emotionally tied to your husband. Think deeply about this as you may be surprised to discover how many different ways this includes. Remember, emotions such as anger, hate, frustration, hopelessness, sadness, and more, are emotions, just as love is an emotion, and they all can tie us to someone.

3. What do you think is the greatest harm, the most hurtful thing, he could do to you, short of death? What is your breaking point?

4. Create a list of all the many ways in your life that you are strong and determined. Think deeply about this and work on this list over a few days. Give yourself credit for everything where you have applied inner strength in your life.

5. Create a list of what motivates you. For example, you may be motivated to maintain an immaculate house, to daily clear the inbox on your desk at work, or to make sure your children have everything they need. Look for the Key Motivators that influence your day-to-day life and write them down. Revisit this list and add to it as you discover more motivators that you implement in your life.

6. **Say this Affirmation**

   I do not need anyone's permission to save my life

   The prudent [one] sees danger and hides herself
   Proverbs 27:12 ESV

   Whether a good day or a bad day, say this affirmation frequently aloud or to yourself. Say it many times, emphasizing a different word each time – **I** do not need anyone's permission to save my life. I **do not** need anyone's permission to save my life. I do not **need** anyone's permission to save my life.

7. **Respect and Reward Yourself**
   Refer to the Rewards List you created in Chapter 2. If you have read this far, created your list of what you are waiting and hoping for, created a list of how you are emotionally tied to your husband, identified your breaking point, created a list of all the many ways in which you are strong and determined, identified your Key Motivators, and said the affirmation, respect and reward yourself.

8. **Insight to Ponder**
   Behavior is an indicator of character. Irrefutable and unchanging character form the core of the truth we face. Accepting the truth, and its finality, and deciding to what extent we will allow a person to damage our life is a deeply personal and difficult decision. It is further complicated because life with him is not impossible every minute of every day. The good days undermine our resolve, cloud our view of the truth, and keep us trapped.

9. **Watch for your personal milestone of growth**
   My Personal Milestone
   I will never forget how depressed, demoralized, and hopeless I felt when I realized I could no longer cope in my marriage. For years, I thought that if I worked harder, humored my husband and covered all the bases in an attempt to keep him calm, somehow life would eventually improve. I reached bottom on the day I knew I had to make changes. Embarrassed, ashamed, and expecting to be treated derisively, I called my family physician and asked for a recommendation of a counselor. To my surprise, the office manager kindly and caringly gave me some names and wished me good luck. I will forever remember the day

I made the decision to find answers and transform my life. It was truly frightening because I did not know what lay ahead.

10. Signs of Healing

Healing is a slow process and, just as with a broken limb, every day repair takes place until the limb becomes strong. Watch for your personal signs of healing.

A sign of Healing

Taking the first step no matter how small, and then the next one and the next one.

9

Survive and Grow Step Two

A marriage certificate is not a bill of sale.

Climbing Back Inside Your Body

It hurts to be a nothing. The pain of hoping that someone will care is excruciating and gnaws away at you, seeps into your bones, fills the cavities of your mind and thoughts, and ultimately numbs you to your humanness. To have no value, to be irrelevant and unseen and to have those closest to us be indifferent to us, is the greatest psychological and emotional anguish a human can experience. A homeless woman once said to me, "The worst part is that nobody sees you. They walk past as though you aren't there." A woman in a miserable marriage knows exactly how that feels.

In a miserable marriage our sense of ourselves as a separate, stand-alone individual with value is limited (if we consider ourselves to have any value at all). Because meeting his demands and needs is the way we keep the peace, our value is similar to ownership; we belong to him and we are his property.

We live on the surface, on high alert like a wild animal sniffing the air for danger, ready to defend ourselves from the onslaught of his rage, sarcasm, demands and all the craziness with which we cope. Or we dissolve into silent lethargy to accommodate the immovable, silent, cold and indifferent stone wall with which we live.

The Most Courageous Step We Will Ever Take

When we reach the extent of our endurance we are in tremendous pain – used up, emotionally drained, feeling as though we are fighting for our life (literally and figuratively). Numb, we can barely think straight but we know we have to do something. It is the bravest of the brave who take on the task of transforming their life deliberately, carefully, painstakingly and thoroughly, without the support of anyone. (Remember, if you or your children are slapped, punched, strangled, shoved, raped, or beaten, get to a shelter immediately!)

Self-Respect is Where Transformation Begins

There is no way to avoid stating that the first step in saving yourself is to acquire self-respect. Many women may say, "Not that same old phrase again!"

No, not the same old phrase, but rather, a redefinition of it. Finding self-respect when you are in a miserable marriage is a treasure hunt with specific clues. It can even be diagramed:

Living underneath his suffocating dominance = No self-respect
Distancing intellectually from dominance = Self-respect begins
Distancing emotionally from dominance = Self-respect grows
Becoming an individual with self-respect = Empowerment

When I read or hear the phrase 'self-esteem' I recoil and wonder if those who advocate improving one's self-esteem picture damaged, tortured women standing in front of a mirror saying, "I have self-esteem, I have self-esteem, I have self-esteem." That approach does not work.

What can transform us is to learn to no longer live merely on the surface, but to climb back inside our body and carefully, lovingly, and patiently develop a deep respect for our body, our mind, our heart and our soul. They are damaged and they need our attention, time, care, compassion and appreciation. Self-respect is a seed that grows into strength; the strength to find dignity, self-value, inner core values and principles on which we will stand.

Self-respect means that we find good things in and about ourselves. Not because we wait for someone to give us positive reinforcement, which doesn't happen in a miserable marriage, but because we work to change our perspective and learn to honor ourselves. Gradually, we recognize that we are valuable human beings, valuable women, not because someone decides to tell us we are but because we discover this truth for ourselves.

Step Two of the Survive and Grow Steps provides the way to climb

94

back inside your body and begin to transform your life. To develop self-respect and self-value (self-love, but more about that further on). And perhaps most important, it is from self-respect and the dignity it engenders, that we can transform our automatically-triggered reactions and responses to our tormentor, transforming our reactions into careful, dignified and appropriate responses, if we choose to respond at all.

Kelly Begins Her Wellness Journey with Step Two

When Kelly and I next meet following the session with the boiled egg, she tells me she feels defeated. But at the same time, she is determined to find a better way to live. She has accepted that she cannot convince Dan to change, "So, I guess it's up to me to make changes because I refuse to continue living with the way things are now."

Kelly Climbs Back Inside Her Body – Part 1

I instruct Kelly to sit up straight but comfortably with her feet on the floor, her hands resting palms up, and to close her eyes.

"There are two parts in this Step. The first is to breathe deeply, exhale slowly, and learn to allow your body to completely relax. Think of your breath as a soft, warm, gentle flow of water that starts at the top of your head and very slowly moves through you all the way to your feet. Think of how wonderful a warm shower feels after a day at the beach or working in your garden.

"Do not strain, inhale deeply but comfortably, exhale very slowly and as you exhale allow each part of your body to relax, from your head to your toes. Think about your body and allow your scalp, forehead, face, neck, shoulders, arms, torso, legs and feet to completely relax as your slow exhale flows down your body. With each inhale and exhale let all the tension in your body flow down, out and through your feet into the floor. Always be gentle with yourself. Your breath should be soft and gentle but comfortably deep.

Training Our Mind to Tell Our Body to Relax and Be Still

"Take your time," I tell Kelly, "and enjoy the feeling of allowing

95

your body to relax. If your mind wanders, gently bring it back and think about your breath as it flows through you. Feel your breath enter your lungs and leave your lungs. Allow yourself to enjoy feeling your breath and your body. Appreciate the breath of life that you are taking in and then letting move through you. Allow your mind to record how it feels to have a relaxed body from head to toe. Appreciate yourself, your body, and this precious time for yourself. Use this exercise to honor yourself."

As I guide Kelly through this simple relaxation technique, I observe her body begin to soften. I also see her struggle and fight against the idea that she should relax. After so many years of not taking care of herself her brain resists doing anything for herself. She has been treated harshly for most of her life so she wrestles with the absurd guilt which engenders, 'Is it OK to relax, to take time for myself and my needs?'

In a miserable marriage we live our lives as soldiers on a battlefield poised for action at any time from any direction. Tension is a way of life and it is damaging to us mentally and physically. Training our mind to tell our body to relax is vitally important in our wellness journey because the ever-present tension with which we've lived for so long constricts our ability to be open to new ideas, new insights and new ways of living.

It is important to note that you may be among those women who spend many hours striving to look beautiful. There is a significant difference between focusing on outward appearance and valuing yourself inwardly. Focusing exclusively on outward appearance can bring its own tension. As you already know, being beautiful externally does not automatically give you a peaceful life and a loving, respectful spouse.

Kelly Climbs Back Inside Her Body – Part 2

Sometimes Kelly strains with a too-deep inhale, but gradually she settles into a steady and comfortable breathing pattern. She is discovering how pleasant it is to not feel like a wound-too-tight spring and she likes the feeling. Her mind is beginning to record how her body and mind feel when they are not held in the grip of constant, relentless tension.

Women have a tendency to breathe shallowly. It is important to breathe deeply throughout the day. Individuals who practice yoga are most likely familiar with the deep breathing and strong exhales that are very cleansing for our bodies.

I allow Kelly plenty of time and when I observe that she is relaxed I quietly say to her, "With your next breath, as you exhale, think only about your feet and focus on them from inside your body. Observe and think about your feet from inside yourself. Structurally your feet are extraordinary. Wiggle your toes and feel the floor beneath your feet. Think about how incredible your feet are. They hold you up, they carry you where you want to go. Appreciate them. Remember, you are not looking at them from outside, you are inside your body feeling your feet."

With her next slow exhale, I instruct Kelly to say this affirmation: 'These are my feet which carry me through life.'

By centering her attention on her feet, Kelly takes the first step in training her mind to focus on specific areas of her body, Body Focus Points© sometimes called chakras (referred to in this book as B-F-P). This is the beginning of the process whereby Kelly will slowly and gradually learn to respect and appreciate herself as a separate, valuable individual who is no longer intrinsically bound to Dan.

The Importance of Learning to Focus

Our minds are filled with thoughts about the misery of our lives and they are like a washing machine sloshing around and around, thinking about him and all the other facets of our up-and-down, crazy-making life. The simple but incredibly important exercise of learning to deeply think about specific B-F-P, such as our feet, helps us develop an alternative – we don't have to think about him all the time. We don't have to let him live inside our heads. We can live inside our bodies and our minds and we can train our minds to not let him in.

This skill isn't developed in one sitting because it requires practice, but it is achievable. Keeping our goal in mind, a self-respecting, peaceful life for ourselves is very important. One step at a time, one step at a time, always one step at a time. Training our mind is the first step that can transform our life.

Body Focus Points (B-F-P) ©

As Kelly continues to breathe softly but deeply in relaxation, and with her eyes closed, I expand the exercise and guide her through the seven Body Focus Points (listed and detailed further below). She centers her mind to dwell on each of them from inside her body. Slowly her attention moves upward from her feet, pausing and breathing into each B-F-P and appreciating each one.

Similar to discovering pieces to a puzzle and fitting them together to create a picture, the seven Body Focus Points help us reconstruct the beauty that is our body and our mind. The beauty that is *us*.

I give Kelly an affirmation tailored to each B-F-P and Kelly says each affirmation aloud or silently to herself as she relaxes into and appreciates the respective Body Focus Points. Kelly takes as much time as she wants for each B-F-P. Several of them touch her deeply, emotionally, and a tear silently flows down her cheek.

This is the process by which Kelly climbs back inside her body and begins to evolve into who she is, a valuable woman who is not merely an appendage to her husband but a woman with inner strength, a loving heart, a good mind, the capacity to love and a finely tuned instinct. Truly a valuable human being, a valuable woman.

The Seven Body Focus Points (B-F-P)

Listed below are the seven Body Focus Points which Kelly learns to breathe into and dwell upon. They are vitally important to our wellness journey. Developing self-respect and inner strength, controlling our mind, clearly observing ourselves and everyone in our life, and developing a deep understanding and appreciation for ourselves is the goal. Most importantly, Step Two provides a foundation on which the wellness journey will expand.

Kelly slowly and steadily breathes into each of the B-F-P, guiding her thoughts to center on them, re-focusing her thoughts if they wander, and saying the applicable affirmations. She begins to appreciate the uniqueness and wonder that is her body and mind, her *self*.

1 – Our Feet

Source of Strength

Comprised of many delicate bones, our feet hold us up, carry us in the direction we wish to go and move us forward.

Meditative Thoughts

My feet enable me to walk the earth. They ground me and symbolize that I am of the earth. My connection to the earth transcends my marriage because I am not owned by another human. I am part of the earth that we strive to protect and treat with respect.

Affirmation

These are my feet which carry me through life and I am grounded in the magnificent earth

2 – The area of our Genitalia, the body parts that define female

Source of Comfort and Strength

They are complex and amazing and should be appreciated. Focusing on this area of her body will play a very significant role in Kelly's transformation during coming months. (Note: This is a deviation from the traditional 'root chakra' centered in the tail bone).

Meditative Thoughts

Woman, wife, mother, daughter, friend. We may discover how little we know about ourselves as we progress through our wellness journey. Repeating family patterns, trying to live up to the expectations of others, trying to be what others tell us about ourselves, asking why I married as I did and made decisions that I made, are part of the mystery of our femaleness which the wellness journey will explore.

Affirmation

I am a valuable and sometimes vulnerable woman

NOTE: Throughout this book the terms female and woman refer to individuals who identify as female. However, the fundamental issues involved also pertain to individuals who identify other than strictly female. The author trusts the wisdom of the reader to best determine what information is helpful to them.

3 – The area of our gut instinct, the Solar Plexus Chakra
Source of Insight and Strength
Our instinct is extraordinary and reliable if we learn to appreciate and listen to it.

Meditative Thoughts
A door into wisdom where discernment can be found. I can learn to trust and honor my instinct and be strong, and recognize when someone intends me harm. My instinct is my partner in my womanhood and my strength.

Affirmation
My instinct is wise and I listen to it

4 – The area of our heart, the Heart Chakra
Source of Comfort
The wonder of our heart. It pumps the blood that keeps us alive and we point to it as the center of love; loving our husband and children, loving our extended family, loving the earth, loving God, the Source, or other.

Meditative Thoughts
Our loving heart can be bruised and broken by the people in our life. Am I giving love where it will be valued, respected, used wisely and be beneficial? Or is it taken for granted? Perhaps not everyone can receive and benefit from the love I try to give. There is a difference between love and loving.

Affirmation
I love, I am loving, I am lovable

5 – The area of our throat, the Throat Chakra
Source of Power and Self-Discipline
The throat area influences the direction of our life because of what we say or don't say. A great deal more about this B-F-P is discussed in Chapter 11.

Meditative Thoughts: We know the results of being targeted by hurtful tongues. The throat chakra is the source of good or bad in our life and when we focus on it, explore it and control it, we can transform our life and sometimes the lives of those around us.

Affirmation
I think quietly before I speak; it may not need to be said

6 – Our forehead, between our eyes, the Third Eye Chakra
Source of Strength, Gratitude and Wisdom
Often considered to be the place where we can connect to the spiritual aspect of life. This is a place to express gratitude for the good things in our life (yes, even in a miserable marriage there are things to be grateful for; our children, our five senses, our ability to love). It is also the B-F-P where we can 'rest' in the presence of being a human connected to the infinite and know that our life is valuable and has a meaningful purpose.

Meditative Thoughts
We can attribute to this 'eye' a connection to the essence of our life. This B-F-P can be a point on which to think about our humanity, life force, God, source of life, whatever suits you best, to derive the deepest relaxation, resting in the knowledge that we are part of something much bigger than ourselves and we can be grateful for life itself.

Affirmation
Thank you for what I have. I am open to grace and inspiration

7 – Above the top of our head, the Crown Chakra
Source of Comfort
With the universe above us we are part of something much bigger than ourselves.

Meditative Thoughts
I ponder the universe above me and experience the wonder that I, a human being on this earth, am part of an unfathomable universe, filled with planets, stars, heavens and mysteries. I know it is beautiful, magnificent, and far beyond my life concerns and worries and I derive peace from the perspective it provides. My life is a speck in time. I end my meditation with renewed courage to go forward in my efforts for a good life.

Affirmation

I am a valuable part of the incredible universe

Note: The above list does not conform to the traditional seven chakra placements on the body. I include the feet as B-F-P 1 because those of us in a miserable marriage do not stand firmly on our own two feet; we are controlled by our husbands. Our feet allow us to move which is symbolically and literally the underlying need in our lives; to take steps, to move forward from our life as we have been living it.

Kelly Begins to Find Her 'Self'

When Kelly completes the Step Two exercise, I quietly say, "Now conclude your practice with this affirmation: I honor myself and I live safely inside my body."

Kelly looks softer and more 'present,' aware, alive and peaceful than when she arrived for her appointment. I tell her the task that lies ahead is to practice daily what she has learned, so that she will become accustomed to being relaxed, aware, and respectful of her body and mind. And to learn to live inside her body with a growing sense of her self-value and the ability to become observant rather than impulsively reacting to outside triggers.

I give Kelly an assignment:
She is to select a place and time where each day she can sit or lay quietly without being disturbed by anyone. (See further below for creative suggestions.) Daily, she is to repeat the above exercises, gently training her body to relax and her mind to focus from inside her body on each of the seven B-F-P; her feet, genitalia, solar plexus, heart, throat, point between her eyes, top of her head, and to say the respective affirmations. If her mind wanders, she is to gently pull it back. Regardless of how many times her mind may want to drift she is never to criticize herself when her mind wanders because it is a normal experience. The important thing is to gently bring her thoughts back to each B-F-P. She is to tell no one about her private time and her Step Two practice. The importance of secrecy is discussed below.

But I Don't Have Time

Practice of Step Two does not have to be time-consuming. Within a few weeks, Kelly will be able to complete her practice in less than thirty minutes, even as little as fifteen minutes in a pinch. But the pleasure of becoming adept at practicing Step Two usually leads to longer times rather than shorter because it feels so good to relax and linger on various Body Focus Points and honor them. The pure pleasure of enjoying the Step Two practice is nurturing and nourishing once it is learned and incorporated into daily life.

Gentleness and Compassion

As she learns these new skills, Kelly's mind will frequently wander and she will guide it back. This slow but steady learning process is the seed of compassion for herself. She will learn to not criticize herself when her mind wanders but rather experience it as an opportunity to treat herself with compassion and bring her thoughts back to the B-F-P on which she wishes to dwell. Introducing the concept of deep compassion for herself is very important because she has been living without compassion for a long time.

Many times, I will say the words, 'gentle' and 'gently' to Kelly because gentleness, tenderness and patience are qualities women in a miserable marriage rarely experience. The beauty of being treated with truly deep gentleness is absent from our lives so it is important for our minds to resurrect and instill this in us. We must learn to be gentle and tender toward ourselves.

Building the Foundation

Step Two is the foundation on which we can transform our life and it requires commitment, determination and patience. There will be false starts, struggle and doubt – can this really make a difference? Yes, but it cannot be done half-way. Commitment and determination are necessary.

Like any life-altering effort, it is not instantaneous. Step Two provides a method by which we can painstakingly rebuild our self-respect, because a healthy appreciation for ourselves is vital to surviving and growing in the destructive marriage we are in. Accomplishing this when no one else appreciates you requires courage. But you are already courageous in your day-to-day life and you can apply this courage to learning and practicing Step Two.

Kelly's Practice of Step Two

The alarm clock's insistent beeping wakes Kelly and she quickly reaches over and silences it. She opens her eyes in the dark bedroom and then quietly pushes back the covers, careful to not disturb Dan, and rolls to a seated position on the edge of the bed. She pokes around with her toes to find her fluffy slippers and slip her feet into them, while she reaches behind her and feels around on top of the blankets for her bathrobe. She shrugs into it and shuffles silently off to the bathroom where she pees and then rinses her face and pushes her hair back out of her eyes.

Switching on a flashlight she keeps in the bathroom Kelly silently goes down the carpeted hallway and into the living room. It's chilly in the house this morning so she turns up the temperature on the thermostat as she goes past it in the hall.

She seats herself in her favorite chair. Well, it's become her favorite chair in the past couple of months anyway, and this early morning hour has become her favorite time of day. Who would have ever thought that could happen? Certainly not Kelly.

As she settles herself into her chair, she tucks the afghan that is draped over the arm across her lap. She nests her hands, one inside the other palms up in her lap, closes her eyes and takes a deep breath, and then another.

She lets herself yawn as a third deep breath overtakes her. She smiles to herself as she remembers how, only a couple of months ago, her mind would whirl like a washing machine, thinking about a grocery list, the most recent argument with Dan, what the kids needed in their lunches, her meeting schedule at work and on and on.

Step Two was very difficult for Kelly to learn but she kept at it until one day it clicked. At first, she fidgeted, felt strange, even weird, and a bit silly, and thought, 'I'll never be able to do this!' and 'I really don't see what this has to do with anything.'

"I don't get the point. How can this help me cope with Dan? I need something now, not in six months! Are you sure this is worth the time and effort? I'm already tired, so how can adding one more task to my list help my life get better?"

To say that Kelly was less than enthusiastic, and more than a little skeptical, is an understatement.

"Not anymore," Kelly thinks, as she straightens her back, raises her chin a bit and settles into an upright but comfortable position.

"I'm past that. Well except for a few lapses, but that's OK."

She's pleasantly surprised at how quickly she has overcome the tendency for her mind to constantly wander when she practices Step Two each morning.

As these thoughts move through her mind, she gently brings them back to her breathing and begins to visualize her breath as a flow of water slowly washing over her, soft, warm and gentle. She breathes deeply and with each breath lets her body relax; first her face, neck, and shoulders, and then her arms, torso, legs and feet.

She relaxes into the comfort of her chair and enjoys the sensations of her body tucked under the afghan, the quiet in the room, the sense of having a world around her that is peaceful. Once in a while she hears the chirp of a bird outside the window, a sound she never before noticed when her morning routine consisted only in dragging herself out of bed and then running in circles trying to get everyone out the door on time.

Kelly takes a deep breath and exhaling slowly she lets her face relax. It feels so good to let her forehead soften, for her eyes to rest, for her cheeks to soften and for her jaw to just drop by its own weight. She never before realized that she clenched her teeth and jaw almost all the time. She takes another deep breath and exhales slowly and lets the breath flow down her body to her feet. With each exhale Kelly feels her entire body relax.

"Who would think that you can relax your scalp and face?"

Kelly inwardly laughs at herself because she had been the world's biggest sceptic when she was told that Survive and Grow Step Two involved learning to become human and that it all begins with feeling your body.

"But that is exactly what has happened. I had no idea that I had stopped even feeling myself as a human being. If I ever did."

Ah, her feet. Never before has she given them any thought unless they hurt in ill-fitting shoes. Now she visualizes her breath washing tension down and out of her body and releasing through her feet into the floor. She slightly wiggles her feet and toes and thinks for a brief moment about the sensation, the physical touching, of her feet against the floor's surface.

She takes another deep breath, slowly exhales the breath down her body and silently says, "Thank you" for her feet and honors them with her affirmation, "These are my feet that carry me through life."

Another deep breath, exhaled slowly down her body, and she rests her thoughts on B-F-P 2. She quietly pauses and thinks about this incredible part of her body and how, from birth, it has defined her female life.

She quietly thinks about how she is unique, how she is different and separate from Dan and, to her surprise, she finds herself honoring Dan's differences too, his maleness.

Quietly she says an affirmation, "I am a female human being, I am a woman, I am a unique individual."

Kelly softly repeats her deep breathing and next places her attention on her solar plexus, the area of her gut instinct. Kelly has experienced times in her life when she sensed something, or had a nagging doubt, or a nudge inside her was questioning a decision she was making, but she had usually ignored these hints because other people or circumstances were telling her what she should or could do.

More than a few times she had doubts about something Dan wanted to do and her instincts signaled danger, and yet she allowed Dan to over-rule. Now she breathes into this place within herself and affirms, "I trust my instinct." At this early stage of her self-awareness Kelly doesn't thoroughly accept the concept of trusting her instinct, but she affirms it anyway.

With her next exhale Kelly focusses her attention on her heart. This is her favorite area because she thinks about all the people she loves. She pictures each one and enjoys the warmth and depth of her feelings for each person—her children, Dan, her relatives and friends.

She pauses, breathes slowly out, and says an affirmation of thanksgiving: "Thank you for each of them and thank you for giving me the ability to love them. And thank you for the love they give to me."

Kelly's next deep breath and slow exhale focuses on her throat, her most challenging body part. She breathes into her throat space and reflects on how the words she speaks influence her life.

Kelly is very articulate and quick to respond verbally in any situation. When she argues with Dan and the situation becomes heated, words can quickly become nasty. She silently says her affirmation which is beginning to change her life: "I think quietly before I speak. It might not need to be said."

She repeats this affirmation because she wants to remember it throughout her work day. She has already experienced the results of silently referring to this affirmation—no longer does she leap into any discussion without asking herself if she really needs to say what she is thinking in that moment.

With her next breath Kelly slowly exhales and focusses her thoughts on the space between her eyes, above the bridge of her nose. Referred to as her third eye, Kelly breathes into it and thinks about the life she has been given. Not her life with Dan, but *her* life, her *life force*, the entity that makes her alive. Kelly believes in God, although she would be hard-pressed to describe exactly what that means to her. She uses this space to think about what it means to be alive. And she has developed an affirmation that she finds peaceful: "Thank you for my life. I am open to Your guidance." Lately, she's found she often offers up silent prayers for her family and herself when she focuses on her third-eye B-F-P.

With another deep breath, Kelly exhales slowly and thinks about an area just above her head. She pictures herself connected to the universe that exists above and beyond her. She is part of that enormity and she is important. She belongs on this earth as it moves through space and time. She silently whispers her affirmation that will become so important to her future: "I am a valuable human and I am part of the magnificent universe."

Kelly completes her morning practice by sitting quietly for a few minutes, just thinking about her breathing and her body and often dwelling on her third-eye B-F-P where she increasingly feels connect to a power beyond herself. Perhaps without realizing it, Kelly is learning to love herself.

10

The Goals of Survive and Grow Step Two

There is great beauty in building something new.

We Begin to Build

Step Two is equivalent to the first stage in building a new house. Bulldozers push dirt, concrete is poured and stark framework goes up. It isn't pretty and it doesn't look like the future finished home. But when the foundation work is completed things start to move along faster and you begin to see what the home will look like. As with constructing a new house, you must be patient with the transformation process and with yourself and remain committed to it.

The Goals of Step Two

All the Survive and Grow Steps collectively move us toward our long-range goal of a transformed life, a peaceful life built on the foundation of inner strength, self-respect and wisdom. Step Two is the step on which every other step depends. The goals are:

- To climb inside our body and look out with an ever-increasing self-respect and clear perspective, and to recognize and accept the realities of our marriage and life.

- To train our mind to relax our entire body because a relaxed body helps us to have a relaxed mind, which gives us clarity.

- To learn to recognize, honor and respect every aspect of ourselves, beginning with our body. As we walk, we can think about our feet and what they are doing for us. We can ponder our womanhood, our instinct, our heart and each B-F-P.

- To slow us down, to train us to stop reacting instantaneously and impulsively, so that we can learn to be discerning and careful in all we do and say, particularly when dealing with our difficult husband.

- To provide a replacement strategy, a method to stop thinking endlessly about him, his characteristics, his manipulation of us, the fights and the heartache.

- To give us the first step in distancing ourselves from his crazy-making behavior—we take the bold step of secrecy and develop inner strength.

- To give us the experience of creating an action plan, by and for ourselves, and carrying it out without our husband's knowledge or permission.

Courage and Determination

True courage and determination are necessary to begin practice of Step Two. It requires that we form an action plan for ourselves and carry it out without revealing it. Much harder than you might imagine because we have been trained to tell what we are doing in an effort to gain approval or permission, an endless game that constantly entraps us.

And we are unsure of ourselves. Can we really take the unfamiliar and bold step to do something exclusively for ourselves? Are we selfish for doing so? Do we really want to explore changing our life?

The decision to learn and practice Step Two indicates how committed a woman is to transforming her life. I once had a woman dazzle me with excuses for why she could not possibly do Step Two. She informed me that her large house did not have any place inside or out where she could be alone. I suggested a bathroom and she told me her husband always stood outside the room and talked to her through the closed door. I suggested that she leave for work a bit earlier and stop at a church to sit and practice Step Two. She stated emphatically that all the churches in her area kept their doors locked. I next suggested a bench in the park near her home, to which she responded that it wouldn't be safe, even though she lived in an upscale area and I knew the park had many joggers and dog walkers early in the morning. It was rather easy to discern that she relished the drama in her life and wouldn't know what to do with herself if she couldn't complain about how her husband treated her. This bright, talented woman eventually died much too young, killed by her food addiction with which she anesthetized herself and destroyed her body. Her denial became deadly.

Determination is the Most Important Attribute

It takes time to become reacquainted with ourselves, to learn to respect and honor ourselves, and to learn to function as an individual with emotions, thoughts and desires that are separate from our husband. We should be respected by everyone, first and foremost by us. But we have to learn to respect ourselves. Rebuilding your self-value while living in the derisive environment of a miserable marriage requires the same determination you utilize to get through every day. Only this time you can direct an all-consuming determination to finally have a better, peaceful life.

If you are reading this book you are perhaps feeling broken, literally and figuratively, and it's difficult for you to imagine where and how you will manage to do anything for yourself or that you can ever have good thoughts about yourself. But the depths of despair can call forth the determination to no longer live as you have been living, and you can go forward. I know this from personal experience.

The Importance of Secrecy in Step Two

Step Two requires that we not tell anyone about our new practice. *Anyone*. Including your best friend who might tell someone who might tell your husband.

For women in a miserable marriage, Step Two may be the first time they make a decision exclusively for themselves and carry it out. Only women in a miserable marriage appreciate the significance of this because the total control under which we live generally precludes us from believing that anything can be ours alone, or that we should do anything without his permission. We fail to recognize the pervasiveness of this dynamic. While many women might have some little secrets (small purchases for example) making the commitment to transform your life and carry out new behaviors is a significant endeavor. It needs to be kept completely private.

Our Downfall—We Still Want Him to Understand Us

Our automatic programmed desire to have approval, understanding or permission from our husbands can undermine our action plan. As mentioned in an earlier chapter, we want approval even from a man who is brutal. Step Two targets this automatic response by requiring that we not ask permission to begin our wellness journey, that we tell no one about it and hold this information in our heart as a first step in learning to nurture, respect, and eventually love ourselves.

We must not break this code of secrecy, a trap we have a history of falling into when he is in a good mood and we let down our guard. Frankly we may talk too much and share too much after good sex. And how many times have we impulsively fallen into the delusion 'If I share my deepest thoughts with him, he might recognize how good, kind and wonderful I am?' Many of us have experienced sharing a personal thought or emotion with our husbands, only to have it thrown back in our face at a later time. Don't fall into this trap.

NOTE: For those who may say, "You can't have a good marriage if you intentionally keep secrets from each other," I remind you that you are not in a good marriage or you wouldn't be reading this book. Interestingly, men are masters of secrecy. Thousands of men have bank accounts (and affairs) about which their wives know nothing.

As you proceed in the journey of the Survive and Grow Steps you will experience the excitement of acquiring new skills. Learning to not share, to protect your privacy and to transform privately, is very important.

Learning to keep a part of us as precious and private is a crucial aspect of climbing back inside our body and becoming a valuable human being. Women can be easily tricked into telling everything and then later very much regret doing so.

Further Caution About an Abuser's Sixth Sense

Men who are abusers, whether physical or emotional, frequently have an incredible sixth sense about the women in their lives. It's almost as though they can see inside your thoughts, so exercise extreme caution. One woman trapped in a physically abusive marriage carefully planned for several months how she would escape. Her abuser maintained a structured daily routine, but on the day of her planned escape she left the house after he went to work, walked a block, rounded a corner, and there he was, waiting for her and ready to pounce. He had sensed what she planned and he beat her severely. Don't take anything for granted. Remember, you are up against a champion and you are just beginning your training. Most importantly, remember the rule: If you or your children are beaten, get out! The first time you are hit, punched, shoved, or beaten, get out! And don't go back! You can transform your life *after* you have escaped severe injury or death at his hand.

If We Don't Control our Body and Mind, Everyone Around Us Will

Inner strength and self-respect begin from honoring our physical body and knowing that we live inside ourselves and are in control of our bodies and our minds. If we don't control them everyone else around us will. We already know how to automatically respond to the demands of others, to be controlled by others. Now it is time to take control of our thoughts about ourselves and to learn to honor ourselves.

It is important to note: What your body looks like is completely immaterial. It does not matter if you are thin or fat, tall or short, your body is an incredible machine and Step Two helps you learn to honor yourself.

Learning to relax our body and becoming deeply acquainted with our body is an important step forward. Daily practice of Step Two helps our minds remember what it feels like to be relaxed and aware of ourselves, our true selves – our humanity – and we can call upon this skill to navigate through everyday life whether at home or elsewhere. Practiced diligently, Step Two very quickly results in change.

Be Patient—Don't Expect too Much When You Begin

Getting started with any task is usually the biggest hurdle any of us face. However, once you prioritize time for yourself and consistently practice Step Two you will start to experience changes in how you view your life, and the everyday events you handle. But don't expect total transformation overnight. Even a small glimpse of the peace you will experience during your Step Two practice is a good start. Keep in mind that your experience of peace will grow deeper and more all-encompassing the more consistently you practice.

The Importance of Affirmations with B-F-P

Affirmations have enormous power to transform our thinking and our lives. Kelly has a difficult time saying, "I am a valuable woman," the last thing on earth she believes because no one in Kelly's life treats her as though she has value and she unconsciously accepts that verdict. Repeatedly saying the affirmation "I am a valuable woman" even though she doesn't really believe it, will begin to plant the belief that she is valuable. Affirmations for each of the Body Focus Points are strong, positive statements that help us honor our body.

Resourcefulness and Consistency

Kelly chose to practice Step Two in the early morning before anyone else in the household awakens. Dan is a heavy sleeper so Kelly is reasonably certain she will not be quizzed about why she gets up early.

For women who are not as fortunate as Kelly, more resourcefulness will need to be applied to carve out private time to practice Step Two. While it is best to practice Step Two at the beginning of the day, any time will be effective provided it is done consistently every day and you will not be interrupted.

It is also important to have a space that is yours even if, like Kelly, it is simply a chair in your living room. However, for women who are in severe situations of isolation and control, and any deviation in routine will be questioned or prohibited, one possible way to create private time and space for Step Two is to do it in bed by laying very still and breathing down through your body. This, of course, increases the possibility that you may inadvertently fall asleep. But a woman who is truly committed to her practice can overcome this tendency.

If you can't practice Step Two at home, then consider alternatives. Remember, you are a strong, resourceful woman or you wouldn't have come this far. Honor this truth and create a space for yourself. I know one clever woman who faithfully practices Step Two (and all of the Steps) in the locker room at the gym where she works out. There is some humor in knowing that her controlling husband cannot invade her space by barging into the women's locker room at a public gym.

When you become adept at Step Two you will be able to do your practice in any circumstance—riding a bus, in an airplane, sitting at the beach, waiting in your car for your kids, even in a business meeting. While you may not close your eyes in all circumstances, the breathing and concentration exercises can be used anytime, anywhere.

Incidentals

As Kelly commits herself to practice Step Two, I suggest that she wear a sleep mask at night. Wearing a sleep mask is helpful because it gives you a sense of being self-contained, shutting out the world, creating your space and helps you focus on being inside your body. Ear plugs can also help you focus on being inside your body. Do not use ear plugs if you have small children you need to hear. But if that is not a factor, ear plugs are an excellent way to help you feel safe and secure inside your body when you practice Step Two and when you go to sleep for at night.

Transformation Action Plan

1. Carefully select a place and time where you can be alone and undisturbed. Be sure you can use this space every day and that you won't be interrupted. Choose a nice space and honor yourself with the location you choose. Place a small plant or vase of flowers nearby or select a seat in nature such as your backyard or nearby park.

2. Begin Step Two by simply learning to breathe deeply and softly, thinking about your breath, and guiding your body to relax. Relaxing your body from head to toe is the most important thing to do first when learning to practice Step Two.

3. Start simply. Perhaps for the first few days all you will do is breathe deeply and comfortably and learn to relax your body. If your mind wanders, gently guide it back to your breath. It may require some time for you to become adept at keeping your mind under control. Don't stop, you can do it, it just requires consistent, gentle practice. Love yourself with your breath and enjoy feeling the life force of your breath. This is your time for yourself. And most important, do not criticize yourself. Even experienced monks started with a restless mind.

4. Gradually add your attention to each of the Body Focus Points described above and say the affirmation for each. Do only one at a sitting if that is easiest for you. Never rush. Give yourself time. Consistent and gentle effort is the key to success. Do the remainder of the Body Focus Points as you progress during your practice. If you find this difficult, just concentrate on gently guiding your mind to think about your breath, and when you are ready, begin to add the B-F-P.

5. Memorize the affirmations and say them, over and over, to yourself or aloud. Do this throughout your day. Affirmations are powerful.

6. Gradually you may find that you can recall your practice at any time, even in the midst of a busy day, by stopping briefly and reminding yourself of how you feel when you are relaxed, centered, and quietly inside yourself. You may notice your impulsive reactions and responses begin to reduce.

7. Gently training your mind to replace thoughts of him with thoughts about your breath and your affirmations is a major accomplishment. Don't hurry the process. If you are consistent, you will become very comfortable with guiding your mind and

116

then you can begin to focus on your B-F-P and affirmations instead
of him.

8. **Say this Affirmation**

   I honor myself and I live safely inside my body

   For you formed my inward parts;
   you knitted me together in my mother's womb.
   Psalm 139:13 ESV

   Whether a good day or a bad day, say this affirmation frequently
   aloud or to yourself. Say it many times, emphasizing a different
   word each time – **I** honor myself and I live safely inside my body. I
   honor myself and I live safely inside my body. I honor **myself** and I
   live safely inside my body. I honor myself and I **live** safely inside
   my body.

9. **Respect and Reward Yourself**

   Refer to the Rewards List you created in Chapter 2. If you have read
   this far, selected a location for your private space, determined a
   time when you can practice Step Two and are learning the
   breathing and relaxation practice, the Body Focus Points, and said
   the affirmations for each, respect and reward yourself.

10. **Insight to ponder**

    Becoming a stand-alone individual is not a severing of the marriage
    bond. It is a recognition that two separate and unique individuals
    are in that bond. When you become an individual with self-respect
    and self-value, you may also develop a respect for your partner's
    uniqueness and his behavior choices. It is respect for your
    individual uniqueness that ultimately leads to clear decisions
    regarding which of his behaviors are, and are not, acceptable.

11. **Watch for your personal milestone of growth**
    My Personal Milestone

    After I learned and regularly practiced Step Two, I experienced the
    effect it had on my life in a particularly clear way. In a conflict with
    my husband I breathed deeply, centered myself inside my body,

and looking outward I realized he was baiting me in the hope that I would 'lose it.' I looked at him as though I saw him through a window, and I did not engage. I also recognized another dynamic in that exchange–very often our arguments began, or centered around, me asking him for something: Asking for help, attempting to find a solution to a problem, seeking his cooperation or understanding. Looking out from inside myself, I realized that he felt little, if any, emotional attachment to me. I observed him from a distance and formed my Rule Number Two: Never ask him for anything.

Rule Number Two: Never ask him for anything.
NOTE: Before you say, "But this is terrible. This is nonsense. Of course, we should ask our husband for what we want or need," let me remind you that we are dealing with reality not how things should be. We already know what we can and cannot expect to receive from difficult men so wishing for him to be responsive to us is the perpetuation of an unchanged life.

12. **Mantra to Remember**
    I look out at him and see him clearly and I choose to not engage.

13. **Signs of Healing**
    Healing is a slow process and, just as with a broken limb, every day repair takes place until the limb becomes strong.
    A sign of Healing
    One day when he is in a tirade you look at him from inside yourself and suddenly see him as a complete stranger, and realize you are becoming a separate, detached, valuable human being.

11

The Powerful Impact of Step Two

It is our mind that chains us or sets us free – Dilgo Khyentse Rinpoche

Distancing, The Great Pause, Replacement Thoughts, and More

Chapter 11 Part A – Distancing

The vital step in surviving life in a miserable marriage is to distance ourselves intellectually and emotionally from our husband and the craziness with which we live. This is an ultimate surrender and 'giving up,' the acceptance that we can only affect change in ourselves and we must release beliefs, patterns and fantasies that are pointless, such as waiting for him to change. Distancing is a necessary but difficult task to accomplish and takes time because:

- Our life is built around endlessly trying to connect with him
- We are in proximity and under his control in numerous ways
- We are emotionally tied to him; he's constantly in our thoughts

We can intellectually distance by facing reality (Step One in Chapters 5 and 6) but a chasm exists between acknowledging the ugly realities of him and our marriage, and deeply, emotionally accepting those realities and taking steps to rescue ourselves.

Step Two is the Beginning of Distancing

Climbing back inside our body enables us to draw back, detach, look at our husband and marriage from a distance, from inside ourselves, and assess our life. It is an experience that only those of us in a miserable marriage can appreciate—to no longer be anchored to him like a boat tied to a dock. We can drift away and look back and see him more clearly. Centering ourselves in our humanity, we can learn to distance ourselves intellectually and emotionally and become a separate individual with self-respect and self-value.

It's similar to viewing a painting by the artist Georges Seurat. When you look from only a few inches away, you see dots. But when you stand back the dots blend together and become a picture. In a miserable marriage you are so enmeshed in all the craziness that you don't see the whole picture, how the dots interconnect. Step Two is the beginning of stepping back, of disconnecting yourself from the emotional entanglement and taking a look at how you fit into the picture by looking out from inside yourself.

Distancing does not mean you withdraw into yourself and become numb to your surroundings (sadly, you may have already done that). Rather, it is a process of becoming aware and respectful of yourself as a human being and looking out on your surroundings with heightened awareness from a perspective of self-respect, self-security, self-knowledge and increased instinctual wisdom. It is powerful but it does not happen overnight.

Regular practice of Step Two is necessary in order to move forward because we do not learn anything from only one experience. It is the regular, repeated experience that truly changes our perspective and behavior patterns.

Intellectual and Emotional Distancing

Our life in a miserable marriage is similar to thrusting our arm into a bonfire. Our natural response is to jerk our arm out of the fire and try to end the pain, repair the damage and let our arm heal. But in a miserable marriage we repeatedly thrust our damaged arm back into the fire.

When we acknowledge that repeatedly thrusting our arm into a fire makes no sense, we step back from the fire; this is intellectual distancing.

When we delve deeper and learn why we repeatedly thrust our arm into the bonfire, we do more than just step back from the fire, we don't even go near it; this is emotional distancing.

Yes, a 'bonfire' (i.e. our husband) can be warm, even charming, but for us it is deadly dangerous.

Emotional distancing/detachment does not mean we are to become unkind or bitter. It means we remove emotional impulsive reaction from

120

our decision-making and no longer allow emotion to cloud our thinking, blind us to reality or select our behavior. Emotional distancing/detachment is the key to extricating ourselves from the effects, the triggers, of our husband's behavior.

Looking Outward, Assessing and Choosing

Healing from the damage and pain of mistreatment requires stepping back from it. Untangling emotionally, disconnecting from automatic surface reactions and viewing your life clearly does not mean you must become cold and hard-hearted. It does not mean that you are to no longer love or become unloving.

Rather, it is paradoxical that by distancing ourselves from the drama we can actually learn to love more thoughtfully and carefully and not expend our love where it will not be appreciated.

We may even look out at our husband with more compassion, recognizing his flaws but also seeing his humanness and life struggles while we simultaneously learn to reject his mistreatment of us. As we look at him from a distance, we discover that we are not responsible for his behavior and he will treat any woman the way he mistreats us because that's who and what he is.

When we stand back and observe our husband with clarity, we can develop a self-protective wariness of his choices and then make our own choice to engage or not to engage.

Step Two helps us recognize that we have value and the right to reject behaviors that harm us. We also learn to recognize harmful behaviors for what they are—seriously destructive.

Stepping Back to View Our World Clearly

Until we stop living on the surface and reacting to whatever comes along, we cannot view ourselves, our husband and our marriage clearly, and we do not make wise decisions. It is not possible to see all the dynamics in a miserable marriage if we are so caught up in it that we never step back and take a good look at it.

Distancing enables us to observe our emotional reactions and responses to him and his behavior, observe his actions and words in a detached way and carefully choose our response, if we respond at all. We can learn to not be automatically triggered by him but to react as independent, valuable women who possess core values that are our own, not a pattern of behavior dictated by him. Step Two gives us a foundation and Steps Three and Four provide us with additional changes we can make to move forward.

Loneliness

Distancing may add to our loneliness. But we are already familiar with loneliness because indifference from our husband is a lonely life. We may share his bed, his children, launder his underwear, tolerate his flatulence, watch endless sports games with him and know that whenever his needs conflict with ours he will choose his needs first, and not compromise. To his way of thinking, compromise is defeat.

Indifference from someone you care deeply about is the essence of loneliness and the reality is, he has already emotionally detached from us perhaps a long time ago. When we accept the fact that we ourselves need to distance in order to save our sanity, we may feel sad. It's another part of releasing and giving up our fantasies and blind hope. As with everything else in our life, we are alone on our wellness journey.

The secret to managing loneliness, and growing from it, is to learn to enjoy being with yourself; to truly enjoy time spent with yourself doing what you want to do. As with everything else on our journey, learning to thoroughly enjoy being with yourself must be developed.

Whether a quiet solitary time reading a book or working on a craft project, taking an energetic hike or strolling through a museum or shopping mall, settling back with popcorn in a theater to watch a movie, or having lunch or dinner in a restaurant by yourself, learn to enjoy being by yourself. Enjoy some time without the tension of worrying about how he will react and possibly prevent or spoil the experience.

You can learn to be your best friend and enjoy being with yourself in every circumstance. How do you accomplish this? By bravely going for the first time to a movie by yourself, by bravely making a dinner reservation for yourself, by scheduling a weekend away at a retreat. Start small and build on your brave experiences. There is a joyous world beyond your isolated life and you can discover it.

Emotional Detachment is Serious

Emotional detachment is serious. When emotional detachment becomes firmly established in a relationship, regardless of which partner first becomes detached, there is little hope that the relationship can ever be resurrected into the passionate or committed style that it perhaps had (or we thought it had) at the beginning.

Because this book is devoted to helping women survive in a miserable marriage it is reasonable to assume that he has already emotionally detached—and we have reached our limit in chasing after him, endlessly trying to convince him to communicate or work on the marriage.

Recognizing the Difference Between Love and Loving

Distancing and emotionally detaching helps us value our love and our loving and to be far less indiscriminate in how we allow ourselves to become depleted.

The nature of love has mystified humans since time began. To care about another human seems to be at least a partial definition. When someone you deeply care about is hurting, you hurt too. This is perhaps another way to express this level of care, of love and loving. Most mothers know about this level of love and when their children hurt, good, loving mothers hurt right along with them. (The damage done to children from unloving mothers is permanent. I deal with this issue in *Keep Walking and Don't Look Back©*)

The offshoot of care is caring as in 'caring for.' Anyone who changes baby diapers knows about 'caring for.' Sustaining that level of caring love into adulthood (where the changing of much more revolting diapers may be involved) is something we don't really want to think about.

When you deeply care about someone you tend to recognize their good points and minimize or ignore their weaknesses, annoying habits or even serious character flaws. Unfortunately, cloaking this under the guise of

123

'the good woman' or 'the saintly woman' can be a form of denial. There is a huge difference between minimizing leaving a wet towel on the bathroom floor and minimizing addictions, untamed anger or being shoved up against a wall.

Which brings us to the issue of loving. Love can be present but the degree to which loving is involved is the glue that holds love together. Volumes can be written, perhaps already have been written, about how men and women express love, i.e. loving.

I once heard a man say to his obese and far-from-glamorous wife, "Hi, beautiful!" No way on earth did that lady define beautiful in the world's eyes but her husband no doubt made her feel beautiful because of his 'loving' of her.

On another occasion I witnessed a woman helping her unsteady-on-his-legs elderly husband onto a stationary bicycle at a gym. After he was settled, she gently pushed his hair to one side in a loving manner as one would with a small child. I suspect this tender 'loving' permeated their marriage for many years. There is very little 'loving' in a miserable marriage—the genuine tenderness that both women and men crave but rarely find.

Women in miserable marriages are tripped up by 'loving.' As has already been alluded to, we do and do and do, often thinking we are storing up points. It is only when we step back, detach intellectually and emotionally and evaluate our level of loving that we can ascertain if we are draining ourselves of our reservoir of loving and allowing ourselves to be depleted by our husband's demands.

It is not unusual for a man to say, "She knows I love her," when he's just told her she's a pile of horse manure or given her a black eye or broken her arm. This is the disconnect between love and loving and those of us in a miserable marriage can only sort it out by detaching emotionally and examining from a distance the convoluted situation we are in.

If someone loves you, they will help you. They will want to help you. They will take pleasure in helping you, not expecting or commanding you to do what they could also do. And they, and you, should be able to reliably expect reciprocity. As the very old song says, "I will give to you and you will give to me, true love." In a miserable marriage the lyrics are, "I will take from you and you will give to me, and you will give to me, and you will give to me…"

Only by distancing intellectually and emotionally can we weigh the love and loving in our marriage.

Chapter 11 Part B – The Great Pause

How many words break our heart or cause us to break someone's heart? How many words do we wish we could take back? How many words satisfy our insatiable need to hear our voice take command, criticize or give our opinion?

Our throat B-F-P can run wild and our voice can cut someone to shreds in a split second via countless media. The power of the tongue destroys wives, husbands, children and families. So important is the use of our voice it is referred to as Right Speech in the eight-fold path of Buddhism and the Bible describes the tongue as holding the power of life and death. Those of us in a miserable marriage know so well the results of being targeted by acid tongues. The throat Body Focus Point is the source of good or bad in our life and when we focus on it, explore it and control it we can transform our life, and sometimes the lives of those around us.

In my Step Two practice I focused on how I used my voice and I recognized some unpleasant truths; how I spoke to others, how quickly I responded, sometimes cutting them off, and I always had something to say, an opinion to give. I didn't hear others because I anxiously wanted to impart my so-called wisdom. I faced the truth that my use of my throat chakra was obnoxious. This wisdom arrived gradually, as described in the next chapter. When I endured the shame of reality, the truth, about how I used my voice, I matured. I wish the people I inadvertently hurt when my voice ran wild and untamed might cross my path again so I could make amends. I hope women who read this book will benefit and save themselves later regret.

The Great Pause—A Moment Between a Thought and Our Mouth

I instituted The Great Pause when I recognized how I misused my throat B-F-P. The Great Pause is a brief moment inserted between a thought and our mouth. Countless times when my ingrained habit to say something was triggered, I stopped myself and said the affirmation: **"I think quietly before I speak, it might not need to be said."**

And then I asked myself, "Does this really need to be said?" For an astonishing number of times the answer was a definite, 'No.'

The Great Pause taught me self-control and self-discipline. The addition of The Great Pause, together with my Step Two practice which slowed me down and reduced tension, became the key to making wiser choices and decisions that transformed my life.

Behind this Great Pause question lay other questions: Is what I am anxious to say vital? Will it add to the conversation? Is it genuinely interesting to others or do I just want to hear myself tell a story or give my opinion? Where is this impatient desire to speak coming from? Does my B-F-P 5 reflect a need to be the center of attention, a desperate need to be heard or understood?

It is humbling when you observe yourself and examine your motives for speaking. I employed The Great Pause in my personal and work life and discovered something; when I wasn't always determined to inject my 'wisdom' I began to carefully listen to what other people said. Very often, what others had to say held value and wisdom.

There is a significant difference between listening with a bobbing head that pretends interest and focusing on, and actively listening to, what someone says, graciously drawing them out and encouraging them to continue. When I stopped trying to argue, use logic, fight for my position or convince my husband about anything and listened from my growing-ever-stronger position inside my body, I heard and learned more about him. Some of it was positive and some of it was not but a more complete picture revealed itself.

The Great Pause gives you the split second necessary to evaluate any situation and your role in it. It is a very instructive experience if you commit yourself to it. The Great Pause is a skill that can transform your life because it not only changes how and when you speak and what you choose to say, it helps you develop self-discipline, self-control and discernment.

The Great Pause requires practice and is a product of awareness of ourselves from practicing Step Two. The more conscious you are about yourself, the more present in your body and mind, the more comfortable you become with not speaking (or acting) impulsively. Eastern traditions espouse awareness, striving for ever-present consciousness which leads to wisdom in every area of our life. At this early phase of the Survive and Grow Steps, adding the practice of The Great Pause is a definitive step forward in transforming your life.

A woman angrily once said to me, "I can't possibly stop and think before I say anything!" I patiently explained that The Great Pause is similar to the split second a tennis player has when a ball from their opponent is coming toward them, to evaluate the direction and speed of the ball and decide how they will swing their racket. Without that split-second analysis they might swing wildly. She looked at me with disgust. This woman did not consider that she might have any flaw and she eviscerated the lives of her husband and children with her acid tongue. They suffered a lifetime of her verbal abuse. How different their lives would have been if she had controlled her tongue. Her family breathed a sigh of relief when she died. I doubt their lack of grief would have bothered her, but her children struggled for years with the scars from her verbal lashings and hateful criticism.

Women, the Throat B-F-P and The Great Pause

With the Great Pause I wondered, 'Do we women talk too much *at* our men?' We often reveal so much because we want them to be interested in us and what we say. But is this unrealistic and part of our fantasy about marriage?

Sharing personal information and feelings with our women friends is life-affirming. But men seem to have very short attention spans. I noticed this in my business life where problems required 'working' a situation, sometimes for weeks. Men quickly bored of the task or subject and moved on whether the problem had been solved or not. They waved away issues if they were discussed more than once or twice.

I observed that most men appeared to tune women out (including their mothers) after about our fourth word. The Great Pause guided me to not say much of what I previously would say and alerted me that I didn't have an attentive audience. I evaluated the importance and priorities of the points I wished to make and condensed them and they carried more weight. The enormous power of The Great Pause comes about through practice.

Chapter 11 Part C – More Empowerment from Step Two

In a miserable marriage, the uncertainties and unpredictable blowups, silent treatment, mind games and more, keep us on high alert. We're always looking over our shoulder wondering what's going to happen next.

The tension we experience is very serious. Research studies correlate illness with living in constant danger. Many women reading this have a personal relationship with blood pressure medication, anti-depressants, weight-control pills, migraine remedies and anti-inflammatories for muscular aches and pains. It is not easy figuratively carrying a two-hundred-pound man on your back.

The breathing and relaxation techniques in Step Two are remarkably helpful when you incorporate them into your daily life. Yes, you can take a deep breath, breathe into one or more of your Body Focus Points and let the tension flow down, out and into the floor. Most important, this allows you to stop and think before doing or saying anything.

Disappointment and Pain

The pain of being rejected or being invisible doesn't go away, but it becomes manageable and diminishes when you have a method to deal with it. When you sit with it and look at it and ponder it as you practice Step Two, it becomes a lighter burden to carry. Perhaps another way to say this is, you can honor the tremendous disappointment that is your marriage and honor and respect the horrible pain you feel, but no longer allow it to debilitate you.

The Importance of Replacement Thoughts

Obsessing about our husband, our marriage, and our hopelessness can eat away at us and make us physically ill. Learning to control our mind by focusing on our Body Focus Points is the beginning of creating Replacement Thoughts. Similar to lifting weights to strengthen a muscle, training our mind to focus can help us learn to 'change the channel' when we start to obsess about 'Why is he the way he is? How could he do that to me? Why does he treat me this way?'

Allowing your mind to endlessly dwell on him or whatever drama is taking place, is poisonous. When thoughts about him occupy your mind you sacrifice your time, your mental health and eventually your physical health. Obsessing about him is a serious matter and should not be ignored.

For your mental health, it is important to not wallow in the misery of thoughts about him that saturate your life with sadness.

Equally important, when you obsess about him you are preventing yourself from developing clarity about your life. Chapter 16 explores this in detail, but developing clarity about your life is vitally important to having inner strength. Allowing your mind to be continuously clouded by thoughts of him is equivalent to lowering a veil over your mind and eyes and missing the realities that are in front of you.

Thinking about your Body Focus Points is one way to begin replacing thoughts about him. Once you have trained your mind, taken control of it and not let it run wild, you can develop more Replacement Thoughts.

Creative projects are an excellent source of Replacement Thoughts, ideally big projects that you thoroughly enjoy working on and thinking about. I know one woman who, in the process of divorce, came into possession of a large, dilapidated doll house. Although she knew nothing about miniatures, she embraced the idea of restoring the dollhouse and threw herself into the project. She filled her thoughts with ideas, plans and research, learned a great deal, and after months of concentrated effort presented her grandchildren with a doll house any child would love to have. She told me she daydreamed about how beautiful the doll house would be and scraped, painted, glued, hammered and wall-papered her soon-to-be ex-husband right out of her mind.

Another, more dramatic example of the importance of Replacement Thoughts is the true story of a soldier who spent years incarcerated as a prisoner of war. Confined alone in a small, filthy cell, every day he 'built' his dream house on the wall by visualizing exactly how he would construct his home when he was free. Board-by-board, brick-by-brick, he sat and stared at the wall and constructed his house in his imagination. Regularly he would be dragged from his cell and tortured but when he returned to his cell, he took up his imaginary construction where he left off. His focused mind saved his sanity and yes, eventually he was freed and he did build his home.

Forgiveness can be part of our replacement thoughts strategy also. The subject of forgiveness is a very big one and is examined in detail in Chapter 21. If you are plagued with obsessing about him, consider taking a look at Chapter 21 now, to learn about forgiveness phrases that can serve as replacement thoughts.

We should not criticize ourselves when we struggle to focus on something other than our husband because it requires practice to stop ourselves and consciously choose something else to think about. With determination and our Step Two practice we can stop ourselves when constant thoughts about him clog our mind. We can switch to healthy replacement thoughts including our Body Focus Points and their accompanying affirmations.

The Beginning of Transformation

As with so much of our transformation process, we must reach into ourselves and find determination and self-discipline. As we begin to find self-respect and self-value, we can recognize that we shouldn't waste so much of our precious life on someone who mistreats us, who has moved on from us emotionally and has stopped caring.

Regularly practicing Step Two and incorporating it into your life is the beginning of dramatic personal change. As detailed in the chapters that follow, the meditative practice of Step Two forms the basis for the incredible transformations found in the remaining Survive and Grow Steps.

Transformation Action Plan

1. Journaling is a very effective way to help us understand and appreciate our journey to wellness. If you have not already done so, purchase a lovely blank book or set up a journal on your computer or in the notes on your mobile phone. Record your thoughts and how your perspective changes as you practice Step Two and the remaining Survive and Grow Steps. Be cautious, your journal should not be shared with anyone or available to anyone to discover and violate your privacy.

2. Record in your journal the situations or circumstances in day-to-day life where you have relaxed your body and mind by using the breathing technique in your Step Two practice.

3. Record events or situations that indicate you are distancing intellectually and emotionally.

4. Record how you utilize The Great Pause as you manage your daily life.

5. **Say this Affirmation**

    I honor myself by giving time and attention to myself

    Come with me to a quiet place and get some rest–Mark 6:31-32 NIV

    Whether a good day or a bad day, say this affirmation. Say it many times, emphasizing a different word each time – **I** honor myself by giving time and attention to myself. I **honor** myself by giving time and attention to myself. I honor **myself** by giving time and attention to myself.

6. **Respect and Reward Yourself**

    Refer to the Rewards List you created in Chapter 2. If you have read this far, are practicing Step Two consistently, and feel you are beginning to distance, and are implementing The Great Pause, reward yourself.

7. **Watch for your personal Milestone of Growth**
My Personal Milestone
As I emotionally detached, I viewed my husband as a stranger I might observe in the boarding lounge of an airport. I could engage in conversation as any dignified, self-possessed, gracious woman might do but I never expected or attempted anything closer. I was never unpleasant, mean-spirited, or cruel. When he indulged his anger, I watched him as I would observe a stranger causing a fuss at the ticket counter in the boarding lounge; an out-of-control stranger in whom I had no interest. His choices of behavior were his and I did not engage.

If he became verbally abusive, I sometimes imagined a huge, clear tube that I mentally lowered down over him and silently watched this 'bug' in the tube shout, fuss and look foolish and then I removed myself from the situation. My new, self-respecting, dignified woman reacted with equanimity, grace, intelligence, intuition and strength and did not engage because it was pointless to do so. I distanced and removed myself mentally and physically from his presence.

8. **Mantra to Remember**
His choices are his. I structure my emotions and decisions to ensure his behavior choices remain separate from me and I protect myself and my children and our futures.

9. **Signs of healing**
Healing is a slow process and just as with a broken limb, every day repair takes place until the limb becomes strong.
A sign of healing
When you look upon him with the same level of interest you would give to a stranger and you accept that you are no longer

emotionally attached to him, and you experience the peace this realization provides.

12

Survive and Grow Step Three

Am I who my parents and husband tell me I am?
Or am I the person I was created to be?

Learning Who You Are Now

Developing self-respect and learning to value ourselves can cause us to ask some penetrating questions: Who am I? What have I become?

Because we live on the defensive, are we what we *have* to be? Or are we who and what we *want* to be? Have we morphed into what life has required of us and lost contact with our inner core being, the uniqueness that makes us truly *us*?

Most of us think we already know who and what we are. It's a harsh reality to bravely examine your behavior and discover the extent to which you've been molded by others, including your husband, his way of thinking, his demands and your reactionary mode to try and keep the peace.

Because it happens gradually, our life slips into habits, patterns and behaviors that suffocate who we are: The woman who loves art but never sees the inside of a gallery because, 'He says it's so boring.' The woman who would enjoy hiking with friends but, 'He doesn't like me to be with them.' The woman who would love to spontaneously go to a movie but, 'He has to plan ahead and hasn't heard of the film' and he never likes any movie she suggests so he will sulk and audibly sigh throughout the film. The woman who can't invite her friends to dinner because, 'He doesn't like them,' and he'll sit like a giant slug rather than be a gracious host.

These women adapt their behavior and subjugate who they are, or once were or would like to be, just to keep the peace. They've learned, have been trained by him, that nothing they say will convince him to give a little, to compromise, to allow himself to be inconvenienced so that she can have or do something she would enjoy. These women give up part of who they are.

Where Do We Go from Here?

Step One taught us that we cannot convince him to change, that nothing we say, no logic or argument we use, will persuade him to change his behavior.

Step Two gave us a daily practice to help us become separate, self-respecting individuals and to detach from our husband and view him more clearly and objectively.

What are we left with? Do we become silent or do we look at our behavior, our responses to him, and search for more answers to help us survive with him?

Steps Three and Four teach us to look at our behavior, alter and expand our repertoire of responses and make changes that will prepare us to move into Part II of this book to build a better life.

Moving Forward and Building on Step Two

Step Three of the Survive and Grow Steps is powerful. It guides us to examine ourselves with our critical eye, the same critical eye we train on others, including our husband.

Why bother? Why examine our behavior in depth?

It's rather fundamental actually: With Step Two we learned to appreciate our humanness and look out from inside our valuable selves so we now need to take a look at our *outer* self.

Kelly Learns Step Three—Exactly Who Is Kelly?

Kelly practices Step Two daily and when we again meet, she tells me she feels changed. She moves through life more slowly, cautiously and with new calmness.

In addition to her boiled egg understanding of Dan, she views him from a distance, looking outward from inside herself and she does not always automatically react to his manipulation, tirades and aggravations.

Interestingly, because Kelly is becoming self-aware, she is beginning to realize that Dan is weaker than she previously thought him to be. Watching him from her more self-possessed perspective, she recognizes that Dan lacks strength, courage and self-discipline to control his behavior or examine himself. The invisible scale that always judged Kelly as the lesser of the two is beginning to tilt toward a more level balance. As she develops self-respect and recognizes her value, Kelly is less inclined to think of Dan as superior to her regardless of how often he ignores her or refers to her as stupid, a bitch, or worse. But he still drives her crazy and she wants more help with how to cope.

"Dan came home in one of his moods and I told him I couldn't take it anymore and we had a big fight. I'm so sick of arguing with him."

"Do you think your goal should be to never get angry or upset with Dan?"

Kelly looks at me, puzzled. "Yes. No. Well, I don't know. He makes me so confused. What do you think?"

"Trying to go through life without any reaction, without any anger, without any emotion, is an attempt to be a mannequin or a robot."

"So, what am I supposed to do?"

"Your reactions and responses to Dan can be selected not automatically triggered. Learning how to respond and react to Dan from a position of dignity and strength can transform your day-to-day life. But examining your current reaction and response behaviors is the place to start."

Survive and Grow Step Three

Kelly settles into a comfortable chair and closes her eyes.

"Breathe deeply as in your practice of Step Two, relax your body and enjoy this time for yourself," I guide her.

"Gently focus on the area of your genitalia, B-F-P 2. Guide your thoughts and rest there. Think about how you picture yourself as a woman and answer these questions: Who are you? What are you?"

Kelly says what I expect to hear, "I am a woman, a wife, a mother, a daughter, a career woman, a friend," the answers most women give, the roles she plays in her life. The labels are nouns, the 'it's' of our life; it's a woman, it's a wife, it's a mother.

"Now, use your imagination and picture yourself seated in a

beautiful theater with plush seats."

Kelly breathes deeply into B-F-P 2, and I continue.

"You are the only audience-member. You have the entire theater to yourself with a perfect view of the stage. A performance is about to begin.

"The actors on stage are you and Dan. In your mind, replay the scene of the fight you had with Dan. Relive it in every detail. Watch the scene carefully, listen to what is said, look at the action, observe both actors as though you have never seen this before. You are onstage as the female actor in the scene and you are also the impartial, observing audience."

I allow Kelly time to create the images in her mind and relive the quarrel.

"What do you see?"

"Dan and I are fighting and we look like crazy people. All we do is talk past each other. He talks down to me like I'm an idiot and I loathe him when he does that. He treats me like a child he can persuade to do anything. I look frustrated, angry and ready to explode. He makes me so mad! I look like a fool screaming at him. I hate that smug look on his face. He plays me like a violin and I look weak. No wonder the kids hide in their rooms. Watching this makes me angry all over again!"

"Remember, you are an impartial member of the audience. Watch and listen to the female character, you, in the scene. Don't let your emotions get in the way, just look and listen to what is in front of you.

"As you watch the scene again, I will say Behavior Defining Measurement Words. Evaluate the female character's behavior in relation to each of these words. Some may apply to her and some may not apply. Ask yourself, 'What do I see in her behavior? What impressions am I forming from her behavior? The most important question to ask is, 'How do I experience her?'"

I slowly say Behavior Defining Measurement Words and watch Kelly's face register her reactions to each word. Some cause her to frown, even grimace, and some cause her to nod her head in agreement. Puzzlement shows for many of the words as she struggles to equate what she sees in her behavior with words she's never thought about in relation to

137

herself.

Behavior Defining Words and Phrases

The chart below contains the words I say to Kelly. It is in alphabetical order because it is important to focus on each behavior and trait individually and to not choose from among a group of similar words. Our behaviors and traits are the combination of these words not merely a few of them, because we use a variety of behaviors and traits in different situations and circumstances. Learning what the components are that make us *us* is vital to our wellness journey.

Behavior Defining
Measurement Word Chart

Abrupt	Dishonest	Loud	Resigned
Angry	Easily Manipulated	Loyal	Sadistic
Arrogant	Empathic	Manipulative	Sarcastic
Articulate	Enraged	Masculine	Self-confident
Aware	Enthusiastic	Mature/Maturity	Self-controlled
Begging	Feminine	Mean	Self-disciplined
Broken	Foolish	Naïve	Short-tempered
Calculating	Frugal	Optimistic	Silly
Callous	Gentle	Passive	Simpering
Calm	Gossip	Patient	Spaced-out
Cheerful	Graceful	Peaceful	Spiritual
Childish	Gullible	Persistent	Steadfast
Churlish	Hard	Petty	Strong
Closed	Honest	Plaintive	Stubborn
Cold	Impatient	Playful	Talks-over
Compassionate	Impulsive	Pleading	Tender
Complacent	Inarticulate	Poised	Tense
Compliant	Intelligent	Pollyanna-ish	Thoughtful
Creative	Intense	Prideful	Tough
Critical	Interrupting	Problem-solving	Unreasonable

Cunning	Intuitive	Quiet	Uptight
Curiosity	Joyful	Reflective	Violent
Detached	Kind	Religious	Weak
Dignified	Liar	Remote	Whining
Discerning	Listener	Reserved	Withdrawn

Facing the Reality of Who We Are Now

This is a challenging exercise because it requires that we remove emotion from the scenes of our life and look only at our behavior and label it. It is not merely a cursory look but instead requires a soul-searching analysis.

Exactly how does each behavior portray us in our life roles? What behaviors that we may admire, are not in our life?

What are the behaviors that currently define us?

We already know our behaviors don't inspire him to change or give us peace, so what are the ineffective behaviors that currently form our responses to life, to conflicts, to reasoning, to problem-solving, to general interactions with all the people we encounter in our day-to-day life?

We can evaluate them and also recognize and learn about behaviors we don't have in our repertoire, and expand our choices beyond the same old triggered behaviors we've used for what seems like forever.

Introspection and Transformation

We rarely step back and observe ourselves. This is an exercise we like to apply to other people. We can pretty quickly and readily point out the inadequacies or pleasant qualities of someone else. It's rare that we take an impartial look at ourselves and honestly describe our own behavior.

We assume we know precisely why we are doing or saying something. But to actually take an objective look at ourselves and define in detail how we look and act goes beyond the 'how others see us' as mentioned in the poem by Robert Burns: *To see ourselves as others see us.*[2]

---

[2] Robert Burns, *To a Louise, On Seeing One on a Lady's Bonnet at Church*, 1786

More important than how others *see* us is the question, how do others *experience* us? And most important, how do we *experience* ourselves? There is usually a disconnect between the answers to these questions.

I know a couple who consider themselves to be the life of the party, but when they depart the other guests breathe a sigh of relief, agreeing about how obnoxious and boorish the departing couple is.

Surface Responses

In a miserable marriage we can define our husband's behavior because he is in our face with it. But what about *our* behaviors? Our surface reactions and responses are patterns that don't move us forward toward a better life so why do we endlessly repeat them?

Because we never take the time to seriously examine them.

If we define our surface responses and reactions they can usually be reduced to a few words because our repertoire is limited: Anger, frustration, submission. But clothed within those few words are more realities that define us and are the impression we make – how others experience us.

Going beneath the surface and defining ourselves by examining our behavior and forcing ourselves to name its components using Behavior Defining Measurement Words is a revealing and transforming experience.

The Compulsion to Always Respond

Behind every confrontation there is an accusation, a put-down, a demand, and much more as illustrated by the crazy-making scenes between Kelly and Dan in Chapter 4. But essential to the drama is Kelly's response to it.

Kelly truly is 'Everywoman' because we all respond when we are attacked. It's human nature to defend ourselves. And most of that defense is in the form of explaining, trying to convince the other party about our point of view, and trying to state the truth and find logic in the illogical. When you are trapped with someone who uses you for his entertainment by goading you into a fight, there is no logic. You end up punching air.

The compulsion to react and respond is exacerbated by today's addiction to instantly react to texts, emails, social media posts, mobile phone messages and more. I know one woman who became emotionally frantic from the constant haranguing she endured via hateful texts from her ex-husband who used their children as his excuse to incessantly contact and berate her.

In desperation she downloaded an app to screen the foul language from his texts. She also devised a simple code system for herself so that she never actually read the content of his hateful texts but responded with a check-mark emoji that acknowledged receipt only. It required self-discipline and determination to train herself to not instantly respond and to not feel compelled to read what he sent and then try to defend herself.

As counter-culture as it may be, women in a miserable marriage or in the process of getting out of one, can learn self-control and self-discipline to not instantly respond. To pause and carefully construct any response that may be absolutely necessary and to reduce the number of messages interpreted as 'absolutely necessary,' because many of them, if not most, are not absolutely necessary. Difficult men in miserable marriages can be as cunning and adept in their manipulations via electronic methods as they are in person.

The Structure of React and Respond

Controlling and crafting our responses (if we respond at all) requires maturing beyond the automatically triggered defenses we leap into time after time. The compulsion to always and instantly respond can be overwhelming; to always respond to insults, injustice, being baited, lied to and so on. Overcoming this impulse is possible by training ourselves and developing an expanded repertoire of behaviors.

There seems to be injustice in learning to not allow ourselves to be ruled by our compulsion to respond. Put another way, why do *we* have to learn and grow? What about him? The answer: Do we really want to continue to be like him, impulsive and uncontrolled? The answer is no.

The question then becomes: How do you handle the insanity of the situation you are in, in a manner that is dignified?

When you finally and forever set aside the deep-seated hope that you can affect change in him, then you can look at your behavior and ask

141

yourself, 'What do I like or dislike about *my* behavior?' This question should be asked and answered with complete independence from his behavior.

As Kelly said, she saw herself as weak and a fool when she watched the scenes of herself fighting with Dan. Now knowing that she isn't going to change him, she can decide if she wants to continue to react and respond as weak and a fool or develop behaviors that demonstrate self-respect and self-value.

Dignity

There is not any dignity in throwing dishes across the room but living with a difficult man can cause a woman to eventually explode in frustration. Only those of us who have lived with the incessant pressure of a miserable marriage fully comprehend the extent to which a woman can be pushed to reaction behaviors that are extraordinarily demeaning and dehumanizing.

Not having a fallback strategy when he increases the pressure leads to the tragedies mentioned in Chapter 8. Women can be driven to desperation and to the brink of destruction, whether of themselves or their tormentor. Finding self-respect and dignity are vital to having a strategy that anchors us in a self-preservation frame of mind.

This raises the question of how much personal dignity is important to us? Is breaking crockery (figuratively or literally) part of who we are? Is it behavior we grew up with? Is it behavior we want to keep as part of who we want to be? What about screaming, sulking, going silent? Are these behaviors we like in ourselves?

These same questions can be asked for each of the characteristics in the Behavior Defining Measurement Word Chart. Is poise, peacefulness, maturity and dignity part of who we are now? Are they qualities we once had or would like to have?

We can choose to have any of the qualities in the Behavior Defining Measurement Word Chart that we wish to have. We can choose among all of them whether ugly or attractive. It's entirely up to us.

It is an enormously important process to evaluate every detail of our behavior, where and when we learned each behavior, why it is part of our current behavior patterns and to ask ourselves, 'Do I want to keep it, replace it, or discard it?'

What about other characteristics we may have once had or would like to have, such as curiosity, enthusiasm, creativity, problem-solving, steadfastness, persistence, optimism, cheerfulness, playfulness? These characteristics go way beyond the basic 'I'm a woman, a wife, a mother.' They speak to our essence, of who we are, once were or would like to be.

When we examine what comprises *us*, we may be surprised to discover character and personality attributes that form our essence, our inner core, which we have discarded just to please or placate someone. Or we may discover attributes of someone else that we have adopted as our own only as part of our effort to cope.

As stated in an earlier chapter, whether we realize it or not we absorb the characteristics of the people with whom we live. While in many instances compromise is a good thing, sacrificing who we are just to keep the peace is going too far. And keeping behaviors that are destructive to our self-respect and self-value also demands too much from us. It is morally corrupt for any man to mistreat a woman and erode her qualities as a human being. But that is the price those of us in a miserable marriage often pay, day after day.

Putting the Puzzle Together Piece by Piece

Kelly will practice the theater scene analysis with each of the roles in her life; wife, mother, employee, daughter. All the characteristics on the Behavior Defining Measurement Word Chart can be evaluated for each role. The goal is for Kelly to develop an accurate picture of who she is now by doing a thorough and perhaps painful inventory of each role. Where she is now will lead her to the most important question of her life: Who and what does she want to be? She'll find the answers to those questions in Step Four in Chapter 14.

Facing More Reality About Him

But first, as part of our work today I ask Kelly to return to her imaginary seat in the theater and to once again watch the quarrel scene with Dan. She is to focus on Dan's behavior but with an alteration. The role of Kelly will be played by an imaginary actress, a stranger in the role of Kelly. Kelly is puzzled. Why put a stranger in her place?

"Watch closely, observe Dan's actions, voice tone, words, everything that I asked you to analyze about yourself when we began the exercise. Most important, evaluate all of his words and actions as performed with a stranger in the role of his wife."

This is a startling exercise and Kelly is uncomfortable. She is critical of Dan when she sees him in his role with an innocent third party. Kelly has devalued herself to an extent that Dan's behavior is more repugnant to her when it is directed at a woman she doesn't even know, a nameless imaginary actress. Kelly admits to herself that she repeatedly participates in scenes with Dan that she wouldn't wish upon a stranger. This unsettles her. Why does she allow something to happen to her that she finds repulsive when she witnesses it happening to someone else?

Kelly is accustomed to Dan being nice to friends and strangers so watching him treat his stranger-wife in the same way he treats her is very revealing. Kelly has been conditioned to accept Dan's two-faced behavior as a fact of life. When that pattern is disturbed via the imaginary actress, Kelly discovers what an impartial witness might think if Dan's mistreatment of Kelly became public.

As we conclude our session, Kelly is unsettled. Here is a new challenge, so I remind her that the growth process is a difficult one with many surprises, some pleasant and some unpleasant.

Kelly's assignment is to watch scenes from each of her roles; wife, mother, daughter, friend, employee, but particularly her relationship with Dan. She is to sit with those scenes and delve deeply into them, evaluate what she observes about her behavior and select Behavior Defining Measurement Words for every aspect of her behavior.

Her task is to identify her characteristics from her outward behavior and to form a definition of who she is now in each of her roles.

She is also to identify where each of her behaviors came from. Did she learn them in childhood, are they family patterns, are they copies of Dan's behavior?

Who is Kelly *now* and how authentic is she? Is she authentically Kelly or a reactive Kelly? Does she even know who authentic Kelly is?

How many versions of Kelly are there in her life? What characteristics has she abandoned in recent years? What characteristics has she adopted, whether or not they reflect who she truly is? Which characteristics does she like and not like?

The Pain of Reality About Ourselves

Step Three devastated me but it also woke me up, like being jolted out of a deep sleep by an earthquake. I thought I had escaped from my dysfunctional birth family but that illusion lay shattered on the stage of the imaginary theater where I watched myself play my roles in life. I never before recognized the problems inherent in my behavior and my personality until I watched scenes from all the roles of my life and evaluated them as an audience member with a critical eye.

I completed the exercise Kelly is embarking on and reached some sobering conclusions. My behaviors largely copied my parents, the behaviors I abhorred and wanted to escape. I didn't realize how ingrained in me were those behaviors, and since my husband came from a similar background, we were like two broken-winged birds trying to fly. I also recognized that over the years I had incorporated into myself much of his disturbing behavior too. I got lost somewhere along the way and I wanted the real *me* back.

13

Where We Came From—Where We Are Going

What we are today comes from our thoughts of yesterday – Gautama Buddha

Original Sin and finding Adam and Eve

We don't know what we don't know. If we are only exposed to one set of behavior patterns, we cannot learn anything else. Teachers face this reality every day where a classroom of children behave the way they experience behaviors at home. You cannot learn how to behave, how to resolve conflicts, in any other way than the one you have seen since the day you were born. Almost all of us grow up in a closed society. Our parents and extended families live and move within a same or similar socio-economic and educational environment. And as has already been mentioned in an earlier chapter, family patterns are virtually impossible to change and very difficult to overcome.

While a common theme of clergy is the concept of original sin emanating from real or legendary long-ago parents, the issue is much closer to home, within the last generation or two. If tossing dishes in the middle of a conflict is the pattern inherited from a previous generation then tossing dishes seems normal to those tossing them. The important question is, do you like yourself throwing dishes?

A problem develops when the pattern, the tossing of dishes, doesn't solve the underlying issues in the conflict and worse, serves to destroy one or both partners in a relationship. This is when one of the partners may reach a point of 'enough' and start to ask questions and search for answers. A family's original sin patterns need to be closely examined if you want to move beyond them.

The sins of the father and mother pass down to the next generation through example. Within some family structures and cultures, behaviors that are acceptable to them may be unacceptable to others. But this book is for women who are no longer willing to unquestioningly accept behaviors in themselves or others that are making their lives miserable. Critically

146

examining those behaviors, identifying their source and determining which behaviors to keep and which to discard, is the key element in Step Three of the Survive and Grow Steps.

Searching for Your Adam and Eve

It requires serious effort to unravel the original sin components in your life but doing so can reveal a great deal about your personality and the life you are in. Learning why you are the way you are and how you demonstrate your personality through your behavior is similar to looking at a road map. Where you are reflects where you've been and where you've been is the environment in which you grew up.

The road ahead can be charted by us if we take a thorough look at ourselves and those with whom we spent our early years. Sometimes we have to turn our back on the road behind us and the people in it if we're going to move forward in a new direction.

Clarity on some points can present itself in epiphany moments and other factors can slowly reveal themselves as life unfolds. The pace is determined by how committed we are to uncovering the details.

The problem lies in the fact that when a belief, pattern or behavior is imbedded in you, you simply don't see it for what it is or how it has impacted your life until you bravely self-examine. Even after you uncover the original sins in your makeup and perhaps assign their origins to the Adam and Eves in your heritage, they continue to rise to the surface and undermine your progress. Self-awareness gives us the tools to respond to these intrusions and keep them under control.

Only with hard work and struggle did I fully recognize the original sins imbedded in me because of my exposure to those behaviors throughout my childhood and adolescence: Criticism, control, judgementalism, arrogance, superiority, willful ignorance, lack of self-control, impatience, coldness, hardness, dishonesty, and absence of tenderness and compassion. I grew up with these, they were the air I breathed, the patterns that surrounded me, and they buried themselves in my psyche. If someone had guided me to identify these at an earlier age, I would have been spared a great deal of hardship and regret. But now as an

147

adult I could look at my life on my imaginary stage and sort out the truth.

I also identified the most damaging, even deadly, judgments from others that affected my beliefs about myself. They were: You don't deserve anything, you are ugly, and you are stupid. These condemnations (perhaps 'curses' is a more accurate term) influenced virtually every decision I made until I identified them and rooted them out.

Coming face to face with debilitating condemnations that influence your life is a startling exercise. I didn't recognize those deadly statements for the damaging power they held until I uncovered them and formed 'I am' statements and actions I could say and take to counter them. Only committed effort enabled me to overcome those curses and to mature and find peace and joy in my life.

It is possible to diagram our past and chart our future. A portion of what I diagramed as my Original Sin Behavior Chart is shown below. It pointed the way for me to learn new behaviors in order to change my life.

Original Sin Behavior Chart

My Behavior	Defining Word	Origin
Instantly finding fault	Critical	Parents: No one was ever good enough
Judging others as OK or not OK	Judgmental	Family & Church; only those 'good enough' were allowed
Know-it-all	Arrogant	Family & Church; everything is already determined and correct
Lack of knowledge	Willful Ignorance	Extended Family & Church; secular knowledge = sin
Angry response to slights	Short-tempered	Family; anger the only emotion expressed

Brusque, thoughtless	Hard	Family; lack of tenderness, empathy, kindness
Acting without careful thought	Impulsive	Parents; lack of self-control

Damaging Judgments

Judgment	Counter Affirmation	Counter Action
You don't deserve anything	I deserve a good life in every way	I carefully make every decision to ensure it is wise and good for me
You are ugly	I am a beautiful human being; a beautiful woman	I take good care of myself in every way
You are stupid	I am intelligent	I educate myself

NOTE: It is important to understand that searching through our current behaviors and discovering where we learned detrimental behaviors is not intended to be a blame game. Blame is pointless on our wellness journey because we are committed to taking control of our life, not wallowing in what others did to us. It is important to accept that many of our behavior handicaps were innocently acquired by us through no fault of our own. Children are powerless to change the adults in their life. When we are sick, we explore what caused our illness. The same applies to behaviors that are no longer appropriate for us.

Not all is bad news. It is equally important to give credit to ourselves for our positive, good points because it is precisely those attributes in ourselves that are overlooked, derided, even forbidden when we are in a miserable marriage. As has already been explored in a previous chapter, many of our truly good qualities are the reasons we are easy targets for mistreatment. But our good qualities are still good. We just happen to be wasting them on an abuser(s). We need to regularly recognize our good qualities and honor, respect and nurture them.

Positive Attributes Chart

Positive Attribute	Defining Words	Origin
I am a loving mother	Gentle, Kind, Protective, Patient	Grandmother
I am a good friend	Listener, Patient, Loyal	Not sure
I am creative with what I have	Creative, Problem-solver, Frugal	Mother

The Impact of Isolation

Isolation is the most influential factor in keeping us trapped in any strata of life. As already noted, we don't know what we don't know, and every circumstance that includes psychological abuse involves isolation in one form or another.

Take a careful look at the Behavior Defining Measurement Word Chart and identify how many of the words don't apply to a woman who is in a miserable marriage because her narrow life is constricted. One of the most crucial goals of the list is to inspire women to stop and reflect on what they *don't* have in their repertoire of behaviors, most likely because they simply don't live in a circumstance where those qualities even exist.

For example, there is very little graciousness in life when your husband (and most likely your extended family) is anything but gracious. What does graciousness even mean when you have none? Causing us to stop and think and reflect on the Behavior Defining Words is an effort to inspire women to expand their horizons and think beyond what their entrapment dictates, what they've learned, and the only behaviors they currently know.

What We Are and What We Think We Are

What I saw in the scenes I replayed in my mind did not match the image of myself I had inside my head. Certainly, my behaviors did not reflect what I thought I was projecting onto the world and I did not like what I saw.

As the audience, I watched two very unlikeable and unsympathetic characters on that imaginary stage but the one of most concern to me was me. I stopped looking only at my husband and pointing out his faults and focused on myself. And while he did need to change his behavior, which I now accepted I could not influence, I definitely needed to change my behavior, my words, my voice tone, everything. When I applied the same scrutiny to all the other roles in my life, I didn't like much of what I saw there either.

With Step Two, I climbed back inside my body and learned to appreciate my humanness, and to look out and not live only from surface reactions. But now I faced a brutal reality about me after viewing myself with detached objectivity. Where did I go from here?

As with Kelly's assignment, I made lists of my personality traits and characteristics. How did they add up? For each one I asked myself: Where did this trait or behavior come from? Did I adopt this trait or behavior to cope and survive? What traits reflected what I remembered from being a child, a time when I was perhaps closer to being myself? Which roles and behaviors in my current life reflected what I considered to be the real me? Had I ever been the real me?

After two weeks, my list included words such as, arrogant, articulate, hard-working to a fault, too trusting, tender (toward my child), impulsive, compromising, gullible, naïve, tough, loud, determined, respectful of authority, intelligent, impatient, and much more. While some of these are perhaps admirable, the combination of them did not portray a woman I wanted to be.

Who We Are Now and Who We Will Choose to Be

When, with bravery, persistence and determination, we *select* our behaviors, the behaviors that we choose to define our core self, behaviors that will transcend every outer circumstance, we begin to transform our life. We will always utilize a variety of behaviors but if we grow to truly know ourselves, our core behaviors can become a firm foundation. Starting

151

from where we are now, we can move on to Step Four and *choose* who we will become.

Transformation Action Plan

1. Practice your breathing and Body Focus Point exercise in Step Two. Then focus on B-F-P 2 the area of your genitalia, your womanhood.

2. Imagine yourself as the only audience member in a theater (or watch from a drone overhead or cameras aimed at you from a variety of directions). Over a period of days, watch scenes from your life. Play each scene carefully and in detail. Watch your behavior and your husband/partner's behavior in each scene. Avoid the tendency to focus on his behavior because evaluation of your behavior is the purpose of the exercise. If your mind wanders, gently bring your thoughts back to the scene you are watching.

3. Slowly and with purpose read the words on the Behavior Defining Measurement Word Chart and evaluate all your characteristics in each scene from your life. Ask yourself how you feel about your personality, behavior, and character traits portrayed in those scenes. Are you happy, satisfied, surprised, or disturbed by what you observe? How do you experience yourself as you watch? Write down your Behavior Defining Words and how you feel about each.

4. Go over scenes numerous times and look for different aspects of your behavior and your husband's behavior that you may have missed the first time. For example, are you trying to be logical? Is he trying to be logical? How do you react to him? How does he react to you? Although you have fought a hundred times and think you know the answers, look again.

5. Next to each Behavior Defining Measurement Word identify where you learned that behavior, and from whom. Ask yourself if your behavior is a choice you carefully make or automatic reactions that

are habits you learned or formed. Delve deeply. Repeatedly ask yourself: Where did this come from? Is this authentic? Is this me?

6. For each of your behaviors that you find unacceptable, write them in the form of an Original Sin Chart. Carefully evaluate each behavior you wish to overcome or discard and identify from whom and how you learned that behavior.

7. Make a final comprehensive list of Behavior Defining Measurement Words. Be honest. Your list may not paint a pretty picture of who you are now but accuracy is more important than pretending. Remember, growth and transformation are a process so be patient with yourself.

8. **Say this Affirmation**

   ### I can look at myself with honesty

   Teach me what I cannot see – Job 34:32 ESV

   Whether a good day or a bad day, say this affirmation frequently aloud or to yourself. Say it many times, emphasizing a different word each time. **I** can look at myself with honesty. I **can** look at myself with honesty. I can **look** at myself with honesty.

9. **Respect and Reward Yourself**

   Refer to the Rewards List you created in Chapter 2. If you have read this far, sat quietly and watched scenes from your life, carefully observed your behavior, identified the Behavior Defining Words that describe you in the scenes, and said the affirmation, respect and reward yourself.

10. **Insight to ponder**

    Learning who we are by examining our behavior is a serious search for truth. We may believe many things about ourselves but examining our behavior to find out who we really are, what we really look like to others, how we and others experience us, is valuable beyond measure.

11. **Watch for your personal milestone of growth**
My Personal Milestone
When I developed my 'Who and what I am now' list I resembled a captain trying to turn a ship; it requires distance and time to make the turn. Sadness enveloped me too because I recognized my immature, narrow and limited behavior patterns had cost me dearly; lost job opportunities, friendships that didn't develop or last, and a poor marriage choice. All might have been quite different if I previously knew what I now recognized about myself. But most important, I accepted that my behavior was my choice to make and I could change my behavior as I grew and moved forward.

12. **Mantra to Remember**
I am my own person. My behavior does not have to be dictated by his behavior or my previous patterns from my past.

13. **Watch for Your Sign of Healing**
A sign of healing
When you recognize the truth about your behaviors and know where and from whom you learned them and continually ask yourself, 'Is this how I want to behave?'

14

Survive and Grow Step Four

I do not need permission from anyone, to choose how I wish to be in my life.

Learning Who You Choose to Be

We do not have to be indefinitely defined by what we were born into or married into. We can examine all the many personality styles, character traits and behavior choices available to us and consciously choose how we will live our life. Survive and Grow Step Four is the most dramatically transforming of all the Survive and Grow Steps and guides us to choose our new life.

Moving Beyond Who We Are Now

Several weeks after she watched scenes from her life and identified words on the chart to describe her current behaviors, Kelly arrives to meet with me. She looks tired. It isn't unusual for Kelly to report that the previous week included Dan's blowups and her efforts to handle them. I admire her persistence because Kelly is determined to keep moving forward regardless of the constant negative pressure from Dan.

"What did you learn from the Behavior Defining Word exercise?"

"In every scene I watched of Dan and me, we were arguing. I'm so tired of arguing. Or he was giving me the silent treatment. Or I was trying to keep things organized for the kids and Dan was doing his own thing. We're like two ships going in opposite directions. The whole situation exhausts me."

"What else did you learn?"

"I'm closest to being myself when I'm with my kids. I'm gentle with them and listen to them and treat them with respect. I'm relaxed and patient. And I enjoy playing with them. I feel like I'm really me when I'm with them."

"Anything else?"

"Yes. I am very competent at work and I feel good about myself but

I'm impatient and rough around the edges sometimes. When I thought about it, I realized that I don't like the hardness I exhibit at work. I must have a split personality. I always seem to have to fight for what I want."

"And?"

"I watched my behavior in many scenes and recognized that I'm a lot like my Dad. He's the only parent I could identify with. My mother ignored me so there wasn't a female role model in my life. When I read the defining words on the chart, I realized how many traits are not part of my life and never have been.

"For example, elegance or tenderness. My parents were hard people. There wasn't any elegance or tenderness in my childhood. I suddenly could see that I don't express my love for my kids in a truly tender way. I'm gentle with them and they know I love them but we're always on a schedule and I'm the cop directing traffic. I feel so much love for my kids but I don't express it to them as much as I want to, by taking more time to listen and tune into them."

Kelly pauses. "I also recognized that even when I'm with my kids I'm thinking about Dan and our situation."

She hesitates again. "I'm not happy about what I saw of myself in those scenes."

Then she shakes her head, "There isn't much of the real me in there."

"What do you mean?"

"The hardness that makes me efficient and decisive is why I get things done but it isn't who I am in my inner core. It is a skill I developed because I have to earn a living. I'm always afraid I might lose my job. I think that is one reason why I fight with Dan, because I'm afraid I can't do everything forever, that I'll burn out and then we won't have a roof over our heads. And I have to try and not feel the hurt I experience from Dan's treatment of me. I realized one morning that I don't have kind feelings for Dan. There isn't any caring in our relationship because I'm always on guard."

"What else did you discover through this exercise?"

156

"I have always loved art and music but there isn't any in my life. I enjoy learning about new things, but Dan is convinced he already knows everything so when I tell him something I've discovered or read he dismisses it as yesterday's news, like he's already aware of it and ahead of me. I would not be surprised if one day he tells me he knows what it's like to go through childbirth. What he doesn't know is of no interest to him so I don't have much mental stimulation outside my work. I used to think of Dan as strong and reliable because he always talked so confidently about everything. Now I realize that I misinterpreted his behavior. I fell for his phony side."

"What does this knowledge tell you about yourself?"

"I was immature when I met Dan. And I'm still naïve and gullible. I accept people as they present themselves and don't discern what is underneath. The more I look at it, I realize I do this automatically."

"Why?"

"Because that is what I learned from my parents. As I watched scenes of myself with my parents, they were giants. I was a little kid when they hollered at me and told me I was stupid. They dictated how I should feel and think. When I watched those scenes, I realized I had to hide my feelings and wishes to survive being a kid. If I complained my mother told me I shouldn't feel the way I did."

"The most important questions are, how did you experience yourself as you watched the scenes of your life? And how do you think others experience you?"

Kelly ponders for a minute and then says, "I'm all over the map. I'm focused and driven at work but emotional, frantic and angry with Dan. Then I'm gentle, patient and loving with my kids. Then wishy-washy and constantly giving in to my extended family. When it comes to femininity all I allow myself are leftovers, squeezing in a hair appointment or running into a shop and quickly buying an article of clothing. I'm like leaves thrown up in the air, all of them falling in different directions."

157

Kelly Learns Step Four—And Discovers the Woman Within Her

Kelly settles into a comfortable chair, closes her eyes, and we embark on Survive and Grow Step Four. Because she is now adept at breathing deeply, centering her attention and controlling her thoughts, I tell her to once again direct her attention to B-F-P 2, the area of her genitalia, her womanhood.

"Take a moment to think about yourself and respectfully honor what you have recently learned about who you are in this place, your life in this moment, at this point in time.

"Acknowledge and honor each of the traits on the Behavior Defining Word Chart that you identified as part of who you are. Some of them you admire, some you don't like, but you can choose what you wish to become. Gently release what you've learned and open yourself to learn more about yourself.

"Think of your life as a blank page. Breathe into your womanhood and slowly and quietly begin to picture yourself as the woman you want to be. Think of this woman as living in your inner core, your essence, and she wants you to become acquainted with her. She may be very different from what you identified from the word chart and that is OK. Delve deeply into the woman you want to be and examine every aspect of her.

"Take your time. Don't cling to any idea. Let the deep awareness of your Body Focus Points with which you are familiar through your practice of Step Two, lead you to an image of who the woman inside you is. Her appearance and behavior may surprise you. Let that happen. The key question to guide you is: If you could be any woman you choose, what would she be? How would she behave?

Behavior Defining Words for the Woman You Choose to Be

"Think about the Behavior Defining Words that do not currently reflect who you are and choose the words that you wish did apply to you. They may be the opposite of what you currently are. It is what you wish to become that is important. What are those words? How would the woman you wish to be demonstrate those Defining Words in her behavior? Think about the entire list and choose all the words you want to incorporate into your behavior. Picture in your mind exactly how you would like to be in your life.

"Go deep and repeatedly ask yourself: Who is the woman within that I want to become? Who is the woman inside of me who has been forbidden to show herself? How would this woman behave if I became her?

"It does not matter how dramatically different from your current life she may be. Reach inside, learn about her, and welcome her.

"Today is just the beginning. During the next several weeks go very deep into each of your Body Focus Points as you do your morning practice, and discover the woman you want to emulate, the woman who is already inside of you and whom you will learn to admire, respect, love and welcome into your outer life.

"When you have a sense of her, look very closely and observe everything about her; how she moves, how she speaks, how she relates to everyone around her, even how she is dressed. Remember, this is the woman who speaks to you, to your heart and soul. Who you choose to be is already in your inner core, the essence of the woman you now choose to become. Your goal is to discover everything about her."

Finding and Choosing Mentors

I allow Kelly time to relax into her thoughts about how she wishes to be as a woman. After a few minutes I quietly say to her, "Now think about several women you admire. They may be famous or not famous, they may be alive or have lived in the past, and they could be fictional characters, but they exemplify the qualities of the woman you have been visualizing, the woman you wish to become.

"Think about their characteristics, mannerisms, and behaviors. These can become yours too. You can incorporate their behavior into your life, your consciousness, your self-awareness. Observe how they move, speak, handle challenges, manage their relationships, and any other aspects of their behavior that you have read about or observed and admire."

The Value of a Mentor

There are many women who are wonderful examples of transformation and they do not have to be held at arm's length and remote from us. We can use information about them and choose to follow their example. We can make a conscious effort and learn to be like them.

Many women who are examples of graciousness, strength, courage, poise, and femininity came from childhood backgrounds where those qualities did not exist. They overcame their backgrounds and grew to eventually be effective in all areas of their life.

Women who inspire us with their behaviors, mannerisms, and in some cases achievements, very often do not have perfect bodies, beautiful faces and unlimited financial resources. Look around you. Identify women whose behavior, self-awareness, physical bearing and powerful presence speak to you and to the woman within you who wants to emerge and be recognized and honored by you.

The value of a mentor cannot be over-emphasized. Even if you will never meet the woman or women you choose to emulate, she or they can be the personification of the affirmation: *This* is who I *am*.

If you are fortunate to have someone in your life who can provide inspiration and guidance to you, then you are indeed blessed. Unfortunately, because isolation in one form or another is so often a reality in the lives of women in miserable marriages, don't be afraid to look for examples of women you can admire and emulate even if the closest you will come to them is reading about them or seeing and hearing about them via media.

Choose wisely. We each need women whose behaviors we admire, with inspiring qualities reflected in their behavior: Strength, courage, persistence, dignity, wisdom, graciousness and many other defining words you may choose. As already mentioned, there are examples of women who rose from nothing and overcame the odds. We do not have to be trapped in behaviors that do not bring peace, dignity and value into our life, even in the reality of living with an impossible-to-please man. Our goal is not to please him, for that is impossible. Our goal is to become a whole, complete, self-respecting and self-valuing woman.

Kelly Meets Her Woman Within

Two weeks after Kelly learned Step Four, she arrives to meet with me. There is an astonishing noticeable change in her. Kelly is always neatly groomed, but today is different. Today it is her demeanor, posture, calm facial expression, steady eye contact with me, and overall graciousness and peacefulness that are strikingly new.

Kelly tells me her story.

"I met the woman within myself during my daily quiet time on a morning following a nasty quarrel with Dan. I sat and thought about that quarrel. I watched it on the imaginary stage and realized that I often try to reason with Dan. I felt broken and vulnerable and, for some reason, my instinct just seemed to be more alert, more vivid, and I noticed details I had not noticed before.

"As I focused on my B-F-P 2 and pondered myself as a woman, an image came into focus that felt deeply rooted within me. Not only in my womanhood but in my heart, my instinct, even my third eye. As I rested in her presence, I realized she looks nothing like me in my current life. She exudes a sense of elegance, calm and self-confidence. She is thoughtful and never impulsive. She is regal and has a presence about her that indicates she does not quarrel with anyone because she does not tolerate nonsense from anyone. She does not respond in a harsh, hurtful way but with composed, quiet, articulate, immovable dignity.

"Not at all cold but rather the epitome of graciousness, kindness, caring, and compassion. Combined with an obvious and extraordinary inner strength. Her soft, vulnerable qualities are not worn on her sleeve as a signal to others that she can be taken advantage of. They are inner qualities that define how she values herself.

"She knows who she is, she respects herself and she chooses wisely on all fronts: Whom she lets into her life, how she reacts to people and life situations, and how she behaves in all circumstances. Self-control, dignity, strength and grace define her.

"Every detail came into focus. Dressed simply but beautifully in a

161

soft evening gown of pale green, she stood on a terrace overlooking an expansive lawn, a property she owns and manages wisely. And she was not alone. A calm and masculine male figure stood slightly behind her.

"Both individuals were quietly confident in who they are, respectful partners, not competitors. I sensed an energy of self-confidence and peacefulness, a strong, quiet, confident peacefulness that radiated from the woman.

"And then I realized that the masculine qualities in the male figure were not those of an actual separate male individual, but are the woman's inner strengths. 'He' was part of her essence not a separate male. I recognized that she honors her inner masculine strength that protects her, trusts her instinct, and gives her discernment and courage. She holds these strengths as part of herself while she simultaneously honors her womanhood.

"This woman does not need to crash through life trying to cope, trying to change things, trying to convince others to love her. She does not try to change them or demand they do what she wants to meet her needs. This woman is dignified and discerning and she chooses her behavior carefully from her repertoire of firm convictions.

"She is not a woman who allows anyone to invade her life and tear it to shreds. She values herself. She has boundaries and inner core values and she does not need to defend herself by shouting and trying to reason with someone. She simply stands strong, quietly and unwavering within her extraordinary powerful female strength."

Kelly and I sit and reflect on this revelation. We are bonded as two women, thinking about what her womanhood can be if she chooses.

Measurement Words to Define the Woman We Choose to Be

How does one carry over this extraordinary experience into everyday life?

I ask Kelly to think about each of the qualities her inner woman embodies and to select the defining words that express those qualities.

"Inner strength. Outer strength. Peacefulness. Wisdom. Femininity. Self-possessed. Self-controlled and clear about her boundaries."

162

The role of the property in Kelly's vision of her inner woman is significant. She owns property and properties have boundaries.

Kelly's wise inner woman is complex and not at all a surface-only, reactionary woman. She does not argue because she does not have to. She knows what is right and wrong in her world and she does not have to reason with anyone about those ethical boundaries. She is too dignified to mindlessly argue or raise her voice in a crass manner.

Kelly's strong inner woman is also soft and tender—she wears a soft flowing gown. And she is a valuable part of the earth; her gown is green.

"Have you selected one or more women as your mentors?" I ask Kelly.

"Yes," she says, and tells me the names of several women who reflect what Kelly discovered in her inner woman. Each of these women is very impressive in her respective way.

Kelly Constructs New Kelly

Kelly can now close her eyes, breathe deeply, and completely relax into her inner woman, her *self*. She connects with her vision of herself daily when she practices her Step Two quiet time, and throughout her day when she stops and reminds herself about the 'new woman' she has chosen to become.

I guide Kelly in how to deepen her connection and truly become the woman she has chosen to be.

"Select the defining words that describe your inner woman. For each word you select, close your eyes and deeply ponder exactly what the behavior is that demonstrates that quality.

"Picture *yourself* as your New Woman and picture yourself using each behavior you select. Take on that behavior, live that behavior.

"If you have selected 'dignity' then ask yourself, 'How does a dignified woman behave?'

"If you select 'discerning' ask yourself, 'How does a woman with discernment behave?' If you have selected 'gracious' ask yourself, 'How does my inner woman demonstrate graciousness?

163

"Dwell on and imagine the behavior that reflects each of the defining words you select for the woman you choose to become. Think about your inner woman and introduce her to your mentors. As your mentor(s) welcome your inner woman, allow them to become you. Welcome them. Welcome *yourself.* This will be New Kelly."

15

The Power of 'I am'

Be transformed by the renewal of your mind – Romans 12:2

'I Am' versus 'You Are'

There is nothing more powerful and empowering in our growth process than practicing 'I am' statements. 'I am' statements are the secret weapons in transforming our life.

'I am' can be placed in front of every Behavior Defining Word and help us decide, 'Is this what I choose to be?' If the answer is yes, we can keep it. If the answer is no, we can reflect on why we are that way and change ourselves by choosing to become the opposite. A loudmouth? 'I am self-controlled.' Impulsive? 'I am discerning.' Timid? 'I am strong.'

There is no limit to how many 'I am' statements we can devise to change our behavior and our thinking about ourselves. Once we select our defining words and place them in 'I am' statements, we can reflect on what behaviors demonstrate each 'I am' quality.

'I am dignified.' How does dignified behavior look? How do you carry yourself if you are dignified? What image do you have of yourself as a dignified woman? Think about a mentor woman who is dignified. How does her behavior demonstrate dignity?

When you breathe into a quality you wish to have, embrace it, absorb it and change your behavior to reflect it. You then become a woman with that quality.

We have already explored the power of strong positive affirmations to change our thinking about ourselves. Now we can become everything that our inner woman and our mentor(s) exemplify by employing the power of 'I am' when we accompany each statement with an image of exactly what that behavior looks like. How does it feel? How do *I* look and feel when 'I am' that behavior? We can take the power of 'I am' and put it in front of everything we wish to be.

'I am' Statements are a Counterattack

Equally important, with 'I am' statements, we counterattack, control, even destroy, the negative messages we've absorbed from others. And we can choose to replace attributes about ourselves that we simply don't like and want to discard. The most powerful 'I am' statements are those that counterattack the destructive negative messages we have absorbed from others.

We've been told we are stupid, 'I am intelligent.' We've been told we are ugly, 'I am' beautiful. Our list can be long but every judgment leveled against us can be turned into a powerful 'I am' counterattack statement.

I guide Kelly, "Place the words, 'I am' in front of every attribute that constitutes the woman you choose to become. Say your 'I am' statements to yourself throughout your day and particularly when you find yourself in any situation that undermines you in holding onto everything you've accomplished in your wellness journey. Your 'I am' statements will support you.

They may alter as life unfolds but there is nothing more empowering than your 'I am' statements. It is a good idea to periodically review your list of 'I am' statements and update them to reflect what is happening in your life."

With careful thought, Kelly develops her list of 'I am' statements and she places the qualities that challenge her most, those she finds the most difficult to believe, at the top of her list.

> I am valuable
> I am strong
> I am intelligent
> I am beautiful
> I am dignified
> I am peaceful
> I am wise
> I am composed
> I am self-disciplined

I am intuitive

I am loving

I am kind

I am self-confident

The Power of 'I am' to Overcome 'You are'

Women in miserable marriages hear many destructive 'you are' messages. 'You're a bitch, you're too stupid to understand, you're a fat cow,' and on and on. Powerful 'I am' statements are the antidote for the poison of those hateful words.

Extraordinarily damaging and destructive 'you are' messages can be imbedded in us when we are innocent children. They influence the choices we make, including whom we marry. Destructive 'you are' condemnations from childhood are incredibly difficult to overcome. But persistent use of strong 'I am' statements can effectively counterattack them and eventually reduce their impact on our life.

Powerful 'I am' statements begin to shape our lives in a new direction. When you become a dignified, self-possessed woman, your behavior is that of the woman you now are—a self-valuing woman. When you plant powerful 'I am' statements into your life, repeat them and behave in accordance with them, you will become transformed.

The woman you become almost always asks some life-altering questions of herself:

- Why would any intelligent, dignified, strong, peaceful woman engage in arguments with someone who is baiting her for their enjoyment?
  The answer: She would not.

- Why would any dignified, clear-thinking, peaceful and strong woman engage with someone who plays mind games, uses and manipulates others for the pleasure of their warped self-importance?
  The answer: She would not.

- Why would any dignified, clear-thinking, self-respecting and self-valuing woman attempt to reason with anyone who is behaving like an un-self-disciplined maniac or a hate-filled vicious human being? The answer: She would not.

A dignified, self-respecting, self-valuing woman with a strong sense and understanding of who she is, does not behave in any manner inappropriate to who she is. Put another way, she does not lower herself, trying to reason with, argue with, or out-shout someone who does not behave in an equally dignified manner.

The New Woman does not ignore problems. She uses her new-found wisdom to continue to grow and find better ways to cope. And she never acquiesces. She plans ahead, she does not bend her principles, she requires and maintains her standards.

The 'I am' Practice

Kelly begins to absorb the 'I am' of her new life, to take in all of her 'I am' statements and make them part of her inner self, her genuine self.

And they begin to be reflected in her behavior. Her repertoire of reactions and responses to Dan now includes those of a dignified, self-possessed woman, not a shrieking, frantic woman living on the surface of her emotions.

Shortly after Kelly defines herself as New Kelly, she no longer reacts to Dan as she previously did. She shares with me the story of the day her life changed forever.

"I came home from a business trip and Dan was in a foul mood. He caught a cold while I was out of town so he didn't like the burden of taking care of the kids. While I was gone, I called every night but he never told me he was sick. If I had known, I would have contacted the lady we hire as a babysitter to help. I guess I'm supposed to be a mind-reader." Kelly rolls her eyes.

"Anyway, he was really going at me saying some nasty things. I tried to reason with him but I know how pointless that is. He screamed something at me and stomped off into the garage and I followed him, just as I always did in the past.

"But when I got to the door of the garage I stopped. It was the strangest sensation. All of a sudden, I thought about how I looked on 'the stage,' like I was watching this scene unfold. And then I thought about my new inner woman, the woman who is dignified and intelligent, and I said to myself, 'This is not how I behave.' I took a deep breath, stood taller and took on all the qualities in my 'I am' list and I literally became my mentor woman, my New Woman.

"I looked at Dan and saw this maniac with the angry, distorted face and heard the ugliness spewing from him, and I turned and walked back into the house, into the kitchen, and calmly and peacefully began to do what needed to be done. I had no interest in Dan. None whatsoever. I felt nothing for him. He was a stranger. A maniacal, disgusting, creature who repulsed me.

"And that was that. I will never, ever, again react to Dan as I did in the past. I am no longer that weak, foolish woman, trying to reason with him or trying to find any semblance of intelligent communication with that man. I am a dignified, elegant, intelligent, reasonable, strong woman and she does not deal with anyone at that level.

"The curious thing is," continues Kelly, "Dan didn't know what to do. When I turned and walked away from him and the fight that he obviously wanted, he was left empty-handed and flat-footed. He literally didn't know what to do with a woman who did not respond like he always expects.

"When I walked away from him that day, it wasn't as the subjugated, hopeless, broken, depressed Kelly he expected. I walked tall, poised, strong and composed, and he could see the difference. He may have even recognized the look of disgust for him on my face.

"I have changed in a manner more thorough and permanent than he could ever imagine. I will never go back to the way I used to be."

Identifying Exactly What You Want in Your Life

Our life is the culmination of decisions that others made for us and, as we mature, decisions we make for ourselves. Unfortunately, many of life's most important decisions have to be made when we are really too young and inexperienced to be making them, including whom we marry. But now, by examining every aspect of ourselves we can ask, 'What do I want my life to be?'

I give Kelly an additional task: To ponder what she would like to have her life become. Not just her new *self*, but her entire life, what surrounds her, what constitutes how she will live. I ask her to close her eyes and tell me what she wants in life, and to preface each desire with the words, 'I will.' Kelly ponders this and then says:

- I will be healed and find wellness
- I will have a peaceful life
- I will be financially secure
- I will be healthy in mind, body, and soul
- I will have good people in my life
- I will have joy, humor, and fun, in my life
- I will have a life of honesty
- I will have a life with love

How do you change yourself dramatically when you've been a certain way for so long? How does any woman, manipulated into being a self-loathing imbecile, awaken a strong, clear-thinking, peaceful and unflinchingly powerful woman inside herself? It takes time and determination, as stated so frequently throughout this book. But the key is, and will remain, the time you take each day for yourself, to reflect and connect with your inner core, your essence.

As part of her daily practice of Step Two, Kelly now pauses at her B-F-P 2—her genitalia—and slowly, carefully, and with deep thought, recites her 'I am' mantra.

Her mantra occasionally changes, with new items added and some subtracted as she identifies particularly deep-seated negative judgements that others, and sometimes Kelly herself, have leveled against her over the years. Her strongest 'I am' statements are those that are the opposite of what she has heard from her parents and her husband. Carefully, Kelly identifies all the negative words that have been spoken over her, the curses one might say, and she replaces them with strong 'I am' statements to rebuke those negative judgements.

Self-Confidence—The Missing Ingredient

Kelly discovers that underlying most of her struggles is a lack of self-confidence. 'I am self-confident' becomes an important statement for her.

She further expands on 'I am self-confident' by asking herself, 'What would I do now, in this moment, if I had self-confidence?' She teaches herself to stop, to become aware of what she is thinking and doing, and then bravely and with determination move forward in a self-confident manner.

This is a significant step because lack of self-confidence plagues women. As already discussed earlier in this book, we tend to ask for permission and can be easily dissuaded from doing what we know is a correct or a prudent action to take, especially if the manipulator in our life is a skilled narcissist.

Developing Self-Confidence

"How do I develop self-confidence?"

This forty-plus-year-old woman sat in front of me, crying and in despair. Her husband recently told her he wanted a divorce. He found someone new so she had been unceremoniously discarded.

She did everything right, just the way he wanted. She never worked outside the home and devoted twenty years to raising their two children, including home-schooling their learning-disabled child. She thought she and her husband were partners in life; raising children, establishing a home, looking forward to a long life together.

Now her shattered life terrified her. Her husband always took care of everything. She did not know how to earn a living. At forty-plus her life capabilities were those of a sheltered teenager.

Patiently and gently I explained to her that she could build self-confidence (which she sorely needed, as she had to find a job) by beginning to do something, anything, that she feared doing.

"Take a route home that you've never taken before. Sign up for a class, a book club, a charity for which you can volunteer, anything that forces you to do what you've never done before."

It is only by taking the initiative, regardless of how terrifying it is, to try something new or alter what we've always done, and experience triumph in our successes, that we can develop self-confidence. And yes, part of the effort is to learn to cope with and recover from our failures. There is no other way to build self-confidence. Like so much of our wellness journey, courage and bravery are necessary.

Kelly Develops Her 'I am' Statements

For areas where Kelly believes she is inept she now inserts positive and strong 'I am' statements that help her move forward to achieve her goals. She certainly does not feel self-confident when she begins to say these 'I am' statements, but that is the most important point: 'I am' statements are often the opposite of how we feel or think at that moment because their role is to help us build a future, and also help us stop dwelling on the past or living as victims.

Just as affirmations plant positive thoughts and beliefs that are often startlingly contrary to what is reality at the time, 'I am' statements do the same thing. So, instead of 'stupid,' the devaluing word planted by Kelly's parents and reinforced by her husband, she says, 'I am intelligent.' Instead of naïve and gullible she says, 'wise and discerning.' Instead of hard and tough she says, 'strong and tender.'

Kelly has a list of qualities she wants in her life, and most of them have ugly twins—negative versions planted by her family and husband. For each of these destructive messages Kelly devises a new 'I am' statement. Her list is long because there are many destructive messages in her past.

Finding Our Inner Core Values and Our Guiding Principle

After I met my inner woman, I pondered her every day when I practiced Step Two and focused on my womanhood. Throughout my day, whether at home, at work, or in public circumstances, I learned to stop, reflect on the woman I had now become and my behavior instantly reflected that change. 'I am' became *me*. Within a few weeks my inner woman devolved into a clear list of Core Values that were me, the *real* me.

These core values transcended any outward situation or aggravation because they portrayed the essence of my humanity, my womanhood. My core values were defined by the Behavior Defining Words I chose to be.

And from my core values I discovered my Guiding Principle: I wanted a peaceful life and would let nothing, and no one, damage that principle. My Behavior Defining Words also described my inner core values. 'I am peaceful' became my Guiding Principle of Peace. I would not settle for anything less than peace in my life.

Most important, the combination of my core values and Guiding Principle changed my behavior because what good would it do me to have these values if I didn't continually behave in the way they required?

My life would never be the same again.

I became a strong, composed, dignified, self-controlled, discerning, tender, loving, self-respecting and self-valuing woman. My behavior reflected this in every aspect of my life. I did not need anyone's understanding or permission to hold within me my core values and how I chose to express them through my behavior, because these were my choices and mine alone to make. My 'I am' statements and affirmations were planted in me and I repeated them to myself in all places and circumstances.

A Guiding Principle

Together, my core values all pointed to the Guiding Principle I chose: Peace.

Grounded in a profound desire to have peace in my life, every aspect of my life and every behavior I exerted were now directed at creating and preserving peace in my life.

Genuine peace. Not peace purchased at the price of my sanity or giving in to anything I did not agree with, but rather peace that emanated

173

from my refusal to accept anything less.

This did not mean life would be easy or that I would in some wimpy way float through life in a dazed state. Quite the contrary. I made difficult decisions, and yes, I made mistakes, but I never lost site of the woman I chose to be. And I kept going. My next step became Step Five in the Survive and Grow Steps, the beginning of living in a new way.

A Cautionary Tale—The Pressure Will Be Increased

When you change your behaviors and patterns, everyone in your life who has depended on your previous behaviors and patterns will not be happy. They liked you just the way you were—pliable, perhaps foolish, easily led, argumentative, the list can be long.

In their world view, if emotional, psychological, and verbal abuse achieve what they want, they assume that if they increase the abuse then you will cave, you will fold, you will retreat back into your reliable, previous response behaviors and patterns.

And they are correct in this assumption until we become so firm in our self-conviction that nothing and no one will move us. This is why daily practice of Step Two is so important to keep us in touch with our true selves, our New Woman.

Abusers are relentless and they don't give up, ever. Remember, we are learning how to cope and stop clinging to the false hope that he will change. As he turns up the heat we must work harder, go deeper, creatively find solutions, but stay on our path. We will slip, perhaps, but climbing back up onto our feet and continuing our journey is now what we are accomplished at doing.

Transformation Action Plan

1. Plan a bit of extra time, or even carve out a special day or two, to focus deeply on your Body Focus Point B-F-P 2 and think about yourself as the woman you wish to become. Try not to hold onto old ideas of yourself, many of which may reflect what you've heard about yourself from others. You may have to do this exercise

numerous times for an image to come into focus. That is fine. Just let yourself relax into the process.

2. When an image arises take a very careful look at all aspects of it. How does this woman look, walk, talk, carry herself and move through life? What Behavior Defining Words are demonstrated in her behavior? Review the Behavior Defining Words Chart and identify all the words that apply.

3. Identify the Behavior Defining Words that describe how you choose to be. Remember, these descriptive words may be very different from how you are currently living your life. The goal is to clarify how you *wish* to move through your life regardless of what you have been told, instructed, ordered, forced to be in your life, or currently believe about yourself. You are looking for your inner core values, your essence, not trying to please someone else.

4. As images and thoughts come into focus remember them and write them down in your journal. Regardless of how long or short, develop a list of Behavior Defining Words that describe what you envision as the woman you wish to become.

5. Once you have developed your list of Behavior Defining Words to describe your New Woman, convert them to 'I am' statements.

6. Ask yourself if your Behavior Defining Words indicate an underlying, all-encompassing Guiding Principle. Don't force this, take your time. It may require some days, weeks, or even months before you arrive at a Guiding Principle that profoundly speaks to you.

7. Think about what you want in your life. Identify each item or area and turn it into an 'I will' statement. Make a list of your 'I will' goals.

8. **Say this Affirmation**

   I am a strong, capable, valuable, woman

   She who is in you is stronger than he who is in the world
   1 John 4:4 ESV

   Whether a good day or a bad day, say this affirmation frequently aloud or to yourself. Say it many times, emphasizing a different word each time – **I** am a strong, capable, valuable, woman. I **am** a strong, capable, valuable, woman. I am a **strong**, capable, valuable, woman.

9. **Respect and Reward Yourself**

   Refer to the Rewards List you created in Chapter 2. If you have read this far, sat quietly, focused on your womanhood and developed an image of the woman you wish to be, developed a list of your Behavior Defining Words, identified a mentor or mentors, developed your 'I am' statements, perhaps identified your Guiding Principle, developed your 'I will' goals, and said the affirmation, reward yourself.

10. **Insight to ponder**

    Developing an image of the woman you choose to be is a remarkable experience. Sometimes this image is so different from how we are currently living our life that it seems surreal. But it is not a fantasy and it is achievable, regardless of how horrible your life may be, because we carry this image inside ourselves, in our essence. It then becomes up to us to demonstrate this image in our outward behavior. The most profound way to accomplish this is through the power of 'I am' statements.

11. **Watch for your personal milestone of growth**
    My Personal Milestone

    My day-to-day life changed dramatically when I became the woman I chose to be. Every interaction I had with my husband, my birth family, and my business associates, took place from the completely new woman inside myself. My husband increased the tension but I did not falter. My new woman navigated from the perspective of dignity, poise, graciousness and clarity. No insult defeated me. I moved away from it because I emotionally distanced myself from it. My new woman did not engage and her strength increased.

12. **Mantra to Remember:**

Everything within you changes when you no longer respond the way he expects you to.

13. **Signs of healing:**

Healing is a slow process and just as with a broken limb, each day repair takes place until the limb becomes strong.

A sign of healing

When you look at him and know that you are no longer connected by any puppet strings he attempts to pull. When you are so completely your own person, with values and behaviors you choose that define who you are, and you view him more clearly than you ever have before.

Part II

Living from Your Core Values

16

Survive and Grow Step Five

*In a theater, when the scrim is raised,
the audience views the scene clearly for the first time.*

Seeing Your World Clearly

When we change our behavior to align with the woman we choose to be, and we view our world through *her* eyes, our perception of our life changes dramatically.

Seeing your world clearly enables you to recognize the bait when he throws it, and make the decision to not bite.

Taking Another Look at The Scenes

There is a startling difference between looking at your life through the eyes of the woman you have now chosen to be, and how you previously looked at your life. Watching the same scenes that you watched in Step Three (Chapter 12), but this time through the eyes of the new you, produces dramatically different results. The woman you are now doesn't react in the same way.

In addition to watching 'old' scenes, you begin to watch the events of your life in real time as they are happening. Gone are the days when you were wound so tight with tension you reacted on the surface with runaway emotions that might explode.

Now you have the strength of character, the self-discipline and the instinct, to step back and observe your life as it is happening. Your detachment allows you to see the action clearly, to delve into it and identify all the nuances you previously did not see. Scenes in your life come into sharp focus, and you ask yourself how you failed in the past to observe the details.

Becoming the woman you choose to be is fundamental to seeing your world clearly. It's like waking up from a very long, interminable dream that you didn't know you were living in.

It also opens the door to move toward wise decision-making. Every minute that you remain the 'new you,' is a moment invested in the transformation of your life. As has been said many times already in this book, it is a process, it takes time and requires perseverance and patience with yourself.

New Kelly

Kelly has changed. Ten months passed since that first day when she tentatively and hesitatingly began her practice of Step Two. She's worked her way through Steps Three and Four and her new demeanor, the New Kelly, is noticeable.

She has matured and is careful, reflective and thoughtful. She measures her words, thinks quietly and speaks when she has something of value to say. Even her voice tone has modulated. She appears taller somehow and she's gained in stature from the changes in her behavior and her increasing self-respect. 'Impulsive Kelly' is fading away and being replaced by New Kelly, a woman who is in control of herself.

"I'm using all of the Steps in every area of my life," Kelly tells me. "And every day I understand more about myself, and everyone and everything in my life. I'm far less inclined to blurt out the first thought I have, whether at home with Dan or in a meeting at work. I think before I speak, and very often I don't react at all. I frequently stop and picture myself inwardly and outwardly as the woman in my inner core essence. And my behaviors in every situation are beginning to reflect *me*, who I am in my heart and soul. The power of my 'I am' statements is remarkable."

Inner Core Values

Kelly has progressed steadily, deeply pondering her B-F-P and life in general during her daily quiet time. And she continually delves into who and what she chooses to be, the woman she chooses to exemplify.

"I know who I want to be now," she says.

And then she laughs and corrects herself.

"No, I know who I *am*!"

182

Kelly recites the inner core values she has developed for herself, the Behavior Defining Measurement Words that describe the woman she has now become, framed as her 'I am' statements: "I am dignified, I am strong, I am steadfast, I am intelligent, I am discerning, I am soft, I am tender, I am peaceful, I am self-controlled, I am aware of myself and my surroundings."

She is proud of her accomplishment. I ask her if she wishes to share with me the name of the notable woman, or composite woman, she chose to be her all-encompassing example and mentor, but she politely declines.

"No, I'd rather keep her to myself. But this I will say; she is one badass woman!"

We share a laugh.

When I first met Kelly—the hunched over, confused, weak, angry and emotionally isolated Kelly, she could never be imagined as wanting to pattern her life after a 'badass' woman.

What Clarity Can Produce

In a theater, when a scrim is raised (a thin veil of cloth between the audience and the stage) the audience realizes they were viewing the scene fuzzily. Suddenly everything is clear, the colors are brighter and the actors detailed. The same is true in our lives. When we develop self-respect, when we step back to view our life from a distance, and when we raise the scrim—the misconceptions and automatic responses—we see everything more accurately and well-defined.

Kelly began to remove the veil that previously hid the details in her life and looked at each scene through the eyes of the woman she has chosen to be. In countless scenes with Dan she now looks at her behavior and realizes her impulsive reactions were the veil that kept her from clearly viewing Dan and his behavior as the complex, cunning and destructive forces they are. And in those scenes, she also observes herself in much greater detail.

When New Kelly takes a clear, unobstructed look at the realities of her husband, her marriage and her life, she recognizes the serious nature of the problems she previously numbed herself from recognizing or accepting. Problems inherent with Dan and also embedded in herself.

New Kelly does not hesitate to identify the details of what makes her crazy, and she writes a list of them, adding to it as she recognizes additional realities. With the scrim, the veil, no longer obscuring reality Kelly now lives her life with a new type of alertness: Not as a soldier expecting attack but as a keen and very careful observer who misses nothing.

Fundamentally, seeing your world more clearly can also mean seeing your spouse and yourself as others see you. One unexpected result of this can be a bit of a shock—realizing that some people around you have indeed recognized the dynamic in your marriage, but they never said anything to you about their observations. Why not? There can be a sense of betrayal involved. Why didn't they try to help by leveling with you? Usually it's because they didn't want to get involved or assumed you wouldn't welcome the input. Nevertheless, this realization is a disappointment; another realization that your life has been far less than palatable, including for those around you.

When Kelly sees her world clearly, she also must process her anger, frustration and the realization that she has been foolish to let Dan use her. These are not easy emotions to deal with and New Kelly applies her increasing wisdom to address them. She identifies the work she needs to do and she takes steps to develop healthy physical activity as a way to burn off some of her anger.

New Kelly Replaces Old Kelly

For several weeks, Kelly completed an assignment I previously gave to her: Step Five of the Survive and Grow Steps.

She once again looked at numerous scenes in her life, just as she did in Step Three, but this time she evaluated every detail through the eyes of her new self, the woman she has chosen to become, New Kelly.

"What did you think when you watched those scenes again, only this time as the new you?"

Kelly laughs.

"After I watched a few, I fast-forwarded them."

"What do you mean?"

184

"I realized the woman in those scenes is gone. She is a stranger to me. I can't imagine myself behaving like that today."

"That's a rather dramatic statement."

"Well, it's true. And I actually laughed several times when I realized that Dan, poor stuck-in-the-past Dan, only knows one way to behave, like a ridiculous fool because that previous woman, the former me, could be depended on to respond in the same old way."

Kelly pauses.

"But it also made me sad."

"Why?"

"Honestly?"

"Yes, if you want to share."

Kelly pauses for a long time and looks at the floor and then she looks up.

"Because if I'd known what I know now, I wouldn't have given Dan the time of day when we met."

We are both quiet for a moment.

"But you didn't know, so you can't be blamed for the past. It's over. Today you can go forward, keeping in mind your new goals."

Kelly straightens her back.

"A lot has changed. For example, I don't argue with Dan anymore. And I've analyzed what I need to do in every area of my life."

"How do you accomplish not arguing with Dan?"

"Arguing pointlessly is not something my inner woman, the real me, would do. She simply would not engage with Dan. There is nothing to be gained by trying to argue with him, about anything. To put it bluntly, he just isn't worth the effort and it leads to demeaning behavior by me, which my inner woman does not do.

"As hard as it is for me to believe, I have complete respect for his choice to be an asshole. But who I am now, the woman I am now, does not waste her time arguing with any asshole.

"If he thinks he is always right, then so be it. My goal is to make sure his behavior does not ruin my life or the lives of my kids. I have quite a

185

few tasks to identify and deal with as I go forward. But I'm sure I'll be able to handle them, no matter how difficult it turns out to be."

"So, how does this play out in your daily life?"

"I have clearly looked at each role in my life through my 'new' eyes, recognized the underlying truth in each one, and developed Rules that I follow in order to live with him and preserve my Guiding Principle, which is peace.

"I know how I arrived at each Rule and they provide me with a firm guideline to follow. When I am with Dan, I pause, analyze what is happening, say my Rules to myself and behave exactly as my Rules require. In all circumstances my Guiding Principle is to protect my inner peace and provide peace for my children.

Rules of Non-Engagement

"I looked clearly at how he won't discuss anything with me and realized that he does that to control me. His satisfaction comes when I get upset. I examined the details and realized that conflict always happens if I ask him a question, or ask him for something, or offer my opinion about something.

"I watched many scenes and noticed something; he always takes an opposite stance to me. Always. There is no logic or reasoning involved, he just automatically says no, or blows up. It's all a game to him and he always has to win. He wins when I get upset.

"The way to avoid getting upset is to not ask him for anything or offer my opinion. I already know how it will turn out, so why do it? Therefore, my second rule is, 'Never ask him for anything.' (Kelly's first rule, mentioned in an earlier chapter is, 'Do not expect anything from him.')

"I also examined, from the perspective of the woman I am now, all the aspects of my so-called relationship with him. Regardless of what subject it might be, any opinion I express is met with derision. Therefore, my third rule is, 'I do not volunteer my opinion.'

"From that came my fourth rule: If he asks for my opinion, I will give it when I have worded it carefully. If he is derisive about it, I ignore him. My attitude is, he asked for my opinion, I gave it, and that's the end of it.

"An additional rule is, I never share my inner thoughts with him. This came about from further clarity in examining what happened in the past when I shared my thoughts, dreams, even my experiences growing up. He eventually throws the information back in my face. It is pointless for me to continue to fall into that trap. My inner woman is much smarter than that and keeps her counsel."

Kelly continues and outlines all of her Rules of Non-Engagement that New Kelly follows in her daily life with Dan. Each Rule evolved from her assessment of the details and dynamics she observed when she viewed the scenes in her life. By looking at each one through the eyes of New Kelly, her careful and clear assessment of the elements of her relationship with Dan that caused her so much grief in the past, helped her devise a strategy for dealing with them.

The goal of New Kelly is clear and concise: To maintain her dignity and achieve as much peace as possible without acquiescing to Dan's unreasonable demands.

Rules of Non-Engagement
And the Clarity from Which They Evolved

The Rule	Clarity
I do not expect anything from him.	It is unrealistic to expect anything from him.
I do not ask him for anything.	If I ask him for anything, he will say no, so it is a waste of time to ask.
I do not volunteer my opinion.	My opinions are always derided.
If I am specifically asked for my opinion, I will carefully give it.	If he derides my opinion, I ignore what he says and remove myself.
I do not make casual comments	Innocent, friendly, comments are derided so they are a waste of time.
I do not argue. Ever.	Arguing is pointless. If safety is involved, I take action and leave.

I do not take the bait.	I recognize when he is baiting me to argue for his pleasure, and I remove myself without comment.
I carefully plan ahead.	He cannot handle spontaneity so I carefully plan ahead for all necessary activities.
I do not reveal my inner thoughts.	Too many times I regretted sharing with him. I no longer make that mistake.
I am gracious if he treats me well.	I allow myself to enjoy the good times but do not allow myself to be fooled by them.
I am never impulsive. Ever.	I do not allow myself to act or speak impulsively in any way or situation.
I will not behave in a way that is inappropriate to my core values, my Guiding Principle, or contrary to my behavior as the woman I choose to be.	
I develop my own outlets for my creativity, spontaneity, joyfulness and fun. I am quietly but firmly steadfast if he tries to curtail these and I ignore his derision.	

NOTE: For anyone who may say, "How do you expect to have a good relationship if you follow these rules?" I remind you that Kelly does not have a good relationship with Dan. Since two people in a relationship must both commit to work hard to make it a good relationship, and Dan refuses to do his part, Kelly is working with what she has. Her goal is to save her sanity and try to provide some peace for herself and her children while they are trapped.

Clarity Comes from Our Body Focus Points

Consciousness is a popular term today and perhaps it means a number of things to various people. From the Survive and Grow perspective, consciousness means being closely aligned with our inner life and not just passing it off as a once-a-day quiet time experience. Rather, it is something to be referenced constantly as we move through our daily activities.

This consciousness grows stronger when we allow ourselves to expand on our daily practice by going deeper into each of our Body Focus Points. As we do, our affirmations may change and become even stronger, or provide us with a mantra that helps us through the smallest details of our life. Clarity results when we deeply examine each B-F-P from the perspective of the woman we've now chosen to be.

Women are Not a Bottomless Pit of Love

Our heart chakra, our love center, is a vitally important B-F-P to dwell upon. Love is a precious commodity and while the universe may be the source of unending love, the reality is that we women cannot love without any limits or we become depleted, especially when we live in an environment where we are not emotionally nourished or replenished.

We know that a gold bracelet or a bouquet of roses does not replenish us beyond the few minutes when we unwrap the gift and feel momentarily loved (gifts are typical behavior of narcissists when they are love-bombing).

What replenishes us are genuine heart-felt kind words, caring words and comforting gestures, and the knowledge that he won't hurt us for the purpose of enjoying power and pleasure. No amount of gold jewelry overcomes the realities with which we live in a miserable marriage.

Yes, there are women who make the trade-off of currency for tolerating anything from a man. That is a choice they are free to make. But this book is not directed at them—until they no longer want to live as a monetary transaction.

When we delve into our heart chakra and examine how we are giving love and to whom, we often see our world more clearly. Clarity comes from breathing deeply and experiencing a 'releasing' compassion for someone who doesn't show us love.

Love Should Not Be Wasted

Dwelling on our heart chakra can also cause us to ask ourselves if we are wasting love. Wasting love is something that those of us in miserable marriages usually do, often for years. Eventually we can run out of our supply.

Of all the mistakes men make with their wives, this is the biggest mistake of all—to ignore the possibility, no, the probability, that a woman who is mistreated will eventually run out of her supply of unconditional love to give. When love for someone is depleted, it doesn't come back.

An often-told Bible story is a metaphor for our love and loving:

A farmer spread seed across his fields and some seed fell on the hard-packed soil of a pathway, some fell on rock, some fell on good soil, and some fell among weeds. Predictably, the seed that falls on rock or the hard path doesn't grow.

When I thought about this story, I realized I continually threw the seed of my love on the solid rock of my husband's heart. I wasted that seed, that love. I also recognized that I repeated that same unproductive exercise with other people in my life. Seed placed on solid rock cannot grow and there is nothing I can do to change that reality.

When You Can No Longer Love, You Can Have Respect and Compassion

I replaced my efforts to love with respect and compassion for the reality that each individual chooses how they want to move through life. My husband chose to be angry and impossible to please. He chose to shout, to withdraw and not communicate. All the efforts to love him and persuade him to become loving were seeds landing on solid rock.

Instead of endlessly trying to change that scenario, I made the decision to respect his choices. Not to go along with him, acquiesce to him or argue with him, but to be the woman in my inner core who remained dignified, intelligent, calm and wise, and viewed his actions from a safe, emotionally detached distance.

Respect and compassion seem to be strange words when applied to an impossible-to-please man. But put another way, because I no longer felt irrevocably tied to him and had no illusion that I could influence him to change, I could exercise respect and compassion for him to make his choices. They were separate from me. His choices were his to make but I did not have to fall, or be enticed to fall, into his traps.

The new me didn't fall into traps from anyone. I stepped back, released my fantasies and surrendered what I could not change and allowed myself the comfort of offering silent compassion for this man who did not know, would never know, what he missed in life.

This is the fundamental aspect of consciousness—moment by moment assessing the happenings in one's life from the deep connection we form with each strong Body Focus Point within us. Including when we surrender our hopelessness to a higher power, much as those in twelve step programs customarily do.

Awareness Brings Clarity

When you are living as the woman in your essence, you are aware every minute of how your life is unfolding, what you are doing and how you are doing it, what you are saying and how you are saying it.

You *become* the woman in your inner core and you live by, and express, your core values—and you find and live by your Guiding Principle. Nothing and no one, not even he, can alter that.

And if you falter, if you slip back into an old pattern, you catch yourself. You do not berate yourself you simply turn toward your inner woman and core values and correct your course. It permeates your life in a very positive way because you are now an observer of his tirades, not a participant.

It is an entirely new way to live. You do not become an automaton. You become a highly alert, self-aware and active participant in your life and you evaluate all of your emotions and your behavior responses through the eyes of your highly valued woman—*you.*

What Do You Do with the Anger?

Most important, when you have clarity you step back and recognize that you *should* be angry with the injustice, the lies and manipulations that plague your life. Unlike in the past, when you automatically lashed out to defend yourself, the new you can evaluate every situation, see clearly, grasp

191

more fully the insidious nature of what you are faced with, and react with caution, care, wisdom and skill.

Remember, as already stated earlier in this book, you are dealing with a professional-level manipulator and psychological/emotional abuser. You are no match until you have completed your training and learned how to cope with the destructive world in which you live. (It is important to insert here an important reality: You will never be able to compete, head-to-head, with a narcissist—especially a full-blown NPD or other individuals who are committed to evil. Don't even try.)

Turning Anger into Strategy

Recognizing and accepting your anger as an appropriate response, but not turning it into impulsive words or actions, comes from clarity and self-observance. It is not achieved early in the growth process but expands over time.

One woman shared with me the story that her narcissistic ex-husband confronted her at their child's sporting event and angrily demanded that she sit with him and his new wife. He caught her off guard of course, the consummate skill of a narcissist, and she defensively launched into a logic-based response: "I have no intention of becoming part of your harem."

A few months later, when this woman had grown significantly, her response in the exact same situation might become: "Isn't the weather beautiful today?" This is a skillful response from a very self-possessed mature woman, a response to which her narcissistic ex-husband cannot relate because she did not take the bait. While he might persist, trying to force her into a confrontation, she can remain neutral, even smile and repeat herself. In truth, no one can force you to say something that is not in your best interest.

Not taking the bait is what Survive and Grow Step Five is about. Seeing your world clearly enables you to recognize the bait, make the decision to not bite and respond in a dignified irrelevant manner.

How important is this? Viewing your life with clarity, studying it, examining your role and changing your behavior can alter your entire life if you are willing to undertake the work required to do so.

An accomplished young professional man sadly shook his head and told me about his frustration with his mother. He loved her dearly but she never did the hard work to move past her difficult childhood and abusive marriage. He said that anger was his mother's response to every event in her life. He would ask her to behave herself if they attended a family get together because she always seemed to be looking for a fight. Her son dutifully did his best to have a relationship with her but he dreaded any event that might cause an explosion—and almost every event did. She lived for decades with inner turmoil and ferocious anger that gripped her relentlessly throughout her entire adult life, and affected her relationship with her son. What a terrible waste.

Connections

Perhaps one of the most important results of seeing our world clearly is to assess and understand the connections we have with everyone in our life. Connections are like threads or delicate wires over which waves of information, mutual support or just acquaintanceship function. Many of our connections involve giving and receiving. Others are only casual, perhaps simply connecting socially, such as we enjoy the same sport or our children attend the same school.

Connections grow, deepen or fade away as our lives mature and alter. The close friend with whom we shared everything as teenagers may no longer fit into our life. Perhaps we have children and she never does so the significance of children doesn't resonate with her. There are countless other examples.

Birth family connections can change with the introduction of in-laws, geographical distances and career paths that vary. Connections with spouses and adult children also widen or narrow as life unfolds. In all examples, it is the effort expended by the individuals in the connections that keeps connections alive. Showing genuine interest in the life of the other person is always necessary. But truth be told, sometimes the connections just wither and die through no one's fault.

When we marry, we are connected to each other in ways that we assume will be uninterrupted, unchanged and not affected by how we alter as people and deal with outside circumstances. Time and life experiences change everyone, including us and the spouse or partner whom we think we know. Often connections between us alter in ways that erode the very foundation of the relationship.

Taking a thorough look at all the ways we are connected, or not connected, to everyone in our life can be enormously helpful to us in dealing with uncertainty, lack of self-confidence, guilt and all the other emotions and decisions involved in surviving and growing. We can find ourselves mired in feelings of guilt if we don't take time to assess how we are connected and accept that connections to others can grow, diminish, wither and end as life unfolds.

Trying to cling to something that is changing is like holding on to a rope that is coated with a layer of ice. It is healthier to mature to a point where one can look at connections with other people and graciously accept that changes are fundamental to life, like the change of seasons in nature.

I know a woman who, severely and regularly beaten as a child by her father and berated incessantly by him as an adult, still struggles to overcome feelings of guilt. Her patience wore thin when he became aged and demented. He passed away a few years ago but she continues to ruminate on, analyze, and strive to attain maturity to no longer be the little girl he mercilessly beat. Gradually, she is reaching the maturity to understand that it was not only OK, but necessary and morally correct, for her to protect herself instead of remaining connected to him like a small child who could not escape the mistreatment. This same maturation process applies to marriages in which there is mistreatment too.

Children and Connections

The arrival of children affects marriage connections in profound ways. Friends without children don't understand how our priorities shift when late social nights are suddenly out of the question. Spouses have a difficult time grasping how motherhood takes precedence over everything, not to mention the impact on the relationship from fatigue and incessant demands from very small humans.

194

"We had a good relationship until we had kids," is a comment I frequently hear. In every case, the woman is stretched to the breaking point because her spouse wants and expects life to remain as it was pre-child. He doesn't understand or accept that the connection between them has been altered.

As we mature and have broader life experiences, we may recognize we have fewer common bonds with friends and relatives. Even the pursuit of spiritual guidance and practice may evolve and send us in directions that others do not understand. The list can be long of how we connect, or no longer connect, with the people in our life.

It is a good idea to put together a Connection Chart that diagrams how we connect with people in our life, including our spouse. For many people our only connection may be a shared activity such as meeting up with an acquaintance for a sport. For others, we may have a connection because of parenting, life style and intellectual interests. And if we are fortunate, we have one or two individuals with whom we can mutually share struggles, good times, insights, and lean on when we need help.

The goal of the connection exercise is to illustrate that there is no right or wrong number of connections to have with the various people in our life, and to help us recognize that people change, including us, and our connections evolve too. It's part of giving us clarity, facing realities that help us choose the future direction of our life.

Connecting as Your New Woman

When you radically change your life, when you become a woman unlike what you previously were, you will need to expend some effort to form new connections. Survive and Grow Step Five (Chapter 16) discussed the importance and value of mentors—women who exemplify what we choose to be. Once we have selected the Core Values to define our new life, we need to carefully expand our horizon to find other women who share our new outlook. Reaching out may be as straight-forward as joining an exercise class, signing up for a college course, volunteering at a charity or any of a multitude of possibilities.

A note: Do not expand your horizon by having an affair—chances are very good that you'll connect with a man who is very similar to the one you are married to.

Sample Connection Chart

<u>Who</u>	<u>Connection</u>	<u>How Deep</u>
Friend 1	We are both mothers, have difficult marriages, have similar ethics	I can tell her anything. She listens and understands and is wise.
Friend 2	We are both mothers, share some life experiences	It is pleasant to be with her but I avoid topics she disagrees with.
Brother	Family. We have the same parents	We are polite but have no common interests. Our lives are very different.
Spouse	Only through our children.	Our prior connections via mutual interests and goals have eroded.
Associates	We work at the same place.	Professional, respectful

Transformation Action Plan

1. Sit quietly and breathe into the woman you now choose to be. Absorb her, enjoy her, understand her, look closely at her, admire her and respect her.

2. Review the Core Values you developed in Step Four (Chapter 14) and apply them to each of your life roles.

3. Watch again the scenes from your life, just as you did in Step Three, only this time watch them through the eyes of the woman you choose to be. How would she behave in the scene you are watching? What would she say, if she chose to say anything at all?

What does she see in the relationships portrayed in the scenes? What is her assessment of everyone in the scenes?

4. Apply the clarity of your new woman, who you are now, to scenes and situations in your daily life. Ask her, 'Why? How did this happen? Why did I end up like this?' Delve into every corner of your behavior and your life by looking clearly through her eyes and apply her character traits, her behavior, her Behavior Defining Words to each situation.

5. Repeat this process every day over a period of several weeks. Begin to practice your new behaviors that reflect the woman you now choose to be. If you inadvertently slip into old patterns of behavior, stop yourself, correct your actions and bring them back into alignment with the new you. Do not criticize yourself.

6. Regularly remind yourself of your Behavior Defining Words by saying them as a mantra throughout your day. Be sure to always use 'I am' with each.

7. Consider incorporating the Rules of Non-Engagement into your life or develop a list of rules for yourself. Memorize them and remind yourself of them whenever you are with your husband.

8. Create a Connection Chart to help you clarify the current nature of your relationships.

9. Record your moments of clarity in your journal. Review them periodically as a reminder of how you are transforming your life.

10. **Say this Affirmation**
   I have clarity in all areas of my life

   Open my eyes, that I may behold... Psalm 119:18 ESV

   Whether a good day or a bad day, say this affirmation frequently aloud or to yourself. Say it many times, emphasizing a different word each time. **I** have clarity in all areas of my life. I **have** clarity in all areas of my life. I have **clarity** in all areas of my life.

11. Respect and Reward Yourself

Refer to the Rewards List you prepared in Chapter 2. If you have read this far, sat quietly and enjoyed being the woman you chose to be, and have brought clarity to scenes in your life, have repeatedly stated your 'I am' defining words, are developing behaviors that reflect the woman you choose to be, and said the affirmation, reward yourself.

12. Insight to ponder

It can be sad and sobering to view your previous life through the eyes of the woman you have now chosen to be. We may feel despondent that so much of our life was lost due to our behavior patterns that were not productive and are inappropriate for the woman who lives in our inner core essence. We should not dwell on the past but instead focus on the future. For the woman we have chosen to be will now provide the behavior and the thoughts we need in order to move forward.

13. Watch for your personal milestone of growth
My Personal Milestone

When I incorporated the Rules of Non-Engagement into my life, I experienced an inner peace. Sitting at the dinner table my husband might scowl and criticize the food I prepared. It meant nothing to me. I did not respond. I asked my daughter about her day and graciously offered pleasantries to my husband as my dignified inner woman would do at a beautifully laid table in a palace. If he chose not to respond I did not press the point as it was immaterial to me. His choices were his. Every day, I experienced more clarity. My new woman reacted with equanimity, grace, intelligence, intuition and strength.

14. Mantra to Remember

As a gracious, intelligent, self-possessed woman, I do not engage with nonsense in any manner from anyone.

15. Signs of healing

Healing is a slow process and, just as with a broken limb, every day repair takes place until the limb becomes strong.

A sign of healing

When you realize that your values and behavior are your sole concern and you do not bend your values or behavior to enable anyone's need for control over you.

17

Survive and Grow Step Six

*The most difficult decision to make is
the one that requires you to take a stand and not waiver.*

Managing Every Decision

Our lives are the product of our decisions. Minute by minute we continuously make decisions that mold who we are, how we live and how we relate to and affect others. We never bother to think about most of the decisions that comprise our daily life.

Becoming our new self, the woman we choose to be, requires that we start thinking about every decision, particularly the decisions we do not believe we have the power, the right or the ability to make.

Many decisions are habits we never bother to examine:

- Open the mail and put the torn envelopes in the trash or leave them scattered on the table until later.
- Take the chance and cut across two lanes of traffic to not miss the exit.
- Go to bed at a reasonable hour or sit mindlessly in front of TV, the computer, or iPhone.
- Yell at the kids to hurry up instead of planning ahead.
- Leave the apple core on the counter instead of taking two seconds to put it down the disposal.
- Buy the gadget from QVC, sign up for a gym membership to be rarely used, buy the candy, the big screen TV, enter into a lease for the 'right' car to impress the neighbors, sign a house loan document with payments you have no idea how you will cover.
- Take the kids to the library or park, or set them in front of video games so you can have time to yourself.
- Pay the bills at the first of each month or after we've received three notices in red ink.
- Eat the leftover cake or throw it away.

- Sit down and talk, and patiently listen to each other without interrupting, or pack the calendar so full there is never any time.
- Get up in the morning and meditate, read inspiring texts, or lay in bed until the last minute.
- Pout and go silent, instead of problem-solving.
- Indulge in sarcasm instead of kindness.
- Argue instead of thinking things through.
- Say the first thing that comes to your mind, or invoke the Great Pause, formulate a response, or perhaps say nothing.

When we live in a miserable marriage, we face a formidable obstacle. Many of the decisions we would like to make, or know we should make, are blocked by the deliberate actions of our husband or, more often, by the sheer terror he has instilled in us that if we dare do anything on our own volition he will make life difficult for us on multiple fronts.

As has already been stated, no one can fully grasp the power he holds over us if they haven't personally experienced a miserable marriage. That is why Step Two is so important; the first decision made by and for ourselves is the hardest.

A great many decisions are put off, made impulsively or never made at all because of fear. Those of us in a miserable marriage are ruled by fear. We know fear perhaps better than anyone. And we are skilled at not making decisions beneficial to us because we have been trained to always put ourselves at the bottom of the family's list of priorities. That is why initiating the Step Two practice is so important. When we learn to manage our decision making our life can change for the better.

As we incorporate our New Woman into our life, a vital question is part of being *her*: What decisions would *she* make? How would she summon the courage to make decisions that are important?

Kelly Continues to Survive and Grow

Kelly has made incredible strides in her growth while living with the reality of Dan. At times she feels she will die from a broken heart, but she has accepted that Dan is who he is and she keeps moving forward. She lives by her Guiding Principle, peace. For Kelly her children are her reason for living, growing and planning for her future and theirs.

But Kelly has an enormous problem, one that her newly-found self-respect and her changes in behavior are bringing to a monumental climax. Kelly must face and deal with the devastating impact of Dan's financial games.

Kelly is honest with herself. She's scared to death of how Dan will react when New Kelly makes major changes. She practices her deep breathing and reaches into her inner core to find the courage to do what she knows she must do.

New Kelly recognizes that it is her responsibility to put the welfare of herself and her children first. The woman Kelly has chosen to be does not passively acquiesce, submissively give-in and pretend there isn't a problem when there is a huge problem—the financial security of herself and her children.

Clarity dawned on Kelly with a gut-wrenching blow when she reviewed scenes of Dan manipulating her. She recognized and finally grasped the financial burden she carries as part of 'old' Kelly placating Dan to avoid his rage. She now understands and accepts that Dan isn't going to cooperate with her to solve their financial problems.

New Kelly is furious when she acknowledges how foolish she has been when she allowed Dan to get away with using her. But New Kelly doesn't do what old Kelly would have done; scream at Dan. Instead, she formulates a plan and carries it out. With her ever-increasing clarity of thinking and her clear concept of how she, the new woman Kelly, views Dan's financial games as the emotional abuse they in fact are, she embarks on a process of preparation.

First, she allows her inner woman to clearly evaluate the situation and what she hears is, "You've got to be kidding me! You let him take money from your account without asking or explaining what it's for? Let's get real!"

And a startling reality thrusts itself into her consciousness. Her entire background trained her to be blindly supportive of men. Inherited from previous generations of women—her original sin line might be one way to describe it—Kelly did not grasp how deeply ingrained lay her behavior pattern to acquiesce to Dan.

Dignified inner New Kelly says to her, "Let's manage the decisions that need to be made."

But some old messages also play in her head and engender confusion. Such as, 'The man is head of the family' exacerbated by memories of her mother always giving in to her father. Kelly reminds herself that her mother did not work outside the home, whereas Kelly is the primary wage earner in her household. As in most of the challenging steps Kelly has climbed in her growth process, she went through a period of time when a battle ensued within her between old patterns and her new goals and realities.

Money, Money and Money

More than any other issue, the earning, spending and saving of money tears marriages apart (some consider sex and in-laws as first and second on the list but I believe money is primary, particularly today when a woman's paycheck is crucial). As noted in an earlier chapter, greater numbers of women than ever before are in the workforce earning a living—not earning extra money or vacation money or money for college educations for kids—women are working to put a roof over the heads of their families, food on the table, shoes on their children and to buy school supplies so their children can participate equally in a classroom.

These women are also attending to the traditional roles of mothering, housekeeping and shepherding the family calendar. Fortunate indeed is the rare woman who has a husband who shoulders the home front responsibilities equally.

For a woman in a miserable marriage, money is the primary problem in her entrapment and it takes many forms. In the worst-case scenarios a woman has no money available to her. I know of one woman whose husband gives her five dollars cash each morning for gasoline to transport her children to school. She dutifully stops at the gas pump every day. Additionally, she follows a budget dictated by her husband and somehow manages to feed a family of four on an allotment that would have been considered frugal twenty years ago.

Other women I know are given an allowance each month that would be viewed as enormous by most women. Thousands of dollars for personal care, clothing and accessories in order to maintain an arm-candy appearance and forestall the aging process which often signals the end of the marriage and replacement by a younger model.

But most women, particularly those who are earning a living, are just too tired or spread too thin to attend to the details of their financial situation. One woman I know concentrated all her efforts on her career and did not have a clue about her family finances until the IRS seized her bank accounts. She erroneously assumed her husband filed their taxes.

Another woman, dealing with the porn addiction of her husband, met with a divorce attorney and discovered the five-thousand-dollar savings account she painstakingly accumulated from a part-time job would not even cover the retainer fee required for an attorney to just take a look at her case.

The stories are endless, but suffice it to say, we women need to become serious about money. The days of having a man take care of us, attend to the family finances and make sure our futures are secure, are long gone.

What can a woman in a miserable marriage do?

- Learn! Learn about your family's current financial state. If you are not completely knowledgeable about the balances owing on your house, cars, credit cards, taxes and any other debts, find out the answers. If you need to do so, call or walk into the banks that hold the credit on your accounts and sit down with someone and get the answers—all the answers. In addition, there are numerous books and online websites to educate you about money, some specifically aimed at women.

- Do not sign anything without reading it first, particularly tax filings. And make absolutely sure you have your own separate copy of everything you sign. Do not depend on his filing system or his willingness to later provide you with copies should you need them.

- I know a woman who, married for thirty years, paid no attention to any financial matters and blithely signed tax forms each year. When her husband announced he had been involved for some time in an affair and intended to file for divorce, this lovely lady who married her husband right after high school and did not acquire additional education or a career and devoted herself to raising her children, did not have a penny to her name. The divorce court decreed that she had five years to acquire some education, figure out a career and learn to support herself. This illustrates what is stated in an earlier chapter; you do not receive points for good behavior as a wife either from your husband or the court.

- Do your best to save some money in an account in your name only. Even if you can only deposit a few dollars try and do so on a regular basis. It is amazing how comforting it is for a woman to know that she has some money that is hers alone even if it is a small amount. As already noted, make sure the account is in your name only and preferably in a bank completely separate from a bank with any joint accounts you have with your partner.

  - Note: Regarding the issue of secrecy, millions of men (yes, you read that correctly) have secret bank accounts. How do I know this?

  - A friend of mine, a staff attorney for a revenue department of a State, spent a significant amount of her career handling the funds received by the State from abandoned accounts—accounts established by men who died unexpectedly and left no arrangements for the funds to transfer to relatives. (No, a State does not have to find relatives.)

  - My own sweet, lovable unsuspecting grandmother was stunned, hurt and shocked to discover when my grandfather died, that he had a secret bank account. For the sixty years she was married to him he had tucked away money she knew nothing about.

- o A young man, engaged to be married, informed his boss (a friend of mine) that he had a secret bank account because, "You never know what might happen in a marriage."

- o A contractor who handles repairs on an apartment complex and requests that payments for services be divided in half and paid via two separate checks so that he can, "Deposit one into an account his wife doesn't know about because she spends too much money."

These are only a few of the stories about which I am personally aware, but you get the picture. The bottom line is, women are notoriously naïve about men and how they view, cherish and protect 'their' money.

- Do not become pregnant. Harsh words, perhaps, but when you are in a miserable marriage bringing an innocent child into the situation is questionable ethically and certainly complicates your position on many fronts, particularly financially. Take every precaution and do not let down your guard regardless of how seductive your husband can be. Use multiple forms of birth control and don't let him talk you into unprotected sex. Not even once.

Kelly Makes Some Tough Decisions

Kelly learns from her intelligent and strong inner woman that yes changes must be made and are going to be made. This is no longer negotiable. Because of her Rules, she never confronts Dan without carefully planning ahead. She watches for a moment when he appears to be approachable and she asks for an appointment with him to discuss their finances.

"What do you want to discuss?" he snarls at her.

"I want to sit down with you in your office at your business to discuss our family finances."

"Well, what exactly do you want to know?"

"I want to know more about what is happening with your business and what has caused you to need so much money from my earnings."

"Here we go again. I tell you what you need to know."

The new dignified, gracious, intelligent Kelly does not lose her self-control. "I think it could be helpful to you if I know more. What day and time can we meet?"

"Oh, for heaven's sake! Tomorrow then, in the afternoon. Come by at three."

Kelly Moves Forward to Take Charge of Her Life

Kelly dreads the meeting she's scheduled with Dan and steels herself to be ready to apply every lesson she has learned about being New Kelly. Determined to remain calm in the face of what she assumes will be Dan's outrage, Kelly is resolved to satisfy her self-imposed responsibility to inform Dan of her plans. She has reviewed the potential scene over and over in her mind, like a football team reviewing their plays, and she is ready for the unexpected. She intends to calmly tell Dan what she is going to do and then she will leave his office in a dignified manner. Under no circumstance will she allow herself to fall into a trap of arguing, explaining, seeking understanding from him or enduring his rage and threats.

Kelly arrives at Dan's office the next afternoon for her appointment and is greeted by her sister-in-law Melissa, the office manager, because Dan's brother loaned Dan money to start the business so Melissa got a job as part of the deal. She isn't exactly a fan of Kelly. They chat meaninglessly for a minute and Kelly asks where Dan is.

"He left. I don't know where he went."

"I have an appointment to meet with him at three."

Melissa looks at Kelly quizzically.

"I don't know if he's planning to come back today."

"Well, I'll wait in his office."

"That's not a good idea."

"Why not?"

"Dan doesn't like anyone in his office when he's not here."

Kelly puts her hand on the door to Dan's office and Melissa looks

207

as though she's going to leap up and thrust her ample buxom body between Kelly and the door.

Kelly sits down and waits. Until four-thirty. Then she says goodbye to Melissa and drives home.

To say Kelly is upset is an understatement. She's furious and hurt. She sits in her car outside the kids' daycare and tries to calm herself. It's one of those times when she wonders if she can take any more. With great effort she breathes into her inner woman, her New Kelly and struggles to overcome the old Kelly who wants to meet Dan at the door and throw something in his face.

With incredible effort and resolve, New Kelly prevails. She picks the kids up on schedule and takes them to their favorite pizza place. She doesn't have the energy to cook dinner and sit across the table from Dan, if he even bothers to come home at a decent hour. Kelly lets herself enjoy her kids and calms down but still has an ache in her chest. When they arrive home, Dan's car isn't in the drive so Kelly moves through the routine of baths and bedtime stories and then climbs into the bathtub to try and soothe herself. She is exhausted from the stress, goes to bed and mercifully falls asleep.

The next day Kelly does what she already decided to do and about which she wanted to tell Dan in a calm and business-like manner, if he had shown up for their scheduled meeting. She goes to a bank where she and Dan have not previously had any accounts and opens an account in her name only. She then gives her new account information to the HR department at her place of employment and instructs them to automatically deposit paychecks into her new account.

Her heart is pounding and her palms sweat because this is significant. Her decision signals that the trust on which she believes a marriage can be built is irretrievably broken.

But Kelly also knows with complete assurance that she is doing the right thing, what she needs to do and must do. How many times did she attempt to talk with Dan about their finances? How many times do you hold a door open and invite someone to walk through it only to have them refuse? Eventually a self-respecting, self-valuing intelligent woman realizes that it's time to close the door.

But her clear understanding and resolution to do what must be done doesn't alleviate the nagging ache in Kelly's stomach because she knows an explosion is inevitable.

18

Survival Requires Strategy

Pretend to be weak [so] that he will grow arrogant – Sun Tzu

It's All About Him

New Kelly noticed something that significantly changed how she attempts to communicate with Dan. When she watched the action of her life on the stage and analyzed scenes from the perspective of New Kelly, she realized how often she tried to use logic and reasoning with Dan and how that never accomplished anything except to make her crazy with frustration.

She also noticed that Dan did not share her enthusiasm for anything. If she wanted to go for a walk on the beach because of a beautiful sunset, he didn't. If she wanted to go to a movie, he didn't. If she wanted to invite neighbors for a barbeque, he didn't. It was endless.

She watched scene after scene and realized that Dan had only one interest in life; Dan. His comfort, his needs, his desires came first. Always. And she deduced the key to Dan's behavior: His expectation, his goal in life, his philosophy of life is to never be inconvenienced in any way.

Surprised that she had not figured this out before, once she recognized this aspect of Dan, Kelly freed herself from the last remnants of feeling inadequate in her efforts to be a good wife. She and Dan were not remotely on the same wavelength.

Dan's self-centered, selfish philosophy of life diametrically opposed Kelly's outgoing, upbeat interest in other people, places and events. Having a meaningful relationship with anyone is at times inconvenient. To avoid inconvenience as a goal in life means isolation and relationships that are superficial at best.

When she drew back the veil on Dan and accepted this reality Kelly felt as though a weight lifted from her. She never would have unraveled this clue to Dan without her determined, committed efforts to step back and examine her life from the perspective of distance that her practice of Step

Two provided her.

For Him, It's All About Winning

And further, she recognized that Dan always has to win. If *he* wants to invite the neighbors for a barbeque, that is OK because he must be in charge of all decisions and choices. Logic has absolutely nothing to do with anything and any concern for her needs or feelings does not exist.

Regardless of whatever issue presented itself, large or small, Dan needed to be the decision-maker, the one in charge, the winner. That is why he never wanted to do what Kelly suggested. Because giving in to her suggestions, wants, or needs would mean he didn't 'win' and wouldn't be in complete control.

Every issue always came back to Dan. How he felt, what he needed, what he controlled, how he wanted things to be done. As basic as this seems, Kelly realized what she had failed to see before—that mutuality plays no role in Dan's life on any front. His life centers exclusively around what he wants when he wants it, and having his own way, on winning.

Compromise or discussion that arrives at a mutually beneficial solution, or just doing what a wife wants because it will make her happy, are loses to Dan. Anything less than winning is wimpy, stupid, unmanly. Winning is powerful and winning in a struggle or a contest is more satisfying than merely walking away with a prize for just showing up.

Kelly was startled when she uncovered this truth. Dan baited her into arguments and fights because he wanted a victory in battle. Battling with Kelly gave him the satisfaction of winning after a contest of wills. That is why he never backed down. Even if he takes the approach of nagging Kelly incessantly to get what he wants, he never took the pressure off Kelly because without an opponent his victories held no pleasure, no satisfaction of control and triumph.

Once she fully recognized and accepted this, Kelly changed how she approaches any problem with Dan. She added a new item to her list of Rules: When dealing with Dan always and only speak in terms of benefits to him, never talk in terms of what she wants or needs or what might be mutually beneficial because that guaranteed an argument would ensue.

211

How Dan will 'win,' becomes her new strategy.

This requires practice and skill, and further implementation of the Great Pause. Kelly steps back and analyzes every situation, thinks carefully, and constructs her response about anything in terms of how Dan can 'win' in his mind. A challenging exercise at first, but after a few times using this approach, New Kelly became very adept at it.

She even found humor in the situation a few times when Dan looked at her in surprise. He didn't know what to do with this New Kelly who didn't argue but pointed out how he would benefit, how he would win. He would turn up the heat to try and push her into arguing but Kelly didn't take the bait.

She validated his decisions and structured any interactions or communications from the point of view that Dan should have what he wants. But never, under any condition, at the expense of her money, peace of mind or the welfare of her children.

It's a complicated process because it appears to be counter-intuitive but it significantly helped Kelly in her day-to-day dealings with Dan, as illustrated further below.

This covered everything down to the smallest detail. Remember, in Chapter 4, the blowup about the visit to a nursery to purchase seeds? This would never happen now because New Kelly wouldn't mention anything to Dan about her idea in the first place.

But if she did happen to mention it and he started to blow up, she would immediately and soothingly say something along the line of, "I know how important it is for you to have the day to yourself." Regardless of how dramatic a tantrum he threw, she would just soothingly repeat the same phrase never expanding or deviating from it.

As wimpy, self-effacing or acquiescing as this at first seems, it actually is a very clever way to put full responsibility for the results of his decision-making back on him. Like everything the key element is to completely accept the realities involved. Yes, life in some ways is lonelier but it's better than endlessly trying to reason or argue with him, which never results in a pleasant time anyway. As noted in Chapter 11 loneliness can be alleviated.

Interestingly, Dan is left out in the cold, so to speak, because he always gets what he wants. And usually that means not being involved with Kelly or his kids. He is, of course, oblivious to what he is missing but he gets to 'win' in every instance no matter how seemingly insignificant, and winning is more important to him than anything else:

- Kelly wants to go out for dinner and Dan scowls?
  "No problem, Dan, I know you would rather be here working on your computer." Kelly goes to dinner at a nice restaurant by herself and enjoys her own company or a book on her Kindle. Kelly quickly discovers these solo excursions can be relaxing and rejuvenating for her.

- The kids want to go to a cartoon movie and Dan hates that kind of thing?
  "No problem, Dan, you enjoy your afternoon." Kelly and the kids go to the movie, have a good time and are relaxed without Dan's tension to possibly spoil the day.

- Kelly and the kids want to go to the beach but Dan hates hot sun and sand?
  "No problem, Dan, I know you'd rather do something else." Kelly and the kids go to the beach without Dan and have fun. Not having Dan along to complain makes the day more enjoyable.

Sometimes, if she allows herself to dwell on it, the situation makes Kelly feel sad. But reality is what it is, so she trains her mind to think about how much she treasures these times rather than torturing herself with wishing Dan could be different.

Imagining Dan being cooperative, a good sport, and going with the flow to have fun with them is just that, imagination, not reality, so she trains her mind to not go there. Most important, she recognizes that her old pattern of giving in to Dan and not doing activities that she or the kids like, just because Dan says no, accomplishes nothing positive and serves to only make her resentful, lonely and hurt. Learning to let Dan 'win' by not arguing with him and simply going ahead without him becomes a healthier lifestyle for Kelly.

The Extraordinary Power in Being Wrong

And once Kelly identifies the 'win' to point out to Dan, she repeats it and does not allow herself to be lured past it into the neverland of arguing or caving in to his games of control. New Kelly never goes along just to get along. What it means is, the game has changed and New Kelly is now a very careful woman.

No longer does Dan's dictatorship send Kelly into a depression that keeps her from doing what she chooses to do. Rather, she lets Dan 'win' and structures her life without him. As paradoxical as it is, Kelly has the upper hand because she is in control of herself and consciously allows Dan to win.

His 'win' means, in his mind, that Kelly has lost, has admitted defeat, has accepted that she is wrong. He does not realize how secure she is in knowing that she doesn't care if he thinks she's admitted being wrong, because she holds extraordinary power by letting him win.

This is a complex dynamic that requires a great deal of personal growth to achieve. Once acquired, there is tremendous peace derived from honoring the other person's choices and structuring your life to no longer be suffocated by his choices.

The Big Picture and Long Timeframe

I know a woman who became adept at the 'let him win' strategy while living with an impossible husband. She coped with his free-wheeling lifestyle, including affairs with multiple women. An incredibly self-possessed and dignified woman, she moved past the pain of his betrayals and developed a fulfilling life for herself as she raised her children. One day she decided to write her husband a letter:

Dear _____,

I know how important it is for you to have the life you have chosen and I want you to know that I respect your right to make those choices.

I think it is important for me to bring to your attention that I and

214

your children do not wait for you to be part of our lives, emotionally or
physically. While you pursue the people and activities that are important to
you, we have a circle of friends and activities that we cherish together. One
day you will discover we are no longer available on the periphery of your life.

With this letter she made it clear to her husband that she fully accepted his right to make his choices. She also fulfilled what she believed to be her obligation—to tell him the truth so that he knew she had accepted him for what he was. Most important, she did not dedicate her life to waiting for him to change. This is a brilliant expression of a woman dealing with reality in a dignified manner.

Another woman I know, literally out-grew (with great effort and commitment on her part, I should add) her controlling, maniacal husband. As her self-control increased, he turned up the pressure. One day, having reached the limits of his efforts to cause her to explode, he implemented what he apparently envisioned as his nuclear option; he told her he was going to leave her. She listened quietly, and asked him if he planned to leave that day or in the morning. Startled, he said he would leave in the morning. She thought about it for a moment and then calmly told him that it would be best if he left then, rather than waiting, because of the impact his leaving would have on their children's schedule. Perhaps cornered, he marched into their bedroom and began packing a bag. As he strode out the door, head high in his 'I'll show her' mode, she calmly closed and locked the door behind him. She later told me that she had one of the best night's sleep of her life, alone and without any fear of his tirades.

A few days later, he told her that he had found a nice place to live and hinted that he might be persuaded to return to her. She calmly told him that since he had found a nice place to live, he should certainly rent it. She told me later that what went through her mind was, "You didn't think living with me in our home was a 'nice place' so congratulations on finding a nice place to live." She let him win. He got what he wanted, a nice place to live. She changed the locks on the house and filed for divorce. She'd reached her limit without one shouted word being exchanged.

Those of us in a miserable marriage have heard many times how something that he wants is good for us. In all circumstances, he knows best. He points out how our failings are the reason for his behavior because we are such-and-such, or we did so-and-so, or we said this-and-that. According to him, his life is always impacted negatively because of us.

In the past, we applied logic and argued, "How can you say that when this is what really happened?"

But now, with our new clarity and strength from our inner woman we recognize his emotional and psychological abusive behavior for what it is, and we say to ourselves, "That's enough, we don't mindlessly argue anymore. We assess the situation, make a decision, and carry it out."

He has to win, so we let him win, or so he thinks. There is an ironic comfort in knowing that we have allowed him to have what he wants, and we get on with our life.

Kelly Stands Strong

A few days after the scheduled meeting with Dan for which he didn't show up, Kelly's cellphone vibrates and hops across her desk.

Dan's calling. It's three pm on Friday—payday—and Kelly knew this might happen. Should she take the call? Kelly practices the Great Pause, breathes deeply and focuses. New Kelly silently says to her: *Yes, take the call with composure just as you would take a call from an irate customer.*

"Hello?"

"Kelly, what the hell is going on? I tried to make a withdrawal from our account and the bank said the account is closed!" Dan is screaming.

Kelly's stomach churns and a duel between Old Kelly and New Kelly begins: Old Kelly who is terrified of Dan's anger, and New Kelly who now guides her life.

Kelly hyperventilates for a second and then pictures her mentor, the woman she emulates, and she straightens her back and proceeds as New Kelly.

New Kelly guides her: *Implement the Great Pause. Say only what is minimally required, state a simple fact only.*

"Yes, it's closed."

"What the hell? Are you crazy? You can't just close our joint account without telling me!"

Dan ratchets up his screaming and Kelly holds her phone away from her ear.

New Kelly guides her: *Implement the Great Pause. State a simple fact without emotion.*

"You were unable to meet with me as planned so that I could tell you in advance."

[Old Kelly wants to yell: *"I was going to tell you, you bastard, but you didn't have the courtesy to tell me, your wife, that you had something more important to do. You didn't even apologize to me!"* As if he ever apologized for anything.]

"Oh, come on! You're not serious! You closed the account because I didn't show up for some stupid meeting you scheduled? Are you completely nuts?"

Kelly pictured Dan, his face red and contorted, screaming into his phone.

New Kelly guides her: *Implement the Great Pause. Does anything need to be said? No.*

Kelly is silent.

"Kelly?"

"Yes?"

"Did you hear what I said?"

"Yes."

"Well?"

Kelly's mentor woman is present, alert, and in control. Calm, self-possessed, strong, dignified, intelligent and, truth be told, contemptuous of Dan. He and his behavior are beneath her dignity. Kelly formulates her response and is reminded to focus on how he can win. Calmly, clearly, and without emotion, Kelly states a fact.

"I know how much it means to you to independently run your business."

[Old Kelly wants to yell: *"I'm sick and tired of never knowing if I'm going to have enough money to buy groceries or shoes for the kids! You take money from the account without telling me and leave me high and dry. I'm not going to put up with this, Dan, do you hear me?"]*

"Come on, Kelly," now Dan is whining, "You know I have to dip into our personal funds occasionally to cover payroll."

New Kelly guides her: *Implement the Great Pause. Does anything need to be said? No.*

Kelly is silent.

"Kelly?"

New Kelly guides her: *Repeat the simple statement of fact. Do not deviate.*

"I know how much it means to you to independently run your business."

"You. Can't. Do. This."

Dan is now speaking in a quiet, slow, dictatorial, threatening, authoritarian tone that always terrifies Kelly.

"This is a community property State so you can't keep money just for yourself. I own half of everything you earn!"

Kelly's stomach turns over and she feels a cold dread. Oh God, I hope he isn't right. I can check with someone who will tell me the truth.

New Kelly guides her: *Implement the Great Pause. Does anything need to be said? No.*

Kelly is silent.

"Shit! Fuck you, Kelly! You're a bitch! I know what you're doing! You are deliberately destroying everything I've worked for! You've always wanted me to fail! That's what this is about! Dan should give up! Dan should get a job! Dan's business is a loser! Where is the account, Kelly? What bank is it at?"

Dan is screaming at the top of his lungs.

Kelly is silent.

"Kelly? Where is the account?"

Dan now uses his soothing, placating tone, like a parent talking to a three-year-old who's holding a loaded gun. Kelly has fallen for this ploy a thousand times.

New Kelly guides her: *Don't fall for it. Stay steady. Remember who you are now. Quietly, firmly, and with dignity, state a fact.*

"My account is in my name only, Dan. It doesn't matter what bank it's at. I have to go now. I have work to do."

"Fuck you, Kelly! Do you hear me? Fuck you!"

Kelly heard Dan screaming as she clicked off and silenced her phone because Dan would call back and nag her endlessly.

She started to shake and cry and thought she might throw up. Making this strong decision petrified her. But her new inner woman told her in no uncertain terms she had just graduated to a new level in her life. She knew she did the right thing.

Kelly thought her heart would break and her mind and body would explode but she knew she still had more to do, more steps to take to deal with the reality of her life.

She called the security department and told them her husband should not be admitted if he showed up at the building. This humiliation tore at her because she could imagine the raised-eyebrow looks in the security office.

Dan did not speak to Kelly for the next two weeks and looked at her with raw hatred. He bombarded her with insulting texts and nasty voicemail messages, trying to push her to lose control of herself.

He nagged her constantly about petty things that needed no communication: "You are going to pick the kids up today, aren't you? I know how forgetful you are," or "Are you going to cook some crap tonight or get take-out?" or "I noticed your car looks like shit so are you going to get it washed any time soon?" Dan excelled at nagging and endless harassment.

Kelly knew he depended on and expected her to follow her old pattern and break down and approach him to plead with him to stop his harassment and ask if they could talk and make things right. And she feared what Dan might do to get back at her. But she remained strong.

It took every inch of resolve and countless silent affirmations but

219

New Kelly resisted her old pattern and didn't approach Dan to try and discuss the situation with him. A regal, dignified, elegant intelligent woman would never do that, certainly not with someone so vile as the low-life individual sending disgusting texts and messages.

New Kelly saw Dan's behavior through her new eyes and viewed him as immature, disgusting and revolting. But her outward behavior never betrayed her inner thoughts. Dignified, always dignified. It wasn't easy but New Kelly held on.

Remaining calm and detached became easier with each passing day. One morning during her quiet time practicing Step Two, she saw an image of herself as regal, composed and peaceful sitting on the top of a high hill while far down below Dan bellowed, waved his arms and contorted his angry face, but she could not hear him. This image stayed with her for a long time.

What originally attracted her to this man mystified her. Well, not really because he could be charming when he wanted to be. And how she could have tolerated his behavior for so long made her sick. New Kelly fully accepted his choice to be silent. He could be silent for a year if he wished, it made no difference to New Kelly. His harassment bothered her a lot, but she didn't allow it to pull her backwards into old, impulsive responses. She said her affirmations a thousand times and focused on taking care of her kids and herself.

Kelly went out of her way to keep life as steady and pleasant as possible for her kids. She felt tired but she also felt stronger than she had in previous times of trouble with Dan—almost as though she had reached the top of a mountain after a very long, tough climb. Perhaps that is where her vision of herself during her morning practice came from.

The entire episode changed her more than she realized. Knowing she had money that only she could touch gave her an enormous feeling of relief. And reminding herself that she had tried, many times, to convince Dan to share information with her and work with her, assured her that she had met her obligation as his wife.

A few days after opening her bank account, Kelly approached the employee advisor where she works, asked for help regarding her retirement plan and made changes to maximize her retirement benefit. She also asked for and received the names of financial advisors the company recommended. She called and made an appointment to meet with one of them. The meeting resulted in feelings of complete terror.

The advisor, kind, patient and in many ways exemplifying traits Kelly had chosen in New Kelly, explained financial details that Kelly had never thought about before. Confident, intelligent, well-spoken and professional, the advisor asked questions Kelly couldn't answer and that left her dazed with the potential for the financial disaster she possibly faced. Kelly had trusted Dan and she didn't know anything about his business, how it was formed, what debt it might have and whether or not there were bank accounts she didn't know existed.

Most terrifying, Kelly learned that debts Dan might incur without her knowledge could be equally her responsibility, even if she played no part in acquiring the loans. She needed information from Dan and had no way of getting it.

The financial planner suggested that Kelly start by bringing to her for review, the tax returns she and Dan, and Dan's business, had filed in recent years. Kelly didn't even know where that information was kept. Never before had she felt so stupid, so naïve, so gullible and so foolish to have trusted Dan.

The financial planner put together a budget for Kelly and commented that she admired how Kelly had managed to make both the first and second mortgage payments on the house, and pay off the credit card debt that had previously been accumulated.

She suggested that Kelly cancel credit cards that were in both Kelly and Dan's names, just in case Dan decided to use the cash advance feature of the cards since Kelly had closed off access to her paycheck and he would be looking for cash.

When she returned to her office, Kelly called and cancelled the credit cards and made arrangements to pay off the remaining balances which, mercifully, were small. She then approached her new bank and applied for a credit card in her name only, just as a safety net should she need it.

She made sure that any communication from the bank would be sent to her electronically or mailed to her at her place of work, not to her home address. When the credit card eventually arrived, Kelly set up electronic use of the card and the actual card never went home with her. She didn't want Dan to know she had it.

Something the financial planner said also caused Kelly to think carefully about how hard she had worked to provide for her family. She and Dan had together scraped up the down payment for their house. But since then Kelly had made virtually all the payments. The financial planner suggested that Kelly might want to consider trying to convince Dan to sign a quit claim deed to the house so that Kelly would be protected from Dan potentially encumbering the property as collateral for a loan for his business. Because Kelly knew that Dan would probably refuse to sign a quit claim deed, she vowed to learn more about how she could protect herself and her home.

Kelly's head pounded with the seriousness of her situation, and the number of decisions she needed to make if she planned to forge ahead as a strong, intelligent dignified woman.

She rued the day she met Dan but that was over and done with and now she had two little kids and needed to keep her wits about her, and salvage what she could. It was a frightening and lonely time for Kelly.

The Struggle with Guilt

It was also a time fraught with bouts of indecision and guilt. Had she done enough to communicate with Dan? Had she failed him by not giving him one more chance? What if she was blocking his potential success? Was she being unreasonable?

She didn't view Dan as a bad person. But in her new-found honesty she admitted that she saw him as weak but wily. Instead of tackling problems with her head-on, he played word games and money games. And those games were destroying her. She also recognized a large element of dishonesty in Dan's behavior. She no longer respected or trusted him.

How could she figure out if she was the one at fault? If maybe she hadn't been a good enough wife, as he would be quick to point out to her. Maybe she just wasn't much in the way of being a woman. After all, she knew women whose husbands took wonderful care of their wives and children, so perhaps it was Kelly herself who didn't know how to be a real woman or wife.

These thoughts ricocheted back and forth with her fatigue and anger. Fatigue because she was worn out from trying to deal with their situation. And anger because she felt used, even stupid for having allowed herself to end up in this

All for One and One for All is Part of the Fantasy

I once heard a woman on the radio who gave shoot-from-the-hip advice to callers, tell a woman that she betrayed her marriage vow if she maintained a bank account separate from her husband. I concluded that the advisor had never experienced being in a miserable marriage. You are not breaking your marriage vow if you have a separate and secret bank account as part of your effort to survive in a miserable marriage. Your sanity and your life are most important.

As already alluded to in an earlier chapter, we women tend to enter marriage with a Cinderella fantasy of our heroic prince taking care of us and protecting our interests, so we include 'financial trusting' with all the other fantasies we have. Mercifully, perhaps the majority of women don't have the challenges those of us in miserable marriages do, but facts are facts, reality is reality, and not taking personal responsibility for our financial health is a disaster waiting to happen. I am an example of this.

Years ago, I conceived of a business idea that became very successful. Some years later an incident occurred that needed to be addressed in writing. My husband, to whom I had deferred and who held a title superior to mine, refused to write a memo to staff because he, "Hated writing memos." I let the matter drop even though I recognized the seriousness of the issue involved. I should have taken the initiative and written the memo myself. I made this mistake from total deference to him. I 'kept my place' as I had been trained to do. A few months later disaster struck and we lost the business. The story would have been completely different if I had done what my instincts were screaming at me to do, if I had written that memo.

There are reams of articles and books about the 'new woman' and how women are taking responsibility for their lives. This may be true but from what I've observed we women still have a long way to go. There is no betrayal of anyone, whether husband or family, in taking control over your finances, keeping separate records, becoming knowledgeable about your household accounts and having funds, including property, that are exclusively yours. Your life and the lives of your children may depend on your financial courage.

As noted, some improvements in society regarding women and money have taken place. However, very recently I tried, in vain, to dissuade a young woman from marrying the alcoholic with whom she was in love. Failing in my efforts, I then tried to convince her to keep in her name as her separate property, the home she had purchased a few years before she met her now fiancé. I failed in that too because she intended to follow the time-worn tradition of being generous to and trusting of her man. I hope it turns out well long term, but I wouldn't bet on it.

Strength in The Face Of attack

Nicholas and Tracy were laughing in the back seat when Kelly turned into the driveway and saw Dan's car, and alongside it a new big silver pickup that belonged to Dan's brother, Carl.

"Now what's going on?" thought Kelly. Tired from a long day, a knot of dread formed in her stomach.

Kelly and the kids entered the house and were greeted by Dan, Carl and Melissa standing around the kitchen island.

Kelly sensed tension. She put her purse and bag of groceries on the island, removed her coat and scooted the kids off to their rooms. She glanced at the aligned threesome and told them she would be right back.

Kelly went into the bathroom and sat on the toilet, breathed slowly, moved through her Step Two practice and then breathed very deeply into New Kelly. She also recited her Rules to herself.

224

She was tired but when she stood, New Kelly took command and she moved slowly and deliberately. Dignified New Kelly did not rush and centered herself in calmness so that she could think clearly and carefully in any situation.

She straightened her back and said her affirmations: "I am dignified. I am elegant. I am careful. I think quietly before I speak. I am regal. I am intelligent. I am self-controlled. I am strong."

She left the bathroom to face the triumvirate in her kitchen.

"Kelly," Carl cleared his throat and looked stern, "Dan asked us to come over and help him explain some things to you about the business."

Kelly practiced the Great Pause and said nothing. New Kelly did not play the role of old Kelly, the helpful little girl who always pretended things were OK and would cheerfully say something such as, "Oh, that sounds good," or some other inane comment. New Kelly stood tall without expression and practiced the Great Pause. Nothing needed to be said and she silently waited for what she assumed would be a three-person attack against her.

Carl cleared his throat again. "Dan says that you don't understand how the business operates."

New Kelly said nothing. New Kelly felt calm and aware that she had no responsibility to help him get to his point. Nothing needed to be said by her.

Dan jumped in. He never had patience with Carl's hesitation. "Look, Kelly, what happened last payday was unexpected and turned into a real problem for us. When you undermined the company by blocking me from tapping into our joint account, it really set us back."

New Kelly guides her: *Implement the Great Pause. Mentally stand back and view this scene as though it is playing on a stage and you are watching the action unfold. Stay calm. He's pulling the routine that everything is always your fault. You undermined the company? What a crock! Hold back on how you so much want to point out the lack of logic in that. Remember, logic means nothing to Dan. It's all about him getting his way, winning. Stay quiet.*

225

Kelly said nothing and her face showed no emotion or reaction. Dan looked a bit worried. This wasn't what he expected. This wasn't how Kelly always reacted. Usually by now she would be pointing out to him how he was wrong and they would be underway on an argument that could get loud. It appears he will have to work harder to get her upset.

"Look," Carl tried again, "we know how it's been hard on you sometimes, having to be supportive."

[Old Kelly wants to yell: *"Hard? Hard? You don't know what hard is, you jackass. Supportive? How noble of you to say so!"*]

New Kelly guides her: *Stay calm. No comment. Remain emotionless and expressionless. You have no responsibility or requirement to say anything to them.*

Kelly's attackers glanced at each other and shuffled their feet. This wasn't exactly going the way they thought it would. In the past, Kelly would be quick to participate in discussion or debate, ask questions, argue, give them her opinion and when the shouting finally stopped, give in to what Dan wanted. Dan tried his go-to tactic; anger, insults, authority, and threats.

"Look, Kelly, this nonsense has to stop! You have no right to cause damage to our business with your stubbornness, with your disrespect of me by blocking my access to our funds! You know nothing about business and you are completely stupid about money! I've, we've, worked hard to keep the business going and now you're intentionally trying to destroy it. I won't let you get away with this! Do you hear me?"

New Kelly guides her: *Step back and view the scene 'on stage.' New Kelly thinks, 'Hear you? By now the neighbors might hear you, you disgusting fool.' To herself, 'Stay calm. Say nothing.'*

Dan slammed his fist down on the counter and they all jumped. He was red in the face.

"Listen you ignorant, self-centered fat bitch, you are not going to get away with hiding money from me! I want access to that account and I want it now, do you hear me? We have a payroll coming up on Friday and I need funds to help cover it!"

226

"Yeah! There are other expenses too!" Carl raised his voice and glared at Kelly.

Suddenly, like a theater scrim rising the entire scene came into clear focus for New Kelly. Completely detached emotionally from these three people and what they were saying or how hatefully they were looking at her, New Kelly did not get down in the mud with these ridiculous, uncouth people. New Kelly stood apart and watched, listened and let her instinct tell her everything she needed to know.

A payment on that shiny new big pickup in her driveway would also be part of the 'payroll,' not to mention Melissa's paycheck for sitting behind a desk cruising the Internet and playing solitaire or messaging on social media all day.

While Kelly scraped bottom some months to buy groceries these three were covering their shortfall from her earnings, including for Carl's expensive pickup. All because she had trusted Dan. She had trusted her husband who put himself and his relatives far above her and his children.

And Kelly saw something else too. Dan was a ten-year-old little boy trying to take care of his not-too-smart older brother, Carl. He had been taking care of spoiled-by-their-mother Carl forever. Her heart actually ached for Dan and she wanted to reach out and tell him it would be OK.

But New Kelly now fully understood that responsibility did not belong to her to alleviate the problems caused by Dan's inability, and lack of interest in, growing up and away from his entangling family.

Her marriage vow did not include perpetually helping people who refused to help themselves, including her husband. New Kelly no longer allowed herself to be seduced by misplaced charity and compassion for Dan.

New Kelly now recognized that she didn't really help these people who cleverly talked her into doing so. They made a fool of her and they thought of her as a fool for letting them get away with it. For the first time Kelly's instincts were razor-sharp and she saw the big picture.

[Old Kelly: *I want to scream at them to get out of my house!*]

New Kelly guides her: *Stay calm. You are not at their low level. Say nothing. The problem you are witnessing is theirs not yours. Remember, logic plays no role in Dan's life. He only wants what he wants, when he wants it. What is your responsibility in this scene? You have no responsibility in this scene, it is their company, not yours because Dan has made that clear. What their company does or does not do is their responsibility, not yours. That is the choice Dan has made.*

And then an epiphany moment occurred. New Kelly looked at the three people attacking her and could see no reason to continue allowing them to mistreat her. She had nothing to say. Their financial problem belonged to them, not her.

She had helped them countless times in the past, usually without being asked and always without being thanked, and she very much regretted her mistake in doing so. But this is now. She already knew from her financial planner that she potentially had horrible problems regarding Dan's business but she would figure out how to deal with those. Dealing with that mess had to wait.

Kelly stood even taller and straighter, her face betraying nothing, and walked away without saying anything.

She went to her kids' rooms because she knew they heard Dan shouting and were probably scared. She also knew they were hungry and tired. She hugged them and assured them they would all have dinner, "As soon as Aunt Melissa and Uncle Carl leave."

Kelly heard murmuring in the kitchen and assumed Dan told Carl and Melissa, "I'll handle it. I know how to handle her. I'll get the money."

The big pickup pulled out of the driveway so Kelly went downstairs where Dan waited in the kitchen. He looked dangerous but he was now in his, "I can talk her into anything mode," which meant his eyes were hard and cold but his voice as smooth as silk.

"Kelly, I love you honey and I know you want what is best for the kids. The business can really take off now and I've been looking forward to finally being able to give you everything you've dreamed of. But we have to get over this one last hump."

[Old Kelly would have said, "*Yeah, yeah, I've heard it all before. If*

228

you're so anxious to give me everything I've dreamed of then why are you paying for...no, correct that...why am I paying for Carl's truck? I've tried to discuss finances countless times with you and you refused."]

New Kelly guides her: *Stay in New Kelly mode. New Kelly does not try to use logic. Logic doesn't exist with Dan. It's only about what he wants when he wants it. Remember, it's all about him, always. This is his old ploy. Don't fall for it. Stay calm. Stay in your New Kelly mode. It's about what he wants, not what he can do for you, and you know that's true. Form your response accordingly. Remember, remain calm and unemotional. Remember, he's always right, he always has to win. Your words and tone must be neutral.*

New Kelly says, "I'm sure you, Carl and Melissa will solve your business challenges."

New Kelly guides her: *You replied in a Dan-oriented mode and didn't at all address what he wants you to do, which is to give him access to your bank account. He always tells you he knows what is best so you validated him. The business problem is his to solve, not yours.*

Dan is enraged and looks threatening. Kelly knows he is like a caged animal because never before has he experienced her saying no to him in an unequivocal manner. Her stomach churns, and she feels sick.

Dan then targets her weakest spot—her love for her kids. He steps close to her face and spits his words at her.

"You raving bitch! You are evil! You're crazy! You're mentally unstable! You should be committed! I'm going to call a lawyer and take the kids away from you! Do you hear me? God damn you, Kelly! You're not a Biblical wife and I'm going to talk to Pastor and get his help to take my kids away from you!"

Dan's threat causes her a moment of panic. Kelly feels tears starting to well up and she fights them. She feels sick to her stomach and her hands are shaking but she pulls her coat and the kids' coats from the closet and calls Nicholas and Tracy to come so she can take them someplace for dinner, and get herself out of harm's way.

Dan, no longer in his, 'I can talk her into anything mode,' roars at her.

"Where do you think you're going?"

Kelly, exhausted and afraid that New Kelly can't hold on much longer, knows she has to get herself and the kids out of there.

"Come on, kids," she held onto her calm voice, "Let's go get some dinner."

Nicholas and Tracy look scared and they quickly pull on their coats.

Dan jumped in front of Kelly and blocked the door to the garage when Kelly and the kids attempted to leave. With an ear-splitting bang, he slammed the palm of his hand against the door making it impossible for Kelly to open it when she tried to turn the knob.

Then something happened inside Kelly. Something drained downward through her and suddenly she viewed Dan as a stranger, a stranger threatening herself and her children. New Kelly experienced a sensation, hot steel rising in her spine, and like a commander of a regiment or the queen of a nation she looked directly into Dan's eyes.

He frightened her and more than any other time in the past she feared for herself and her children. But a warm heat seemed to move up from her feet and into her chest. As clearly as though it was written on a placard in front of her she remembered that her iPhone held the number and address of a local shelter for abused women and children. In a flash of understanding so deep it was palpable Kelly knew that if it became necessary, she would take herself and her children to that shelter.

Shame and humiliation washed over her but she pushed them aside because knowing she had a place to go to protect her children and herself gave her comfort. And strength.

With a voice she had never heard come from herself before, Kelly very quietly and firmly said to Dan, "Get. Out. Of. My. Way."

Dan looked caught off guard and surprised. He dropped his hand and stepped aside. Kelly had never before been this unemotional and unflinching and he had no response in his repertoire except anger and threats and Kelly didn't appear to be cowed by them. This time.

Kelly took the kids to dinner and none of them ate much. They were sad. Their life consisted of one roller coaster ride after another of Dan's anger.

Emotionally detached, she felt like someone looking at a diorama in a museum. New Kelly felt nothing for Dan except disgust and contempt, not even worth the energy to shout at and certainly far beneath her new dignity.

New Kelly simply did not fight or argue because she knew who she was and a screaming maniac no longer matched her self-image and self-respect.

She also recognized that she still had some compassion for Dan, for his immaturity and fear of failure. But she no longer possessed a blind, fools-errand compassion for his inability and unwillingness to address problems. Her previous misplaced compassion and misplaced love cost her far more than what was appropriate and she knew that compassion had just died, right there in her kitchen.

Kelly looked at her children through new eyes and saw perhaps for the first time, the damage being done to them from the crazy-making household in which they lived. She wanted to cry in frustration, anger and self-blame for failing to recognize the truth of her situation months, no years, earlier.

A terrible battle raged inside her, with one part of her wanting desperately to go home and start hitting Dan, kicking and screaming at him that she hated him and wanted him out of her life.

But that would accomplish nothing except to play into his hands.

"You're crazy," he would shout at her and terrify her with his threat to take her children away from her.

No, she would not let him 'win' that. She would not lose her hard-fought-for dignity.

She knew she still had a tough road ahead of her but she had already made progress. She would extricate herself and her kids from the madhouse no matter how difficult or how long it took.

She now had one purpose in life. Somehow, to take one day at a time, to analyze everything in her life and day by day make decisions that would provide the best she could for herself, Nicholas and Tracy until they were grown or until she could afford to get them all out of the mess.

She moved beyond heartbreak, her emotional detachment from Dan complete. She felt as though one weight had lifted from her shoulders while another one of heavy responsibility descended.

19

Persist

Action breeds confidence and courage - Dale Carnegie

The Courage to Make Difficult Decisions

It is excruciatingly hard to face the reality that he isn't going to change—Kelly did that months ago. And facing the reality that you've trusted someone who is at best cavalier about your welfare and at worst uses you and possibly considers you a fool for letting him get away with it, is beyond difficult to accept.

But when you have turned the corner and become a new woman, a woman with inner core values, courage comes to the surface. The more you look at your situation with clarity the stronger you become.

Yes, the situation is dreadful and yes, you possibly could have foreseen it but be gentle with yourself. Some men are very clever and the impossible ones are cunning. They attract and cling to empathic, kind, caring women who trust them and whom they can take advantage of. You are not alone.

Planning—No Impulsive Reactions or Impulsive Decisions

When you become a strong self-respecting woman (and yes, that takes time) you can start to make the decisions you need to make. Jumping at impulsive decisions, such as filing for divorce before you have carefully planned, is a huge mistake as well as not consistent with a new woman who develops her skills. (If you or your children are physically beaten, don't wait! Get out immediately!)

Priorities

Securing yourself financially should be at the top of your list of priorities. And your physical health should rank right up there also. Too many women sacrifice their health and appearance because they live with men who never have a kind word to say to them, or worse, constantly berate their appearance. As a new, strong, self-respecting dignified woman, find a way to get to a gym or just walk around the block. Make some friends, walk, talk, play together and get out from under your husband's derision at least once in a while. Ideally on a regular basis and once a week at least. As you increase your dignity, grace, poise, self-respect and self-value, he will look smaller and smaller to you.

Develop your rules of survival as Kelly did, and always follow them. Remember, your goal is to survive and grow and in the end triumph, not to wait for him to change.

One woman I knew, married to an incredibly controlling man for over fifty years, bravely decided she would join an exercise class at her local senior center. Throughout her marriage, isolated from any social life, she never had any lady friends and so her husband derided her mercilessly about going to the senior center, "To be with women who complain about their husbands!" he snarled at her.

But she persevered and looked forward each week to the after-exercise coffee klatch where she made friends who shared their lives and laughter. She continued these friendships after her husband died. But she passed away less than two years after her husband so she only had that short time to enjoy some freedom and a life of her own. How sad.

Another woman I know became her 'new self,' raised her children to adulthood and for ten years navigated quietly and persistently through everything she needed to learn and do in order to leave her extremely controlling husband. She never indicated that she had emotionally detached. She made daily decisions and carefully created a life for herself. When the day arrived that she announced she had rented an apartment and was filing for divorce, thanks to her planning their funds had already been divided between them down to the penny, and she moved on without any drama. This lady exemplified what was mentioned early in this book; she learned to swim before she attempted to swim the English Channel.

Make decisions one at a time. Use your problem-solving capabilities and your creativity; they are still inside of you if you tap into them. Make one decision at a time and chip away at what needs to be done to secure a decent life for yourself.

Yes, it's difficult, so difficult that only those of us who have lived it can appreciate how hard it is. But one decision at a time, no matter how small, can help you move forward. Let the new inner woman you have chosen to be make those decisions from her inner core of wisdom, knowledge, grace, poise, strength and courage. And remember, you do not need his understanding or permission to make decisions that help you survive and grow. And secrecy is allowed, necessary even, if you are to secure a future for yourself. It is not wrong or a sin to protect yourself from death whether emotional, spiritual or physical.

Determining Responsibility

We are inundated with conflicting messages about just how much we should do to help others, particularly our husbands.

'Go the extra mile, you reap what you sow, what you give will come back to you one-hundred-fold,' and so on. On top of this is the terribly confusing concept of endlessly forgiving (Chapter 21 deals with this). So how do we draw a line, set a boundary, know how far our responsibility to our husband extends? Are we to endlessly go along to get along or give and give and give until we are completely drained?

Responsibility to Recognize a Problem

And what about trying to convince him to meet you half-way? To go to counseling, to make mutual changes? To try and understand each other's needs? Why do most couples never get beyond this tug-of-war?

The answer: Because he doesn't see any problem.

He's content with the way things are (which is always unbelievable to her) so she thinks he is in denial and he thinks she is just…well, a complaining, nagging bitch who doesn't recognize how lucky she is to have him and 'how good she has it.'

He isn't in denial because he truly doesn't see any problem so 'the problem' is entirely hers to solve, or not.

How do you know when you've done enough, made sufficient effort, tried to the last degree?

How Far Does Responsibility Stretch?

I once heard a story told by a Buddhist monk that forever helped me in determining just what is my responsibility and what isn't.

A woman met with the monk because she was concerned about whether or not she handled a situation ethically and appropriately.

Her story: She and her extended family planned a vacation to a far distant city, and upon arrival they would need a multi-passenger van for transportation.

The woman carefully planned weeks ahead, discussed their need with a representative of a rental car company and made a reservation which was confirmed.

When the woman and her family arrived at their destination, tired after a long flight, she went to the rental car counter to get the van and was told it was not available and she and her family would have to hire a taxi to take them across town to where the van was located.

The woman told the monk that she dutifully went outside to hire a taxi but as she stood at the curb waiting, she decided this was not the correct thing to do.

She returned to the rental car counter and told the attendant that she had already met her responsibility by making a confirmed reservation far in advance and that it was now the rental agent's responsibility to get the van so that she and her family could drive it.

"Did she do the right thing?" she asked the monk, or had she allowed her fatigue and annoyance to get the better of her?

The monk carefully explained that yes, she did do the right thing because we each have responsibilities that are ours and ours alone. But our lives intertwine with others who may choose to meet their responsibilities or not, and as a result affect our lives.

We must stand back, the monk patiently explained, and evaluate where and how we meet our responsibilities and where and how others in our life meet, or fail to meet, their responsibilities. It is appropriate and correct to expect others to meet their responsibilities and for us to require that they do so. It is also correct and right for us to not be taken advantage

236

of. And for us to say, 'No.'

The Art of Saying, "No"

Those of us in miserable marriages are accustomed to hearing 'No.' What we are not accustomed to, perhaps don't even know how to do, is say 'No.'

Instead of saying, 'No,' we automatically launch into the whys of how we want to, or would like to, or need to, or should say, 'No.' And then we back down and don't say 'No' anyway. It's part of our desire to be understood and to have permission from someone for us to make a decision based on what we want or need. And our tendency to assume that we are *supposed* to do whatever anyone else needs or wants us to do.

When we grow and become self-respecting, self-valuing women and overcome the need to always have permission, then saying, 'No' is easier and ultimately becomes comfortable. But like everything else we need to learn, we can learn the art of saying, 'No.' It just requires practice. And doing it the first time.

I will never forget when I learned that I could say 'No.'

Having been raised in a family where I could never, under any condition, disagree or say no, I became the ultimate pleaser, the perfect go-along to get-along accommodating female. After all, isn't the old adage true that 'If you're nice to others they will be nice to you?'

It requires maturity to recognize that many people are perfectly happy to 'let Georgia do it' if Georgia never says no. And the harsh truth is, they don't appreciate or admire Georgia. They only feel triumph that good ole Georgia is dumb enough to take on more. Their attitude is, 'If a woman chooses to be a fool, well then, why not let her be a fool?'

The phone rang and a breathless, 'I'm just so overwhelmed and rushed' female voice proceeded to tell me she desperately needed someone to volunteer for such-and-such task at my daughter's school.

My mouth opened and I almost uttered the words, "Well, I'm really busy right now so I don't know if I can afford the time," when my New Woman took over. I invoked the Great Pause, evaluated the situation for two seconds and then I calmly and politely said to the caller, "No." And

237

nothing else. No explanation, no excuse, just that beautiful simple little word, 'No.'

After a split-second of silence, the caller said, "Oh, OK then. Thanks," and hung up. I sat there holding the phone and soaked up the reality of what happened in that short phone call. I realized how my New Woman, the self-possessed, self-aware and self-valuing woman could make a decision and calmly and clearly say, "No."

And it carried weight. It required no excuse, no explanation, no seeking of permission to say, "No." That caller did not argue with me or try to persuade me to do what she wanted. I graciously but firmly said, "No" and that was that.

It's amazing how little things can change our life but that phone call proved to be another milestone in my growth. Self-respecting women value every aspect of their lives; their time, their energy, their love, and they are never door mats. If they discover they've been a door mat for someone they change the situation, and quickly.

Saying No Doesn't Always Require the Word 'No'

Saying 'No' can be accomplished in many ways and becomes easier with increased knowledge about ourselves. It is very satisfying to no longer be the always-flexible, go-along-to-get-along type, the reliable one to be depended on in all circumstances. And it is an incredibly accurate measure of the level and status of our self-empowerment—the extent to which we are taking responsibility for our life.

How many times have you agreed to attend a social event, contribute to a charity, take on one more task, without first thinking through each of those decisions?

When your Core Values are in place, and you recall them when you are faced with making a decision, you can categorize the decision and determine if this is really what you need to do, want to do, will enhance your life or the life of someone you deeply care about, or is it just taking up space in your life because you're panting like a puppy dog looking for someone's approval.

Selecting what we will do, how we will spend our time and

238

resources, is a way of saying, 'No' to much of what can drain our life. This includes all the times we might pointlessly argue. As Kelly demonstrated, saying 'No,' firmly and unwaveringly, can change your life.

Transformation Action Plan:

1. Sit quietly and breathe into the woman you now choose to be. Absorb her, enjoy her, understand her, look closely at her, admire her, and respect her. Carefully examine how she views your life and begin to identify the decisions your New Woman, who is strong, intelligent and self-respecting, needs to make.

2. What decisions do you need to make to secure your financial future? Do you know how much money you have or he has? Do you know where the bank accounts and investment account information are located? Do you have copies of the tax filings you have signed? Do you have a copy of the deed to your house or the lease for your rental home? Make a to-do list and assign dates by which you will take action to carry out what needs to be done.

3. What decisions do you need to make to improve your health and your appearance? Do you need to form some new friendships? Do you need to develop some interests for fun? Do you need to pursue talents and interests that you have perhaps set aside because he didn't like them or want you to participate in them? Make a to-do list and assign dates by which you will take action to carry out what needs to be done.

4. What decisions and actions do you need to take to improve your home, your social life, your education? Make a to-do list and assign dates by which you will take action to carry out what needs to be done.

5. What decisions and actions do you need to take to protect your children? What actions do you need to take to secure help for your children, such as a child psychologist to help them cope with your

crazy-making household? Be realistic. Can your husband set you up to legally take your children away from you? Be alert. Don't do anything impulsive (if your physical life is threatened then immediately take action and get out!). Make a to-do list and assign dates by which you will take action to carry out what needs to be done.

6. **Say this Affirmation**

I can identify the decisions I need to make
and I have the courage to make them

Be strong and courageous and do the work
– 1 Chronicles 28:20 NLT

Whether a good day or a bad day, say this affirmation frequently aloud or to yourself. Say it many times, emphasizing a different word each time. <u>I</u> can identify the decisions I need to make and I have the courage to make them. I **can** identify the decisions I need to make and I have the courage to make them. I can **identify** the decisions I need to make and I have the courage to make them. I can identify **the decisions** I need to make and I have the courage to make them.

7. **Respect and Reward Yourself**
Refer to the Rewards List you created in Chapter 2. If you have read this far, sat quietly and enjoyed being the woman you choose to be, have developed lists of decisions that reflect the woman you now are, and said the affirmation, reward yourself.

8. **Insight to ponder**
Courage in the face of hate and hatefulness is daunting. And making decisions, even small ones, that defy the structure someone has placed us in, can be terrifying. But the first decision is the hardest. And yet, it is that action which provides the cornerstone for our New Woman because it shows us that yes, we can do this, and if we can do this, then we can do more. We can keep going

240

forward.

9. **Watch for your personal milestone of growth**
    My Personal Milestone
    Faced with devastating financial losses, much as those Kelly
    potentially faced, I made some of the most difficult decisions of my
    life. I thought my heart would break when I accepted that I could
    no longer play the part of the submissive wife who left matters in
    the hands of my husband and trusted him. I sought qualified
    professional financial and legal advisors and found the courage to
    do what needed to be done. Like jumping off of a very high cliff, I
    knew I could never turn back.

10. **Mantra to Remember**
    His choices are his. I structure my emotions and decisions to
    ensure his behavior choices remain separate from me and I make
    decisions to protect myself and my children and our futures.

11. **Signs of healing**
    Healing is a slow process and just as with a broken limb, every day
    repair takes place until the limb becomes strong.
    A sign of healing
    When you look upon him with compassion as you would a
    stranger, and you profoundly accept that your responsibility is to
    take care of yourself and your children, not assuage his ego by
    endlessly helping him rather than requiring him to help himself.

20

Survive and Grow Step Seven

Wisdom is an elegant and poised woman,
mistress of the house she built – Proverb 9:6-1

Learning to be Wise

I did not see Kelly for several months, but she calls me occasionally when she wants to share what is happening in her life. The last time we met, she had just established her bank account and cut Dan off from accessing her money. She told me about the confrontation with Dan and his relatives and acknowledged that her relationship with Dan changed from that point onward.

"I did return to the house," Kelly says. "I knew Dan would cool down and turn his attention to how he could get revenge. Now we've settled into largely ignoring each other but not in a nasty way. I am always polite and formal and, of course, follow the Rules that I established for myself (see Chapter 16). I make sure my kids have what they need and whenever Dan pays attention to them, I encourage them to have fun.

"When Dan is in a good mood I respond in a cordial way and we've even had some pleasant times together. That's the challenge of coping with him. He can be decent, even funny and pleasant but it never lasts and can change in an instant.

"I'm cautious, of course, because I know his good behavior is always temporary and I never delude myself into thinking he's changed.

"He can be incredibly verbally abusive, often without any warning. Some of the things he's said to me are unbelievable. Thank God, I now know how to completely ignore him, tune him out and walk away. It never occurs to him that his abuse keeps me anchored in my determination to survive, grow and ultimately get away from him."

Kelly shakes her head.

"I repeatedly say my Rules to myself whenever we are together and remind myself to not fall into the old traps. I can silently and peacefully say my Rules whenever we are together regardless of where we are or what we're doing. My rules help me maintain my dignity, even when Dan annoys the hell out of me.

"My constant mantra is 'dignity'. I don't think Dan knows what to do with a dignified woman. He would prefer the screaming, maniac Kelly."

Kelly laughs ruefully and somewhat sadly at this bizarre fact.

She now recognizes an abuser's behavior—Dan's behavior—for what it is and puzzles over the idiocy of anyone thinking they gain respect by continuing and increasing abuse. Why would a man want his wife and home to include anger and chaos? It no longer matters to Kelly because she won't play that game. Her Guiding Principle is peace, and she isn't going to give up on that.

"We took a short family vacation and had a good time. Dan only pouted once and I immediately took the kids into a nearby shop. If he had persisted in his dark mood, I would have taken the kids to a local park and ignored him. He seems to understand now that I don't respond or have anything to do with him when he rages over nothing or launches into an unprovoked attack. I had a set of keys to the rental car with me at all times and would have taken the kids and driven away if he went off on us. Fortunately, he didn't blow up this time.

"Oh, he hasn't changed and he still is an asshole, but he stands there looking like a fool because he's raging by himself. When he starts one of his explosions, I and the kids are gone in a split second,"

Kelly snaps her fingers to emphasize her words.

"We go to another part of the house, outside for a walk, or if he's really in a rage I put the kids in my car and drive away. I make sure I always have cash in my wallet.

"Yes, it's hard on the kids and me, but I am not going to subject the kids or myself to his craziness by staying there and tolerating Dan raging at us. Physically separating ourselves from his tantrums is the only way to deal with this situation and it demonstrates to the kids that we shouldn't put up with his bad behavior. I hope it is a lesson they take into their adult life and avoid people who behave like their father.

243

"The whole situation makes me angry and frustrated, but it is what it is. As I've said before, I can't afford a divorce attorney although I'm doing my best to save some money, and I don't want the kids with Dan in unsupervised visitation.

"So, I'm still stuck. I would get us out of there right now if I could. But I know what my kids' lives would be like if they had to be alone with Dan for days at a time. He would be ranting and raving at them and make their lives miserable. Until they are older, they need me in the picture to protect them and to provide a loving, tender, kind and compassionate alternative to Dan's crazy-making narcissism. I worry especially about Nicholas. Without me to provide balance, I'm afraid Nicholas will turn out to be just like his father.

"I have my goals and nothing is going to stop me from striving to reach them."

Kelly pauses. "But I do have a limit. If Dan ever, and I mean even once, hits me or the kids, I will tell him he has to leave the house to cool down and then I'm going to call a locksmith and change the locks on the doors."

Kelly looks up at me.

"And yes, if I can't get him to leave the house, then the kids and I are going to a shelter and I'm filing for divorce. If Dan starts to take his anger out on the kids, holler at them over nothing or berates them the way he's always berated me, the same applies. That is my limit. And even without much saved money, I'll manage somehow.

"By the way, I followed your advice and selected a child psychologist for my kids to meet with regularly. Thank God, my health plan through my employer pays quite a bit of the cost. They really love meeting with Doctor Judy, the lady psychologist, and having her in our lives is an enormous help. She never betrays a confidence, of course, but when I ask her questions about the kids, she is very helpful and explains how they are handling what they see of the relationship between Dan and me. I've also been told that it's a good idea to have an expert advocate for my kids when I divorce Dan. Dr. Judy will have insight into what is best for Tracy and

Nicholas.

"Dan and I disagree quite often about decisions involving Nicholas and Tracy, so I ask Dr. Judy's advice and I tell Dan what she says. Of course, he ridicules her, but he did meet with her once so I think she saw through his phony effort to impress her. Thank heavens we have her in our life!

"Dan didn't think the kids should meet with a psychologist but since he isn't paying for it, it isn't any of his business. I calmly pointed out to him that he and I could go to counseling too, but of course, he just laughed at that idea."

Kelly pauses for a long time.

"You know, it's really sad. If Dan would commit to doing the work to look at himself, just as I've done, and if he would work with me so that we could solve our problems, we could have a good life. I would be willing to be patient while he wrestled with why he is the way he is."

Kelly pauses again.

"But the truth is, Dan likes the way he is. He doesn't see anything wrong with the way he treats me and the kids. This is the hardest thing I've had to accept, that he not only doesn't care about the damage he does, but that he is actually proud of it in some sick way."

Kelly shakes her head and looks defeated.

"But I have accepted that reality so I have to put myself and my kids first.

"One rather interesting thing has been added to my life and that is the impact of meeting with the financial planner. She has been helpful and guided me to set up a book-keeping system so that I make note of every expenditure, particularly purchases and expenses for the kids. I file and save receipts for everything. She, the financial planner, helps women in my situation and she pointed out that I should keep a record of everything because Dan is not fulfilling his responsibilities. Eventually he needs to account for his decision to be a deadbeat dad while still married to the mother of his children.

"Can you believe this? She showed me how to prepare an invoice to

245

give to Dan at the end of each month. That's right, I actually prepare a detailed invoice for his share of everything; house payments, utilities, car payments, insurance, and all the expenses for the kids."

Kelly laughs, shakes her head.

"Can you believe it? My knees were knocking the first time I handed him a monthly invoice, but I calmly told him that this is what he owes me for the household and for our children. And what's even more astonishing, one month he actually gave me a check for part of what he owes."

Determination

I must confess that it is difficult for me to picture Kelly—the wounded broken Kelly I first met—calmly handing Dan an invoice for money he owes her.

But I can picture New Kelly standing tall, strong, dignified and silent when Dan no doubt roared in anger and protest against her having the audacity (his word) to provide written proof of his failure to support his family. His belief that women should make no demands and have no limits regarding men's behavior is still firmly entrenched in him.

I can now, however, imagine New Kelly calmly turning and walking away while he shouts his protests into the wind.

The Journey Never Ends

Kelly faithfully practices Step Two and utilizes all the other Steps, to assess her life, her roles and how she reacts in any situation. Frequently throughout each day, she continuously evaluates what is happening in her life and implements the Great Pause. Additionally, she shares with me the wisdom she has already found, and tells me she expects to experience more insights and inspiration to help keep her going forward.

She becomes discouraged at times, stumbles and indulges in a self-pity party every now and then but, overall, she keeps her goals firmly in mind: To keep her sanity and survive living with Dan and provide a peaceful, orderly household for her children, until she can get them out of the situation.

She wants her children to experience her as a strong, dignified, courageous woman who contrasts sharply with their unreliable and emotionally unpredictable father. It's certainly not an ideal situation for her children, but her goal is to not divorce and put her children into the hands of Dan without her oversight, the inevitable result if she divorced without careful planning. Plus, as she readily admits, she can't afford a skillful attorney and she hasn't completed the financial preliminaries to protect herself. Kelly is on a mission of personal survival.

The Building Blocks of Wisdom

Kelly has reached an important point in the constructing of a better life. She has identified the building blocks on which she bases her life:

- **Priorities**
  Kelly identified what is of primary importance to her. She lives her life with her priorities always in mind: Her sanity and the safety of her children and herself. Her Guiding Principle of peace, is the basis for her priorities.

- **Respect**
  She has self-respect, and she recognizes that others, including her husband, do not live by the same code of respect and behavior that she has chosen. She accepts the choices that others make, even when she disapproves of them, and she no longer craves or needs understanding or permission from anyone in order to respect herself.

- **Acceptance**
  Kelly accepted what she cannot change, and is changing what she can.

- **Limits**
  Kelly has limits and she is perfecting the art of saying, 'No.'

- **Distancing**
  She accepted that emotionally and physically distancing herself from individuals whose behavior is harmful to her is OK, necessary

and healthy, even though societal tradition may criticize or condemn her for doing so.

- **Taking action**
  Kelly carefully analyzes what she needs to do and takes action. She no longer needs permission or approval from someone else to move toward her goals. She no longer passively waits for 'something' to change.

Seek and You Will Find

Wisdom doesn't just happen. It is earned the hard way, from life experience and from actively seeking information and expanding your horizon in order to learn.

As a well-known speaker has said to thousands of women when she refers to the Bible verse John 5:8, "Get up!"

In other words, get off your backside, stop feeling sorry for yourself and take action. Learn and make changes. The changes may be small, even seemingly insignificant at first, but one by one they add up and lead in a new direction.

One action to take is to determine to become wise. Wisdom comes from learning everything you can about yourself, your husband, and your situation.

My Search

After I began my Step Two practice and experienced how my life began to change, I craved more knowledge. I wanted to learn everything I could about the how and why of my husband's behavior, my behavior, how other people lived their lives and what I could do to improve my life.

Many times I experienced extraordinary coincidences that placed a helpful book into my hands or I overheard someone say something that struck a chord with me, or I saw a quote, read a story in the news or met someone who mentioned something that made a light go off in my mind. I discovered that it is true that when you take action to change your life, when you push against the walls around you and actively seek knowledge, you find it. You seem to draw it to you.

The key word is 'seek.' My hunger for information and for a better life caused me to take actions that helped me find what I needed and I attracted helpful information and people into my life.

Being Open to Receive What Comes to You

I had to break out from the invisible and impenetrable walls that surrounded me. Those walls were my childhood conditioning that everyone other than me always knew best. That I should unquestioningly do what they said or told me to do, and I should not venture beyond what they approved in my life.

Those authorities were my parents, relatives, husband and clergy, and the message inculcated in me was unequivocal: I did not have the wisdom to make my own decisions so I should keep quiet, not question and do whatever they told me to do.

I grew up in a structured religious tradition that emphasized following detailed rules. Activities such as reading the Bible or other spiritual or informational books for the pleasure of learning, did not have a place in daily life. We memorized tracts and followed what we were told. Questioning and discussion were not allowed and fear played an integral part. Going to hell for all eternity served as the deterrent for all transgressions, including questioning what any authorities said. Prayer consisted of rote recitation of memorized tracts, not unstructured heartfelt communication with a higher power.

None of this provided a foundation for learning but rather for accepting without question, for toeing the line and for being controlled by authority, including by a husband. I joked that my childhood education prepared me for a woman's life in nineteenth century Victorian England. But it wasn't a funny joke. The concept of accepting mistreatment as somehow unavoidable, even noble, is repugnant.

I began to explore, beginning with the 'whys' of my husband's behavior and my reactions to it. I recognized that social isolation bred into us the behavior patterns we both had. Our respective families did not socialize outside a narrow socio-economic, family-only framework.

249

Anyone, including school teachers, who represented a refined or more successful economic and social behavior style, were suspect and not to be trusted. Perceived as causing children to rise too far, which would result in children looking down on their parents, education beyond the basics was discouraged. Parents, husbands, and clergy already had all the answers to life, so why go beyond reading, writing, math and the Church's rules?

Seeking and questioning were anathema to everything I experienced growing up. By exploring I strayed into potential heresy. But I learned that the ultimate product of isolation and narrow-mindedness is control.

Control over human beings is the goal of and product from isolation, lack of education and ignorance. When education is defined as training someone to follow rules then questioning does not and cannot take place. It is a narrow definition of education when questioning and debate are removed and disagreement with dogma is punished in one way or another, including with the threat of eternal damnation.

My hunger for a better life pushed me beyond the limits of everything my childhood taught me. When I began to actively seek knowledge and a better life, I defied what I grew up with and which my husband's controlling behavior perpetuated. Pushing against ingrained patterns is frightening.

Wisdom Comes from Many Sources

On the day when I arose early and began my Step Two practice, I did not know my life would be forever changed. Day after day I went deeper into my Body Focus Points and my thoughts as I pondered each B-F-P. I discovered my value as a human, and also how that value had been violated by people who influenced my life. As I developed my core values and changed my behavior, I became a different person, a more complete individual, a healthier woman.

My 'new woman' had a hunger for more knowledge, more wisdom, and my instincts became finely tuned. I sensed, I knew, I lived fully in the moment and became acutely aware of what happened around me. I learned to listen, look carefully and watch.

I heard words of wisdom, often from people the world would scoff at, or judge to be of no value; the lady who had very little education or money yet she spoke volumes of wisdom about the value of the children in her care; the young woman who overcame drug addiction and unbearable loneliness; the young man seated next to me on a bi-coastal flight who shared how he had been a gang member—a gun held to his temple by an enemy didn't fire when the trigger was pulled, and how that brush with death forever changed his life.

The stories are endless about information and people who happened to cross my path when I began to actively seek a better life. And this wisdom didn't come from rich, famous or well-known people. I realized something of infinite value; all of the extraordinary people I met escaped death, whether figuratively or literally. And this described my experience too.

Fleeing from death applied to my flight from a life of mistreatment, and the anger, frustration and hopelessness the mistreatment engendered in me. Everything changed when I took the initiative, when I examined my life and my behavior, when I pushed beyond what I had been told could be my only destiny; that I should keep my place, not question and submit.

I discovered that my childhood training to never seek knowledge outside the narrow confines of my socio-economic, education and religious background left a rich buffet of information untouched. The world is alive beyond measure with information and I was hungry to learn. I explored books, online sites, teachers and researchers that delved into the various problems that my husband and I displayed in our behavior. The issues of abuse were examined in detail by knowledgeable researchers. I could learn on many fronts and I did. Once again, I could face the truth and not be destroyed by it.

When it Crosses Your Path, Look Closely, Choose Wisely

I stood in a bookstore perusing the shelves, looking for I knew not what, when a book fell from the top shelf and landed at my feet. I picked it up intending to put it back, but first I took a look. I'd never heard of the book or the author but I purchased it and a week later began to read it. The author exemplified a person who had many flaws but changed his life and then decided to share what he learned from his efforts. Did that book fall from the top shelf because I sought knowledge and wisdom? I sometimes think so, as more and more coincidences entered my life of seeking.

Other visits to bookstores and online searches enlightened me to the fact that countless people had searched, or were searching, for answers and guidance for their lives. My resources expanded rapidly.

So many people experienced pain, weakness, shortcomings, injustice and trauma. As flawed people they were searching. They admitted to their need for more wisdom and shared their journeys. Unlike so-called perfect people supposedly without error, whom I had been raised to believe without question, these flawed individuals were honest and revealed and explored their problems. The message felt reassuring. I was not the only damaged person who sought something better.

I observed that many individuals who claimed to have all the answers were themselves imperfect, sometimes even irresponsible in their behavior toward other people. There seemed to be a correlation between how convinced they were they were 'right' and how much damage they did to others, often in secret. I recognized they were afraid to explore beyond what they already knew because they could not allow themselves to be challenged. They were less sure of themselves than they pretended and did not allow themselves to self-examine or explore beyond their self-imposed wall, because doing so might undermine the façade of wisdom they pretended to have.

And pretend they do. When I employed my 'step back and watch the action on the stage,' I saw people who blustered and raised their voices to drown out others but were without substantive wisdom. I faced the uncomfortable truth that I came from a family of ignorant, obnoxious big-mouths and I had been one myself until recently, because that is all I knew how to be.

When I explored beyond perceived limits, I moved away from the people who imposed them. We had little in common because they wanted

252

to be narrowly focused and I wanted to explore. Exploring did not automatically mean falling into error. That was the great divider, the lie, I had been taught; that if you questioned you would be condemned, even damned.

But I knew that I could examine and select while those who might criticize me were afraid to look beyond their walls lest, they feared, they would be tainted, their beliefs might be challenged, that they might fall into a trap from which they could not escape.

Selecting What Helps in Each Situation

Gradually, through my morning practice of Step Two, I delved deeply into what I needed in order to survive. Together with the Great Pause, I incorporated guidelines into my daily activities and thought processes, guidelines that helped me survive and grow.

From a variety of sources, I added to my repertoire of daily practice. I could call upon mantras, inspirational scripture from a number of traditions, and helpful words and phrases for any situation.

Standing in a slow-moving, annoying check-out line, I can say to myself, "All ways, living love," repeating it and emphasizing each word, because we are each an example of love and when you look upon others in that manner you discover patience within yourself.

Every morning I recited my Daily Guidelines which are listed below (followed by a discussion of each). Whenever any situation occurs, I recall and apply the applicable section or phrase in my Guidelines. They inevitably apply to every aspect of my life.[3]

Daily Guidelines

I begin with gratitude

Thank you, Lord, the Universe, Source, for everything I have. I am open to your inspiration, guidance and grace.

---

[3] The phrase 'all ways living love' and the Daily Guidelines below, are adaptations of, and in part reprinted from, *Handbook to Higher Consciousness* by Ken Keyes, Jr., Fifth Edition, Copyright 1975 by the Living Love Center

My addictions

I am freeing myself from my security, power, sensation, abuse, and poverty addictions:

- I recognize how my addictions influence the choices I make.
- I accept life's choices, no matter how difficult, as an opportunity to overcome them.
- I am committed to living life without these addictions.

Living in the present moment

- I have everything I need to fully experience life in the present moment.
- I accept responsibility for how I experience life each moment.
- I accept where I am now in my journey.
- I respect myself for my commitment to continue to grow.

My relationships with others

- I am careful and discerning in all my interactions with others.
- I observe with compassion the suffering of others. If I can, I help them, and if I cannot, I pray for them.
- I do not act unless I am centered and focused.
- I release the thought that I can convince others to change.

My relationship with the world

- I calm my mind and my thoughts and focus on the present moment.
- I observe life as unfolding on a stage and I observe it with interest.
- I love everyone unconditionally, including myself.
- I am open to receiving blessings in my life.

Daily Guidelines in Detail

Beginning with gratitude

There are many things to be grateful for. I can see, touch, taste, smell, speak. I have a place to live, I can see the sky and trees, hear birds or the voices of children. I have occupation, I have clothes to wear, I have transportation. In addition to material possessions I am grateful for gifts such as inspiration, guidance, intuition and my ability to love.

My Addictions

I am freeing myself from my security, power, sensation, abuse and poverty addictions.

- I recognize how my addictions influence the choices I make.
    - o Day by day, minute by minute, I make choices. Each choice I make can add to, or free me from, my security, power, sensation, abuse, and poverty addictions.
- I accept life's choices, no matter how difficult, as an opportunity to overcome them.
    - o Day by day, minute by minute, I stop myself and evaluate how the choice I am about to make strengthens, reduces, or eliminates my addictions.
- I am open to living my life without these addictions.
    - o I do not have to be bound forever by any addiction.

Security Addiction

Addiction to security versus growth can keep us in bad habits, an unhealthy relationship, job, neighborhood, family and our own self-destructive behaviors. Familiarity can be comforting, even if we know it isn't good for us. Attachment is another word for security. What am I holding onto, clinging to or failing to take action about because I just want to stay safe, secure, the same or not rock the boat?

Power Addiction

Craving and enjoying power is an addiction that takes many forms; bossing other people, taking advantage of our superior strength and power over children, spouses, employees and service providers. Wielding the power of money over other people ('I am, of course, better than you because I have more money than you do'). Striving for positions of influence for the personal power involved. Our power may take the form of stubbornness, irritability, refusal to listen, recklessness, impulsiveness, procrastination and other forms of behavior that control and negatively affect ourselves and others. Our refusal to examine ourselves or a situation and instead remain entrenched in our position because we don't want to yield or give an inch of our power away. Addressing this addiction requires examination of our motives, and asking ourselves, 'Why, am I doing this? Why am I making the choice to behave, speak or think this way? Am I just satisfying my addiction for power?'

Sensation Addiction

Sensation of the senses—food, alcohol, sex, pastimes that are a waste of time or resources, procrastination, body pleasures of all types. Anything in our life that satisfies the senses. Addiction is the important word. What sensation satisfiers do I have in my life that are in reality addictions?

Abuse Addiction

Do I experience abuse in my life because I have experienced so much abuse that I have no idea what my life would be like without it? In how many ways do I allow myself to be abused? Do I repeatedly choose the same type of mate, job, stay connected to destructive family, or other life choices that involve a form of abuse of me, whether overt or covert? To free myself from this addiction I must first examine the nature of my abuse addiction, where it came from (its roots) and then consciously make choices that say, 'No,' to each form of abuse, or the people who are the source of the abuse, and remove myself, including geographically, from the abuse. It is my choices and the actions I take that overcome abuse addiction, not waiting and hoping the perpetrator of the abuse will stop abusing. Self-respect and self-care break this addiction.

Poverty Addiction

A mindset that I should not have sufficiency, or don't deserve to have enough, or that anything I acquire will be taken away from me because I don't deserve to have it in the first place. Do I make choices that drain my resources instead of adding to them? How does my poverty addiction show itself? Do I shop to anesthetize myself? Do I stay in a low-paying job because it requires too much effort to make substantial changes in my lifestyle, training or education, or I would need to geographically move, which I may not want to do? Poverty addiction plays out in a multitude of ways but its source is how we think about and picture ourselves moving through our life financially. Poverty addiction is learned from family, community and religious messages that we internalize as guilt about wanting or having financial comfort.

Living in the present moment
- I have everything I need to fully experience life in the present moment.
  - I live consciously, moment by moment, and think carefully before I act or speak.
- I accept responsibility for how I experience life in the present moment.
  - Moment by moment, I accept full responsibility for how I react and respond to anything or anyone who helps me or hurts me, and the decisions I make in each circumstance.
- I accept where I am now in my journey.
  - Day by day, moment by moment, I accept that I am a work in progress and I will never be finished. I accept that I am continually growing and changing and when I disappoint myself, I evaluate what happened, learn from it and continue to move forward.
- I respect myself for my desire to continue to grow.
  - I accept the challenge of the task to change and grow.

My Relationships with Other People
- I am careful and discerning in all my interactions with others.
  - I continually evaluate my relationships with others, whether casual acquaintances or close friends, chance encounters, or relatives by birth or marriage. I am not bound to them as to a

co-joined twin but as a fellow traveler through life. Both I, and they, are individuals. I have the right, and obligation, to choose to what extent I allow anyone to help me, hurt me, or harm me, and I have the right, and obligation to remove myself from any interaction with anyone who covertly or overtly harms me, or tries to destroy me, whether physically, mentally, emotionally, or spiritually.

- I observe with compassion the suffering of others and if I can, I help them, and if I cannot, I pray for them.
  - My ability to be compassionate (have empathy for others) is a gift that I nurture but do not squander. I evaluate each encounter or interaction with others and determine if I can and should help in a material or emotional way, and if I cannot, I pray for the individuals involved.
- I do not act unless I am centered and focused.
  - Day by day, moment by moment, I stop myself in all interactions with others, or situations that present themselves in my life, and I do not act or speak unless I am centered and focused, and then I carefully choose every aspect of my behavior.
- I release any thoughts that I can convince others to change.
  - I honor and respect the choices that others make, and I respect myself for rejecting bad behavior from others that harms me.

My Relationship with the World
- I continually calm my thoughts.
  - My thoughts can be like a washing machine, sloshing back and forth. Moment by moment I stop myself, calm my thoughts, breathe deeply and focus on what is happening in the moment.
- I observe life as unfolding on a stage in front of me.
  - All of life is unfolding every day, like a play taking place on an enormous stage. I am one of the participants and I stand back and watch the action as a non-judgmental observer of life and my role in it.

- I love everyone unconditionally, including myself.
  - Unconditional love does not require that I have no limits or guidelines for my life. Unconditional love respects the fact that everyone continually makes choices that affect others. I respect the choices that others make and I accept that I do not have to, nor should I, allow myself to engage with, respond to, or remain in the presence of anyone who intentionally harms me overtly or covertly. My unconditional love takes the form of respectfully accepting others but not ever believing that I am to accept their bad behaviors or unconditionally subject myself to destructive behavior from others.
- I am open to receiving blessings in my life.
  - The world wants to bless me and I accept all my blessings.

21

Woman's Wisdom

*Caesar and Napoleon could only wish they had the power
of a woman's intuition.*

Wisdom's Insights

When a woman begins to examine her life, inner conflict is
inevitable. And when you add to the equation the gaslighting that usually
takes place in a miserable marriage, i.e. the game of, "No, you
misunderstood," (which impossible men excel at using to confuse us) much
effort and time are required to learn to become wise and most important, to
trust our instinct and insights.

As with every other skill mentioned in this book, learning to trust
your instincts and your female 'knowing,' is something that every woman
can acquire and learn to respect.

Wisdom About Conscience

As has already been stated, when you daily practice, moment by
moment, not just once in the morning, a deep awareness of yourself, your
behavior, your thoughts, your core values that reside within you, the people
around you come into focus more clearly. When you can accept yourself
and others for who and what they are, not what you wish they were, you
can make better decisions and move through life with purpose. Including, if
necessary, leaving behind people whose behavior harms you.

We often struggle with guilt about separating ourselves from harm.
We can't fully accept that some people are not motivated to be kind or
honorable, and we feel guilty about taking wise steps to protect ourselves.

Those of us in miserable marriages have experienced the mind-
boggling confusion of living with someone who says and does hurtful
things without ever showing any sign of remorse. And all of us have
experienced the empty, 'I'm sorry, but *you* shouldn't have made me...' so-
called apology from a manipulative spouse. How can they so blithely hurt

wives and children?

Because they see absolutely nothing wrong with their behavior.

Not every human has a conscience.

Dr. Robert Hare of the University of British Columbia devoted his professional life to the study of individuals whose behavior strongly indicates they simply have no conscience—not any sense of right and wrong.

A burden can be lifted from you when you accept that you may be attached to someone who has no conscience, or who has the ability to turn their conscience on and off like a light switch.

No, you're not crazy. You're attached to someone with a deadly significant character flaw and it cannot be fixed. No one can grow a conscience or develop one, or be persuaded to acquire one. Individuals without a conscience or with a flexible turn-on-turn-off conscience, cannot and will not change.

Women, children, indeed anyone who crosses their path, are merely collateral damage in their unwavering conviction that they are always right, always entitled, even very special humans. Nothing you say or do will change this.

This is the most significant issue facing women in a miserable marriage. It is incredibly difficult to accept that someone has no conscience. Serial batterers, for example, cannot be repaired because they have no conscience. Michael Groetsch further clarifies this in his book, *He Promised He'd Stop*. If you are with a batterer, get out now!

Developing the wisdom to recognize and accept a husband's lack of conscience can save your sanity and your life. And knowing deep in your soul that you not only do not deserve to be mistreated, but you have a responsibility to not encourage it by tolerating it.

This is the ultimate female wisdom about the mistreatment of women by men: That we have a *responsibility* as women to not tolerate it, excuse it, pander to it or cover it up. We have a responsibility to be wise about mistreatment and that wisdom means recognizing it and removing ourselves and our children from it.

It is our job to introduce peace and love, which we are uniquely equipped to provide. But not by having endless patience and tolerating the intolerable. But rather, by setting standards, setting limits, and not being a door mat or punching bag.

As has been stated throughout this book, waiting for him to miraculously change is simply not realistic. If we are going to sacrifice our lives, then it should be for a worthy cause, not to a man who is cruel and questionably possesses a conscience.

Wisdom About Compassion

Perhaps more than any other human capacity, compassion is the element missing in our lives. Compassion is the food a human spirit thrives on. Having someone who looks at you and says, "You seem to be hurting," is like the sun breaking through the clouds after a heavy rainstorm. But in a miserable marriage there is little, if any, genuine compassion.

And worse, when you live without any compassion for you, you can lose your ability to be compassionate toward others. Because, as has already been explored earlier in this book, what and who we live with gradually becomes a part of who we are also.

It is important to note here that a goal of the Survive and Grow Steps is not to remove compassion for your spouse from your life, but to learn how to moderate that compassion so that it isn't a reason to be used, abused and ultimately drained by a spouse who has no compassion or empathy for you. Compassion, like love, is a precious commodity that must be nurtured, respected and dispensed wisely.

The wisdom to accept his lack of compassion is vital because lack of compassion can be deadly. Knowing completely that he has no compassion for you, and accepting it, makes you far more cautious about your safety and the safety of your children.

Wisdom About Empathy

It's hard to believe that someone can look directly at a person and fail to recognize they are tired, sad, hurting emotionally or physically ill. Yet those of us in a miserable marriage have experienced this lack of empathy from our spouse.

One week after the Caesarean birth of our child, my husband looked at me with scorn and announced, "Just because we now have a child doesn't mean I am going to lower my standards." He wanted to make sure that I intended to prepare the specific sauce he expected to be served with dinner. My struggle to recover from surgery and take care of a newborn meant nothing to him. As has already been explored in this book, a woman's emotional and physical needs hold a low priority in a miserable marriage because empathy is almost always completely lacking.

The wisdom to understand and fully accept the seriousness of lack of empathy is vital for our survival. Living with someone who has no empathy, no ability to be empathic, is deadly. Lack of empathy dehumanizes anyone exposed to it, as exemplified by the horror of the holocaust.

Wisdom About Control

Controlling other people is an intoxicating experience. Countless times throughout history, including now, people look at countries, or areas within a country, shake their heads and say, "How can they let their people live like that (in poverty, crime, poor health, filth)?" The answer is very simple, really. Inevitably there is someone, often buoyed by military ferocity and the advantage of wealth, who with the wave of his or her hand can bring death and destruction to many.

Conscience and compassion are not involved. But the wave of a hand to move armies and keep people under their heel is more exhilarating than all the alcohol, drugs and sex the world can provide.

As ridiculous as it may seem, that same rush of power is the thrill behind every controlling, abusive husband in the simplest household or the most impressive mansion anywhere in the world. It is an exhilarating 'high' to demand, yell, or strike out and have a wife and children unfailingly bend to one's will.

Wisdom unveils the truth about how you are controlled when you step back and thoroughly recognize the many facets of control in your life.

Wisdom About the Role of Entertainment

Closely related to control is the entertainment provided by making another human dance to your tune. The husbands in a miserable marriage enjoy witnessing their wives trying to do everything they can to keep him happy and prevent his blowups. But it is a completely hopeless effort because he enjoys the drama and the dance. Regardless of what you do, he will instigate and perpetuate the frustrations, the quarrels, the drama, the chaos, the gaslighting. The game never ends.

It does not require much time in a relationship for clever men to assess what pushes your buttons, what upsets you, what sets you off, what confuses and frustrates you. Pick any of these terms because they all apply. Abusers (particularly narcissists) often deliberately cause discord and upset because it is entertaining, although they would never admit they do this. (I did hear one man admit that he enjoyed goading his wife until she became distraught).

The more upset she becomes the more satisfied he is. And when she yells, he can yell louder or add physical threats to the scene. Like drugs to an addict, an upset wife is a balm to feelings of self-worth for these men. After all, if she is out of control then he views himself as in control and therefore far superior to her.

And a slight variation on this theme is also common; the enjoyment of seeing an empathetic, people-pleaser woman twist herself into pretzel shapes to try and cater to her husband's needs. These husbands can make a woman dance, so to speak, by constantly changing their needs and wants so that she is never done, never quite 'up to the mark' in meeting his needs—in reality his need to enjoy her endless efforts.

Wisdom arrives when you recognize the game for what it is and no longer fall for it. When you no longer provide his entertainment.

Wisdom About Inconvenience

Exercising a healthy conscience and compassion are, in truth, inconvenient. Caring for the people we love is, frankly, not the most convenient course in life to follow, but it does usually have many rewards.

Empathetic women are champions at absorbing inconvenience in order to meet the needs of their family and they are the ideal target for controlling, narcissistic, mean-spirited men.

Those of us in a miserable marriage know that our spouse is to never be inconvenienced. If we inconvenience him, we will pay. So, we bend our lives to avoid inconveniencing him. We explain, we try to pick the right time, we cajole, we hope this time he will be a good sport and not ruin the evening, the dinner, the vacation. We're relieved if, 'This time he wasn't so bad.' But we know the bottom line is, he is to never be inconvenienced, never to be asked to give a little.

If a woman complains or makes any demands, she is affronting the controlling man's belief in his right to have a stress-free, demand-free life. The primary rule for an abuser is, he can be 'stretched' by his boss, his friends, his favorite sports team, but never is he to be asked to stretch his beliefs, his schedule, his life, for anyone in his personal life—except for his best male friends for whom he will accommodate all of the above regardless of the cost to his family.

I know a woman who each year painstakingly makes all the plans and arrangements for a family vacation. Every detail must include thorough consideration of what her husband will need or want in order to try and avoid his blowups or sulking if something doesn't go according to plan or isn't to his taste, liking, or demands.

She shared with me that, one year, when they arrived at the beautiful tropical resort she had reserved for their stay, management had failed to follow her specific request for a luxurious ocean-view suite, and instead assigned her family to rooms without a full ocean view.

She immediately knew this would result in a ruined vacation for herself and her children. Her husband would pout and sulk for the entire week after sarcastically pointing out her obvious stupidity and incompetence in failing to book rooms with a view equivalent to his impeccable standards.

Mercifully, when she appealed to the management, they were able to reassign their rooms to an ocean-view location. Otherwise, she faced days of emotional abuse and misery instead of a pleasant time with her family. This intelligent and interesting woman invested fifty years of her life trying to never inconvenience her husband.

Wisdom About Forgiveness

I have lost count of how many times I sat in a church pew gritting my teeth and listening to a preacher say, "You have to forgive in order to heal."

That is a cliché, probably taught in every seminary, but it isn't exactly true. You have to heal in order to forgive and both of those tasks are on-going and simultaneous. They require time, sometimes years, and are a process that you move through slowly and painfully. Sometimes the forgiveness is never over and done with completely.

The misconception is, that forgiving relieves pain and to a large degree that is true. But the missing part is that it takes time—often a great deal of time—for the pain to diminish. A one-time event of thinking or saying, "I forgive," does not remove the pain.

Sadly, when the dictate that 'You have to forgive in order to heal' is laid on people who are already in terrible emotional pain, it becomes one more burden, one more weight, added to the weight they are already carrying. It almost becomes a judgement—'since you aren't forgiving whoever hurt you, then you are at fault.' And here we go again, one more thing about which we are inadequate and incapable.

It's easy for people to say, "Forgive and forget and move on." Individuals who dogmatically say this may have had to forgive the dry cleaners for ruining their best shirt or shrinking the living room drapes. Or they're pretending they have forgiven someone. Forgiveness is more than simply a one-time, 'I forgive,' event. Especially when the destruction of a human being is involved, whether emotionally, mentally, spiritually or physically.

When you've been damaged, sometimes irretrievably damaged, you don't easily forgive nor do you ever completely forget.

What exactly do these people mean when they lay the burdensome dictate on others to, "Just forgive," or, "You have to forgive in order to

266

heal?" Have they ever really stopped and asked themselves what they intend when they let those words roll off their tongue like they are reciting the Pledge of Allegiance? Are they suggesting that if you simply say, "I forgive," then all is said and done?

I suspect they really haven't given it much deep thought. Or they are simply among the legions who just want to, 'Put it all behind us,' because whatever is the cause of the need for forgiveness is too uncomfortable, too ugly, too hard to believe.

It is perhaps safe to say they are most likely far removed from the realities with which those of us in a miserable marriage live or have lived. Sadly, however, they cause great pain for the damaged souls who are already struggling with the issue of forgiveness.

What, Exactly, Are We Forgiving?

What, exactly, is it that we may decide to forgive? It's relatively easy to list the transgressions we've suffered in a miserable marriage—they're largely found in the 'Who We Are' section of chapter two.

But the real pain behind that list is the knowledge that he won't try, that he refuses to even consider examining his behavior, that ultimately, he simply doesn't care about the pain we felt.

We are forgiving much more than just the destructive actions. We are forgiving the refusal of someone to address the problems that are preventing us from having a relationship with them.

That is the greatest pain, beyond the very real pain that occurs every time they hurt us. The greatest pain is from their failure to care enough to want to face and address the problems in the relationship.

That, then, touches the real core of what we are faced with forgiving: Their *choice* to not even consider that they may be at fault. Forgiving someone for the choices they make is as difficult as forgiving the behavior their choices translate into.

I have never met a woman who wanted to go through a divorce. I have never met a woman who was planning to divorce when she entered a marriage. But without exception I have heard women say that they believe their marriage could have succeeded, "If he would have just talked about the problems." The sadness in their voice when they say this conveys the agony they feel because he refused to try and save the relationship. As one woman said to me, "I never thought my life would turn out this way."

Refusal to face the problems, talk about them and seek solutions is a betrayal that is hard to forgive—harder perhaps than forgiving the individual hurts that eventually add up to the ending of the relationship.

How Do We Know When We've Truly Forgiven?

How do you know when you have truly forgiven?

It is when you arrive at the end of a long journey of healing and you can honestly say that you genuinely wish the best, good things in fact, for the perpetrator of your torture. Then you know you have forgiven and it is complete, because it is no longer burdening you. As already stated, it can take a very long time, and sometimes never happens.

Alternatively, you can feel that you have forgiven when you heal to such an extent that you truly and totally don't care, when you have no emotion whatsoever for or about the person who hurt you. When you very rarely think about them and, if you do, it is a non-event, a passing and unemotional thought.

No emotion includes no animosity. The opposite of animosity is peace, and when you arrive at a place of no animosity you find peace. This is a state of forgiveness that takes a very long time to reach and it is the true sign of being healed. Sometimes we never fully reach that point, and that is OK too and it's out of our hands. The most important thing to keep in mind is, if you have healed and arrived at a place where you respect and value yourself, you can consider practicing safe forgiveness.

Safe Forgiveness

Safe forgiveness is when you remove yourself from the actions of someone whom you may eventually forgive. Safe forgiveness means that you have, over time, evaluated the harmful behavior of someone and said, "Enough," and then you stay away from the damaging behavior, both literally and figuratively. Only by staying away, far away, from your tormentor/abuser can you heal.

This is particularly true when it involves someone you deeply love, or have deeply loved. When you arrive at a place of self-respect and self-love such that you no longer allow yourself to be damaged (the goal of the previous chapters) then you can formulate a forgiveness that might be summed up as a silent message we say to ourselves; "I love you but not enough to let you destroy me."

Remember the analogy detailed in Chapter 11, equating our entrapment as similar to thrusting an already-burned arm back into a bonfire? The more distant you become from the fire, the more protective of your already-burned arm you become, the easier it is to heal and to eventually consider forgiving.

This is one of the most difficult tasks in life because it requires that we move against the dictates of family and society and remove ourselves from the source of abuse. Family and societal structure locks us into repeated abuse, often for decades, as tightly as any prisoner has ever been chained in a dungeon.

Rooted deep within safe forgiveness is complete acceptance of the choices the other person makes. They choose to hurt and damage, it is not a figment of your imagination, and you no longer deny it.

Safe forgiveness is when you accept their choices as theirs, and you consciously, clearly, and without explanation to anyone, permanently remove yourself from the bad behavior, abuse and damage.

Most important, safe forgiveness is strong and uncompromising and based on self-value. You do not owe anyone an explanation or excuse for removing yourself physically, emotionally and geographically from the bad behavior and the person(s) who perpetuates it.

The further you step back, and watch the scenes that include the perpetrator (the process detailed in Chapters 12 and 14) you can increasingly step back, further back, and further back. Allowing the other person to be who they choose to be, and making sure you are safe from them in every aspect of your life, is part of forgiving.

Just as we have to learn, painfully learn, and accept that we cannot change anyone except ourselves, we can gradually forgive by distancing and by practicing safe forgiveness. There is tremendous peace to be found in practicing safe forgiveness, knowing you are a forgiving person, and are safe from the person you may eventually forgive.

Interestingly, the further you can remove yourself from the abuser the more quickly you will heal and potentially arrive at forgiveness. You simply cannot heal or forgive if you allow yourself to continuously be damaged.

Within a family or societal structure, distancing from mistreatment is almost always completely misunderstood. If you distance yourself—refuse to subject yourself to even the remote possibility of the perpetrator abusing again—you will inevitably be judged as 'unforgiving' or having 'not forgiven.' You will be the bad guy because you are unwilling to play your part, refusing to go-along-to-get-along and upsetting the family structure.

This, unfortunately, is the price you have to pay and is part of the basic injustice that is built into miserable marriages and abusive birth families. A great deal of courage, steadfastness, and ideally a thick skin is required to withstand the family forces arraigned against you when you refuse to risk your hard-won self-respect and self-value.

An affirmation that can be very helpful in these situations is: "I forgive [you, him, them] but you may not be part of my life."

Endless Forgiveness

But what about the Bible admonition that we are to forgive over and over again?

Hearing preachers expound on this concept always causes me to feel tremendous compassion for the many people who are deeply hurt by those words. The misinterpretation is that you are to let someone hurt you over and over and forgive them each time.

In my healing I discovered that deep, true forgiveness can happen when you finally reach a state of mental, physical and spiritual health. Along the way, just as healing takes time, forgiveness creeps into the healing process.

Healing first requires facing reality, followed by acceptance, and then a change in behavior by us, which leads to emotional and physical detachment. But events and memories resurface (often countless times) that cause us to relive the pain.

With our new-found ability to control our thoughts and replace ugliness with good thoughts, and to take protective actions, we can move further away from mistreatment. To 'forgive over and over' pertains to the reality that we frequently re-experience great pain when memories rise to the surface, often when we are over-burdened, tired, discouraged or facing new challenges.

Unfortunately, each time memories cause us to re-experience the pain of mistreatment, it is cumulative. That is, we experience *all* the pain from *all* the times of abuse. And every time the memories and pain resurface, we relive the abuse and, once again, we can perhaps choose to forgive a little bit more. Whenever a memory surfaces, the affirmation, 'I forgive,' can be helpful in moving healing and forgiveness forward.

That is the point of forgiving seven times seventy; to forgive when we re-experience the pain, not to place ourselves in a position where we actually foolishly endure a repeat of the abuse itself. It is not an exaggeration to say that we experience the abuse over and over again because the memories are so vivid for so interminably long, so there is certainly no need for us to endanger ourselves by remaining in a situation where we may be, or are, actually mistreated.

With our new skills, we can implement actions to no longer let the memories defeat and destroy us. Each time we may forgive a little bit more, or not.

I have found that it does help to say the words, "I forgive," whenever the memories resurface. Interestingly, the words, 'I forgive,' can become a part of our effort to stop obsessing about our husband. Just as we learned early-on to use replacement thoughts, the words, 'I forgive,' can become a very effective replacement thought.

Forgiveness is not a one-time event because our minds store the memories of everything that happens to us. To forgive over and over is not at all the same as allowing someone to actually hurt us repeatedly.

Referring back to the story of the monk who advised the woman

271

who rented the multi-passenger van (see Chapter 19) we have a responsibility to our mental, physical, and spiritual bodies to remove ourselves as the target of mistreatment. We have a responsibility to not allow someone to hurt us repeatedly and forever. If there is a responsibility to forgive (and I'm not sure forgiveness is indeed warranted in every situation) then forgiveness can flow from the healing process. I can attest that forgiveness is helpful, but you arrive at that destination after a long journey and for those who never reach the end of that healing journey, it is OK. Don't burden yourself with condemnation because you cannot forgive a horrible destructive offense.

Transformation Action Plan:

1. Sit quietly with the woman you have chosen to become, your 'I am' woman. Make a Wisdom List of everything you have learned in your journey to date. Do this over a period of days, adding to your list as you recognize areas in your life where you have experienced startling, profound, or peaceful wisdom insights.

2. Focus on the woman you have chosen to become and think carefully about her wisdom. Create a clear picture in your mind of yourself as your Wise Woman.

3. Describe yourself in detail as your Wise Woman. How do you behave, speak, move, dress, communicate with others, select the people you let into your life, avoid people who damage you, and take care of yourself physically, mentally, and spiritually?

4. What areas of additional knowledge and wisdom do you wish to add to your life? How open are you to continuing to grow in wisdom? Be honest with yourself.

5. Record your progress of wisdom in your journal.

6. **Say this Affirmation**

   I seek wisdom because wisdom strengthens me
   ...when you listen, you may learn something new
   – His Holiness, the Dalai Lama

   Whether a good day or a bad day, say this affirmation frequently aloud or to yourself. Say it many times, emphasizing a different word each time – **I** seek wisdom because wisdom strengthens me. I **seek** wisdom because wisdom strengthens me. I seek **wisdom** because wisdom strengthens me. I seek wisdom **because** wisdom strengthens me.

7. **Respect and Reward Yourself**
   Refer to your Rewards List you compiled in Chapter 2. If you have read this far, sat quietly and created your Wisdom List, have imagined yourself as your Wise Woman, described your Wise Woman in detail, have identified areas where you wish to increase your wisdom, and recorded your wisdom journey in your journal, reward yourself.

8. **Insight to ponder**
   So much is demanded of us. Seeking wisdom can seem like another task, another burden. But the desire to be wise can be turned into seeking, which draws wisdom to us in many forms. Becoming alert to the wisdom around us, and trusting our instinctual nature when we hear, read, or see wisdom, constitutes seeking.

9. **Watch for your personal milestone of Growth**
   My Personal Milestone
   A day like any other day, I went about my business of work, errands, and attending to life's details. As I walked along a city sidewalk, filled with people going in every direction, I suddenly experienced a profound sense of 'knowing' that I had arrived at a level of self-understanding, of self-acknowledgement, and of my life's values and priorities that no one would ever take away from me.

10. **Mantra to Remember**

   My wisdom is mine, just as every other human has their own wisdom. Mine has been hard-won and will continue to grow for the rest of my life.

11. **Signs of healing**

   Healing is a slow process and, just as with a broken limb, every day repair takes place until the limb becomes strong.

   A sign of healing

   When a deep sense of your self-value emanates from the knowledge accumulated through the journey of a lifetime, regardless of how long or short.

22

Survive and Grow Step Eight

Strength and dignity are her clothing and she laughs – Proverb 31:25 ESV

Living with Strength and Grace

Unlike the other Survive and Grow Steps, Step Eight is a culmination of the previous Steps, a coming together process of everything that has been learned. With Step Eight there is no turning back, because life is unfolding and we are committed to living a healthy life.

To do this requires that we become accustomed to, comfortable with, and protective of our strength, courage, wisdom, and dignity. And to live with grace. Step Eight provides us with guidelines we can carry with us in every part of our life, and above all else, honors our womanhood.

I have not seen Kelly for a few months and I hardly recognize the woman in my office. She has a new hair style, has lost a bit of weight (although she was never overweight) and looks toned, healthy, and calm. In fact, she actually looks content. When she provides me with an update, it's rather startling.

"Yes, Dan and I still live together, but largely separately. I have a schedule built around my work and my kids and I don't know what he does most of the time, nor do I care. Since I stopped arguing with him about anything, he knows that when he tries to bait me, I'll just walk away from him, so I'm not fun anymore."

Kelly laughs, with just a tinge of sadness.

"When he is in his charming mode, then I respond graciously, and we even laugh sometimes and enjoy each other's company but in a superficial way. It's always a surface thing. I never, under any circumstances, let down my guard and fall into the trap of sharing details of my life.

"I have completely accepted that he has zero interest in me as a person, a woman, a fellow human being. I am just part of the furniture to him, even if we're having a good time.

"Of course, he still explodes in an instant, so I'm always prepared to remove myself and the kids. When I look back at how totally he controlled me because I naively told him everything, and then he would slam the trap door shut, it makes me sick. But that was then and this is now.

"Yes, sometimes I wish things could be different, and when he's not tearing into me about something and things are calm, I still wonder why life can't be settled and peaceful. But that just isn't the way he is. Underneath the good times is the brooding, simmering, unpredictable, unreasonable Dan. I no longer delude myself, thinking he's going to miraculously change. I'm now a realist and recognize that he likes the way he is. *He* thinks he's great.

"No, I haven't filed for divorce because I did my homework and divorcing would probably mean I would have to pay him alimony. What an insult that would be! I'm the one who's kept a roof over our heads while he plays at running a business, but I would have to support him while he texts or communicates online with women! Finding out that possible detail cost me a few hundred dollars, to talk with a divorce attorney."

Kelly rolls her eyes.

"I have a woman friend who thinks I'm crazy for not divorcing Dan, but I don't want my kids around him when I'm not there to protect them. If I'm not with them, he'll do to them exactly what he does to me. Now, at least, I can tell him to stop, and get the kids and myself out of there.

"I've heard and read enough stories to know that divorce court judges almost always award joint custody, so my kids would be forced to be with Dan alone. I don't want that to happen. Those judges are just like everyone else. They don't have a clue about how these men are."

Kelly shakes her head and looks disgusted.

"Dan hasn't filed either and the only thing I can deduce is that he is basically too lazy to try and rebuild a life, figuring out where to live and so on. This way he knows he has a clean house and food on the table. I think he also may have met with an attorney and perhaps found out that divorcing me would mean he might be required to disclose the actual finances and value of his business to the court, and that scared him.

"I make sure he knows what he has to contribute each month. I maintain a detailed record of all expenses and give him a spreadsheet that states exactly what he owes me for everything. To my surprise, some months he actually gives me a check for some or all of what he owes. No, I'm not naïve enough to think that eventually the court will award me re-payment. It's money I'm investing to keep things together for the kids until they are old enough to not scare me if they are around Dan alone.

"Yes, we still sleep together sometimes, but no sex. I can't stand the thought of him touching me. Letting him use me for sex would be completely dehumanizing for me. I'm no longer the dumb blonde he could manipulate into doing what he wants. Besides, he seems to like the arrangement. He comes home when he wants and spends almost all his time in his den, and then he crashes for the night on the sofa in there.

"The kids seem to be accustomed to him being there, but not there, if you know what I mean. That does make me sad, particularly for Nicholas, as Dan is an absentee father even while he's under our roof. But I already know what would happen if I tried to talk to Dan about becoming more involved with the kids. He'd just tell me in great detail about how everything wrong with our lives is my fault.

"I continue to make decisions I need to make, even some seemingly small ones that are important. I painted my bedroom, the so-called master bedroom, pale peach and made it look feminine to reflect how I now feel about myself. I also had a handyman install a lock on the door. I need to know that if Dan goes off on me and I can't get myself and the kids out of the house, I can lock us all in my bedroom. Get that? *My* bedroom."

Kelly smiles at me, a bit of sadness showing in her eyes.

"Since I gave up trying to convince him to communicate with me in a civil manner, I just stopped caring. It's all part of the 'he always has to win' reality. Since nothing I ever did or said measured up to his standards, then why on earth would he want to have me in his room, or his life?"

Kelly laughs again,

"Dan should have what he wants, right? Me out of his life so that his world is perfect. The irony is, with him out of *my* face, my life is far better.

"We are basically civil, formal and polite, to each other. Since I will not engage in any of his nonsense, being somewhat civil is the only alternative left to him. Oh, he still looks at me as though I'm a piece of garbage, and he still does the silent treatment thing, but so what?

"We have a schedule. I prepare dinner each evening at a set time and if Dan wants to join us, great. If not, then so be it.

"We still sometimes do things as a family, but I make absolutely sure that I plan ahead to avoid surprises that trap us with one of Dan's blowups. If I think he can't be trusted to behave, then I drive my car separately. I make sure that I and the kids can always get away from him if we need to. He's not as quick to be threatening as in the past because he knows I don't respond, but he's still skilled at catching me off guard so I have to always be vigilant. I never take anything for granted.

"In public I go along with the phony, 'He's a great guy' routine but I don't stand there and let him put his arm around me and I certainly don't look up at him with a deer-in-the-headlights 'Oh, my big hero' stupid look, as I used to do. Let people think what they want to think. I know the truth.

"Besides, I am completely comfortable with the real truth, that no one will ever understand or believe what it is like to live with Dan. It took me a long time to fully accept the basic injustice of the situation, but I have accepted it. There is no way on this earth that anyone will believe me if I try and tell them how he treats me and the kids, so I carry the secret inside of me as my 'knowing' that I am doing the right thing to protect myself and my children.

"After I saved up enough money, I paid for the services of an attorney and she helped me figure out ways to protect myself from Dan's financial messes. Interestingly, when I cut off his access to my salary, Dan and his buddies had to figure out how to survive. From what I understand, they laid off people and are now doing the work themselves. I wish I had the money I wasted on those parasites, but that is in the past.

"What is my life like now? Well, it's sad sometimes, and there is some loneliness, but I now realize how loneliness defined my life when I spent all that time trying to convince Dan to stop being psychologically, emotionally, and financially, abusive.

"I have goals. As long as we can maintain this formal atmosphere, then I may stay with him until Nicholas and Tracy are fourteen. Why fourteen? Because in our State, that is the age when children can choose which parent they wish to live with. I don't want them to be with Dan unsupervised while they are little, because I don't trust him. He would scream at them if they do anything that upsets him, and anything can upset him, so they need me to protect them from that. Also, I don't like the porn trash he looks at on the computer.

"I am also realistic, however, and I recognize that harm *is* happening to Nicholas, Tracy, and myself, by living with this arrangement. Dan's dark moods, anger, and nastiness is taking a toll. My responsibility is to make the tough decision to get the hell out of there sooner if I can't take it anymore or if the kids start acting out because of the situation.

"There really isn't a good time to divorce, is there, when children are involved? What a mess! How two so-called adults can turn the lives of innocent children upside down is inexcusable, but when the situation is intolerable, something has to give, some action has to be taken. At least, with me in their lives, my children are seeing first hand that a woman can set and maintain boundaries of behavior. If Dan blows up over anything, I and the kids get out of there. I always have some cash in my wallet and gas in my car. Always.

"What will I do if Dan decides to file for divorce? I'll accept and deal with it to the best of my ability. I certainly will not beg him to change his mind. I've begged and pleaded with him enough already, to try and save our marriage, and he refuses to meet me half way. I'm completely finished with that effort. I've met my responsibility to try and get him to work on our marriage. Now I put my kids and myself first.

"As to my future, I'm focusing on my kids and when I'm ready to move on from Dan I will, but not until my kids are secure and older. Dan does have a responsibility to them and my attorney told me how I can do my best to see that he provides what he should.

"I was a very weak, naïve, and unknowledgeable young woman when I met and married Dan and I now know that I would never give him a second look from my New Woman perspective. But I married him and have two kids so I choose to live with that reality. Oh, if only I had known that I could sit down and actually make a Connection Chart and understand what I wanted and needed in a relationship! But I can't undo the past.

"Yes, it's hard, sometimes very hard. It is what it is, and I'm never again going to be the simpering, foolish, weak woman that I was when you and I first met. I like who I am now. I don't know what the future holds, and yes, I get scared sometimes, but I knew I would die, figuratively if not literally, if I didn't make changes. I'm not a basket case anymore. I'm a strong, courageous, intelligent woman with responsibilities and I know what I'm doing and what my priorities are."

The Journey to Healing

It is difficult to describe what life feels like when you know you are healed from incredible pain, mental agony, and the paralysis of the fear of loneliness. There are a number of milestones in the healing process:

- When you thoroughly and deeply no longer care if the other person understands you, your decisions, or your life choices. It is *your* life for which you are responsible.

- When you no longer have any desire to explain, reason with, or attempt to acquire understanding from the other person.

- When you truly stop caring about 'making the relationship work,' accept life as the beautiful adventure it is, and you watch the action unfold with curious detachment because you refuse to let someone destroy you for their entertainment.

- When you forget—when memories of the person, the history, the past events, no longer invade your thoughts. And if they do rarely crop up you briefly nod to them and replace them. Eventually it may surprise you to realize how many days, weeks, months, even years, go by without you having a thought about the person or events that once so greatly affected and nearly destroyed you.

- When you are one hundred percent comfortable with no longer reacting, or behaving, in the way(s) you formerly did. When your new way of life is so well-ingrained that you would have to actually 'work at' being or behaving in the way you once did.

- When you enjoy life in your new capacity, on every front, and in every circumstance that occurs.

- When you enjoy being with yourself and are careful and selective about whom you let into your life.

The Wellness Journey to Triumph

To look back and see how far you've come—no one else can fully appreciate the obstacles that were overcome, the discouragement and disappointments that weighed you down, the memories that sometimes rise to the surface and need to be respectfully and tenderly released.

But the map of the journey can be lovingly and gratefully acknowledged. From start to finish, here are twenty rungs on the tall ladder to wellness and triumph:

1. **Disbelief and Denial**—The blow-up was just a mistake, a misunderstanding. It was an anomaly. It was due to unusual circumstances and outside pressures.

2. **Pain**—It hurts. I wish the hurt would stop. I wish it wouldn't happen again.

3. **Anger**—Stop it! You treat me badly, so I'll treat you badly back!

4. **Reaction**—I *have* to respond!

5. **Withdrawal**—I won't say or do anything. I'll be as small as I can be.

6. **Protection**—I discover myself. I hide my discovery.

7. **Inner Discovery**—I am far more than who you tell me I am.

8. **Inner Wisdom**—I do not have to respond. I choose not to respond or engage.

9. **Clear Vision**—I see you with a clear vision. I look at you for the first time.

10. **Inner Strength**—I choose to make my own decisions about what is happening.

11. **Outer Peace**—Your behavior and my behavior are separate from each other.

12. **Enhanced Vision**—I see far more than just the action happening in front of me.

13. **Awareness**—There is far more to my life than these encounters.

14. **Inner Peace**—I discover what my principles are.

15. **Courage**—No one will take my principles from me. No one.

16. **Movement**—I choose my behavior and the woman I choose to be.

17. **True Peace**—I survive a challenge to my principles and I stand firm.

18. **Escape**—I am not bound to any other human being. I choose my life.

19. **Joy**—Life is incredible, now that I am able to see it.

20. **Life**—I have found my life.

Survival Requires Maintenance and Vigilance

I am strong but also fragile because I have been through so much, but have come so far. And I am always becoming stronger. Maintenance requires:

- **Observation**—I do not stop observing my life.

- **Maintenance**—I am valuable. I enjoy maintaining my life well, in every regard.

- **Awareness**—I stay alert.

- **Diligence**—I am valuable, strong, but fragile. I do not take chances.

- **Strength**—I do not let go of my principles.

Transformation Action Plan

1. Sit quietly with the woman you have chosen to become, your 'I am' woman, and think about how you have changed since you took the first Step of the Survive and Grow Steps.

2. Congratulate yourself on each of your accomplishments and appreciate the hard work you've invested to achieve your goals.

3. Make a list of any and all commitments to yourself that you wish to achieve in the future.

4. Sit quietly and love yourself, your children, your life. Make a list of everything you are grateful for.

5. **Say this Affirmation**
   ### I treat myself with great respect
   Treat yourself with great respect in every aspect of your life

   Whether a good day or a bad day, say this affirmation frequently aloud or to yourself. Say it many times, emphasizing a different word each time – **I** treat myself with great respect. I **treat** myself with great respect. I treat **myself** with great respect.

6. **Respect and Reward Yourself**
   If you have read this far, sat quietly and thought about how you've changed, what you've accomplished, made lists of your commitments to yourself for the future, and what you are grateful for, reward yourself. Choose an item from the Rewards List you created in Chapter 2.

7. **Insight to ponder**

   Women are the personification of courage, yet it is most often not acknowledged by anyone. Be proud of your courage, even if you are the only one who recognizes just how courageous you are to be navigating through your difficult life. Respect your courage, honor it and honor yourself.

8. **Watch for your personal milestone of Growth**
   My Personal Milestone

   So many times, I felt sad when I wanted so much for our life to be happy but I knew I could not make it happen. We were two very different people with vastly different priorities who had come together for who-knows-what reason, and maybe we both did our best. But it could never work unless we both were willing to say, 'Let's figure out how we can try and meet each other's needs.' I profoundly understood the sentiment of the serenity prayer: "God, grant me the serenity to accept the things I cannot change."

9. **Mantra to Remember**

   There are some things in life we will never understand.

10. **Signs of healing**

    Healing is a slow process and, just as with a broken limb, every day repair takes place until the limb becomes strong.
    A sign of healing
    When you recognize you will carry a certain sadness within you for a long time, but you release it and allow it to diminish.

23

Dignity in the Face of Defeat

You never really know what is in another person's heart

Kelly called me one morning and asked if I could squeeze her into my schedule that day. Her voice sounded unsteady so I moved some appointments to accommodate her. I hadn't seen her for a number of months, although we would text back and forth every now and then.

When Kelly arrives, she looks as nice as the last time I saw her, a professional, well-groomed, poised, and dignified woman. We exchange pleasantries for a few minutes and then she brings me up to date.

"I came home a couple months ago and the garage door was open so I got scared because Dan's car wasn't in the driveway. I knew I closed the door when I left that morning. You hear stories about break-ins, or innocent people stumbling into a robbery-in-progress, and I had the kids in the car, so I called the police. They came right away, which caused a sensation in the neighborhood, of course. I also called Dan and he didn't pick up so I left a voicemail.

"Anyway, the policemen checked the house and everything seemed OK and they didn't see any evidence of someone having been in there, so they left and we went inside. It's a creepy feeling when you know something isn't right."

Kelly pauses and takes a deep breath.

"I looked around and saw an envelope on the kitchen counter, with my name on it in Dan's handwriting. I opened it and it held a note with one line that read, 'I'm leaving.'

"Dan had been really upset with me the day before, because I refused to fight with him. He kept nagging and nagging at me about a purchase he wanted to make. He'd been really awful for the previous several days and I had to hold onto 'New Kelly' (Kelly uses her fingers to indicate quotation marks) to keep him from making me crazy. It's been tough at work lately and I just didn't have the strength to put up with much more

285

from Dan.

"On the previous evening, when Dan was ragging on me, I made an excuse to the kids and had them sleep in my bed with me that night, and I locked the door of my bedroom. The next morning, like every morning, I concentrated on getting myself and the kids out the door on time and Dan didn't say anything. Then we came home to the open garage door and you know the rest of that story."

Kelly pauses again.

"After I read the note, I walked around the house, trying to think about what to do. He took some clothes and his laptop and several other items from his den. I fixed the kids' dinner and went through the evening routine in a bit of a daze. After they were settled, I called Dan's cell and it went to voicemail so I left a message, telling him I had read the note.

"I went to bed and slept peacefully. Strange perhaps, but emotionally I felt as though a corner had been turned and nothing would ever be the same again, and it was OK.

"The next morning, I called my office and told them I wouldn't be in, and I kept Nicholas and Tracy home from school and we went for a long walk. I gently told them that Daddy had decided not to live with us anymore and they asked a lot of questions and started to cry. I held them and told them I loved them and I wasn't going anywhere and we would be a team forever."

Kelly paused and held back some tears.

"I still hadn't heard from Dan, so I and the kids had a quiet day and went through the usual evening routine. They kept asking me if Daddy would come home and I told them I didn't think so but that he still loved them and they would get to see him often. I'm not sure they really understood that, but I didn't know what else to say. They wanted to sleep with me and I said yes.

"The next day I had what I guess you might call a delayed reaction of anger. I could have killed Dan. My two little kids wanted to know about their Daddy and I had to go to work. I did my best to reassure Nicholas and Tracy that everything would be OK and we all needed to do what we do every day.

"I told their school about our situation so they could be sensitive to the kids if they misbehaved because they're upset. I then called Dan's cell and told him to stop being a jerk and call me so we could work out details. I called his office and no one answered the phone."

Kelly pauses for several minutes.

"To make a long story short, it turns out that Dan and Melissa have been in a relationship, having an affair, for the past couple of years. Dan's entire family is in an uproar.

"I didn't know until about a week after I got the note, but apparently Carl found out about the affair and showed up at the office one day threatening to kill Dan and Melissa. I've been told that Carl refuses to go into work and he threw Melissa out of their house. Thank God, they never had kids.

"I'm not sure what Dan's going to do without Carl at the business because, although Carl isn't the sharpest tack in the box, he does do a good job and Dan relies on him."

Kelly pauses.

"But none of that is my problem."

Kelly sighs and shakes her head.

"And to think I trusted Dan and that low-life crowd of buffoons. And worse, he's the father of my children! How could I have been so stupid?"

Kelly is silent and stares at the floor.

"When I heard about the affair, I called a locksmith and had him change all the locks on the house. I also packed up Dan's things, and I mean *all* of his stuff, and paid a delivery company to take it to his office.

"I also called the attorney I met a while back and filed for divorce. That took a major chunk from my savings. The really bad part is, the attorney thinks Dan is entitled to half of the value of the house, so I either have to sell it or figure out a way to pay him as well as the mortgage payments. If he demands his entire half in one payment, then I'll have to sell."

Kelly pauses.

"So, for all those years I struggled to make the house payments I essentially provided a savings account for Dan. This really sucks."

Kelly looks at me.

"Why don't we women know these things? Why don't we know about how the real world works regarding what men, and women, can get away with in wrecking marriages, and lives, and hurting their kids?"

I tell Kelly that I don't have the answers and from what I've witnessed myself, I don't see much hope that the situation is going to change anytime soon.

"Dan came to the house a couple evenings after he'd left the note and I let him in because I knew the kids wanted to see him. They were so happy and ran and jumped all over him."

Kelly shakes her head again.

"How any man cannot see that his children love him and need him, and see the joy in that, is totally beyond me. He is the most selfish person on earth. The kids were devastated when he told them he wouldn't be staying, and then he left.

"He didn't speak to me, of course, but as he went out the door, I told him I had taken steps to file for divorce. He actually looked surprised. Honestly, did he think I would just pretend everything was OK and wait around for him while he and Melissa had their fling?

"He rented an apartment but Melissa isn't living with him, which I suspect didn't go according to his original plan, if he had a plan at all. The last I heard, Carl is trying to persuade Melissa to make their marriage work and he asked her to move back home.

"Since I filed for divorce, we're sorting out the details, which is a nightmare. I'm not sure what's going to happen regarding my house, but I'll try and hold onto it because it's home for me and my kids.

"They've visited Dan for a couple of sleepovers at his apartment and they didn't like it. He isn't prepared for them, and taking care of them isn't something he's accustomed to, so they were bored and didn't like the take-out food he gave them. All they did was watch TV, which upset me when I found out.

"According to my attorney, I'll have to get used to this because the court will probably give Dan shared custody. So, my kids have to suffer because I picked a complete loser as my husband and their father."

Women Supporting Women

Kelly asks me if she can see me regularly as she navigates through her divorce and I, of course, agree. There will be many months ahead of back-and-forth wrangling, and mounting expenses, as she attempts to communicate with Dan via intervening attorneys. Even the simplest task of arranging the children's schedules becomes fraught with difficulty and nastiness.

Along the way, Dan acquires a girlfriend who moves in with him. Nicholas and Tracy don't like her.

To further complicate matters, Dan's girlfriend has a child, a boy named Anthony, who is a couple years older than Nicholas. Every few weeks he joins Nicholas and Tracy in sleeping bags on the floor of Dan's apartment where he kicks Tracy until she cries and Nicholas shoves Anthony in retaliation, and then Dan screams at all of them.

Kelly gets a full report when the children return home, and she despairs when she hears about Dan screaming at them, and also about Dan's girlfriend smoking what she suspects is pot, in the small apartment while the kids are there.

Her attorney informs her there is nothing she can do about the situation because there is no evidence the children are in danger.

The divorce process unravels and plunges into a wasteland of technicalities, rising costs and frustrations. Dan plays games with the information he is supposed to provide about his business and income, when he gets around to providing it, delaying and elongating the already-painful process. Straight answers from Dan prove nearly impossible to get and he seems to enjoy the confusion he causes.

Dan's girlfriend moves out of his apartment a few months after she moved in, and Nicholas and Tracy, who grew fond of Anthony, wonder why he isn't visiting anymore. Their world seems to be one uncertainty after another.

Then Dan demanded that the house be sold and insisted that only a realtor he selected could be given the listing. Kelly cooperated fully while finding it heart-breaking to sell the home she lovingly created for her family, and her garden in which she'd invested so much time.

With the help of her financial advisor, Kelly found a small, rather dumpy, house she could afford to rent and put all her energy into cleaning it, painting, and turning it into a decent and cozy home for herself and her children.

Kelly managed to keep her head above water and fortunately her employer helped her by not requiring that she make out-of-town business trips. A few months into the divorce process, with her frustration reaching the breaking point due to Dan's lack of cooperation in the legal matters, Kelly suddenly realized she was making the same mistake she made for years with Dan.

Namely, she assumed he could see the logic and mutual benefit in dealing with the legal procedures as efficiently as possible. Once again, she faced the reality that Dan needed to win on every point and winning in this case meant making life as difficult for Kelly and the kids as possible.

When she stepped back and released her anger and frantic emotions about the stress and financial burden he caused her, she chalked the entire situation up to Dan's intractable selfishness. She reminded herself that viewing Dan as a stranger and distancing herself from the manipulations he attempted, would help her maintain her dignity and strength.

She adopted a cooperative attitude, particularly regarding the children. She made it very easy for Dan to avoid his responsibilities because she learned to play a 'long game.' She didn't want the children around Dan and his parade of girlfriends, so she cultivated a measured, neutral tone and always said, "Sure, OK, it's fine," whenever Dan wanted her to keep the children on the days or weekends scheduled for him to have them.

The clarity Kelly previously learned to cultivate about Dan became enormously helpful. When she moved past the emotions attached to the frustration of the excruciatingly slow legal divorce procedure, and accepted the reality that Dan wasn't, and had never been, what one would call a devoted father, she recognized he only wanted the kids in order to upset her. He knew they would carry stories back to Kelly about the inadequate sleeping arrangements, take-out-food, endless hours in front of the TV, and his girlfriends, and Kelly would become frazzled when she heard them.

Kelly's clarity told her that Dan would eventually become tired of this particular game because he hated being inconvenienced, and having two little kids underfoot when he now could live a bachelor life constituted a big inconvenience.

So, she was careful to never make Dan feel guilty about his gradual lessoning of interest in maintaining his schedule to see the kids—Kelly realized that he would eventually lose interest in the children overall, which was harmful to them but nevertheless the reality Kelly foresaw.

And Kelly turned out to be correct. As the months went by, more frequent texts or calls came from Dan, asking if she could 'take the kids.' Kelly always said yes, in a neutral manner, neither positive nor negative, but letting Dan off the hook of his shared custody and lessoning the exposure of her kids to his new lifestyle.

Kelly disciplined herself to never make negative comments about Dan to her children or to someone else in front of them. Not an easy goal, nevertheless, she exercised the Great Pause and carefully answered any questions the children had about the situation.

She did, however, give Nicholas a cellphone and instructed him to call her immediately if he and Tracy became scared when they were with Dan. Most important, Kelly created a secure and happy, home in their new quarters so that the children looked forward to coming home after school and being with her. As heartbroken as Kelly felt about the mess her life turned out to be, she kept her focus on her priorities and goals.

Bar Stool Psychology of Divorce

Not infrequently, Kelly would meet with me to vent about her frustration with the divorce process.

"It took two minutes for me to get married to this creep and it's taking several *years* to get out of the marriage!"

Kelly just could not believe how convoluted, inefficient, and downright nasty and abusive the legal process is.

"He left the marriage! He left a note, for God's sake, telling me he walked out. So, why doesn't he want it to be over quickly and not cost so much money and involve so many arguments?"

I explain to Kelly that her experience is not unusual and, in fact, some divorces take years to finally be settled.

In many situations, while the marriage can be legally ended in a relatively short time (six months in many States) the division of assets, child custody issues and spousal support matters can take many months of back-and-forth wrangling. (That is why, in Chapter 8, it is mentioned that women are rarely well-prepared for the realities of divorce.)

Women will say, "But he hates me! For years he made it clear that I wasn't good enough for him so why doesn't he want the divorce to be over and done with quickly? I don't get it."

The Bar Stool Psychology of Divorce

To which I explain what I term, 'the bar stool psychology' of divorce.

To understand 'the bar stool psychology' of a miserable marriage divorce, you must keep in mind his concept of 'winning,'—his insatiable need to win, as discussed in Chapter 18.

The best way to understand how this applies to the divorce process is to picture him sitting on a bar stool at the local pub, nursing a drink and telling a woman who just happens to be sitting on the bar stool next to him, about his sad life.

As he bends low over his drink and shakes his head in mournful hopelessness, he anticipates that his companion will nod her head in sympathy and perhaps reach out her hand to touch him in a soothing, comforting manner. 'Poor, misunderstood man who has been so badly used,' she will silently imply with her tender sympathetic touch.

Because the tale he will tell is, that his wife filed for divorce and he just doesn't understand why she did that to him.

After all, they were married for (fill in the blank) years and have perfect/high achieving/talented kids and he worked like a dog to make sure they had a good life. Everybody knew he worked long hours. She had her own car and plenty of clothes, and she spent money like water, so what could have been her problem? He did everything for her. Just two years ago they went to Hawaii and that cost a pretty penny. (Never mind that her salary paid for much, if not most, of the cost).

What he conveniently fails to mention, of course, is that she worked too, both at a job and at home, and he made life so hellish that eventually she couldn't take it anymore.

But that is beside the point. In his world, because *she* filed for divorce, *she* is the quitter, she is the one who complained. *She* dumped him, an innocent man!

His story is pathetic and he plays the mortally wounded man-child perfectly. It goes over well and there is always a woman willing to extend sympathy, and more. Always.

Interestingly, in our society it is still somewhat frowned upon when a man summarily dumps his wife, the mother of his children (particularly when they are young) and files for divorce from her because he wants to marry his masseuse, the wife of his best friend, or just wants to take off on his midlife crisis Harley.

Our same crying-in-his-beer fellow on his bar stool does not evoke quite as much sympathy if he cavalierly says, "Yeah, I dumped the bitch. I filed for divorce because I'm tired of her nagging me to pick up the kids or my underwear. Who needs it, ya-know what I mean?"

That version of the story causes the woman next to him to move a few bar stools away.

No man wants to be the bad guy, ever. So, he often sets up the process so that his wife will eventually lose her patience and file for divorce herself. Countless divorces are the result of this male strategy—he pulls away, he's tired of the same woman and routine, he wants to be young again and have options, he's everything that drives his wife crazy and he knows what he's doing. Does he actually plan for his wife to eventually file

293

for divorce? In most cases probably not, but when she does it's the gift he's been secretly, even subconsciously, wishing for. He's free at last! (In a few cases, a man will be genuinely shocked and run to a counselor who will ask if his wife ever begged him to go to counseling—answer, yes—and a ethical counselor will tell the guy, 'Sorry, but it appears you're too late.')

And forever after, he can point to how *she* filed to divorce from *him*! He can chant this refrain to friends, relatives, even his kids, for the rest of his life. He may go so far as to maintain that *he* never wanted to divorce *her*, but *she* insisted on divorcing *him*. It's a classic case of what politicians employ as plausible deniability.

And when he creates chaos in the divorce proceedings, his sympathy story acquires more pathos.

Now he can slowly shake his head and elaborate on the months in court and the money he's spending because, "She wants everything I own!"

But the most important point to make here is—he is innocent in his mind. Always.

And the more angst he causes in the divorce process, the better he likes it. Because it is a new, improved, enticing form of battling to win. He now even has support! He's validated. His attorney agrees that, "She doesn't deserve a thing!

"My attorney said not to worry. We'll crush the bitch!"

He may be further supported by friends, even his employer. I know of several instances where men entering the divorce process arranged to be demoted to lesser-paying jobs so that family court would award alimony and child support based on a lower financial earnings report. These men miraculously were promoted in their professions a few months after their divorce was final.

Lastly, as tragically sad as it is, the ultimate 'win' for an abusive man is when his wife or partner commits suicide. Now his bar stool lament is raised to a new and improved level.

Suddenly, his story is, "I can't believe she did it."

"To do this to me and the kids. How could she be so cruel?"

The level of sympathy he engenders from family, friends, and the audience to his bar stool distress, is ennobling and very satisfying to him.

And better yet, together with the expressions of sympathy are the judging and condemning of her and her selfish action in taking her life.

"There obviously must have been something very wrong with her," everyone says.

And he sadly nods his head in agreement and says, "Of course, something wasn't quite right about her."

But him? Oh, he's fine, just the way he is.

'Poor man. He really needs the love of a good woman.'

24

Epilogue

Impermanence is a principle of harmony. When we don't struggle against it, we are in harmony with reality. – Pema Chodron

Where Do We Go from Here?

Rosa, a beautiful woman—calm, poised, articulate, graceful, and one of the wisest women I've ever met—told me her story with quiet dignity and authority.

"Be sure you include this!"

She sternly orders me, knowing that I am writing a book.

"You don't recognize you are in one [a destructive relationship] especially when you're raised in it [that type of environment].

"Until you learn to recognize it, you don't have a clue. I thought, 'I'm not understanding him. He's so good.'

"I wanted a different home style than I had as a child. I wanted a peaceful home for my children. I married him to get away from home. I never should have married him. I went from one slavery to another slavery, from one type to another.

"I didn't think of him as being abusive to me as long as he was a good dad to the kids. The kids were the main thing. I wanted them to have a father. I protected them from seeing it. For ten years. I made sure that he only hit me when the kids wouldn't see.

"Did the kids know? I don't know.

"But now I know that I was depressed. There were days when I went to bed and stayed there, not cleaning my house. I thought I was just tired. I now realize it was serious depression.

"He was jealous and I thought jealousy equaled love, that he must really love me because he got so jealous. Now I know that love equals acceptance, not false jealousy.

"The first time the term abuse entered the picture was when I went to a social worker who said, 'You have to leave him.'

"I didn't know it was something people didn't go through [being hit]. I thought it was just normal.

"During the last few years of my marriage, I listened to other women where I worked. I really began listening and said to myself, 'That doesn't sound like what I have. That doesn't sound like my life.'

"My family said, 'Why are you unhappy? He's a wonderful husband. He takes care of the kids and takes care of the house. What's the matter with you?'

"He was so good in front of people. He was the life of the party.

"I never talked to anyone. I had been taught to keep secrets.

"My whole hope was to just get the kids to a certain age so that then I could kill myself because there must be something wrong with me. I needed to raise my children until they could take care of themselves.

"But then he broke my rule. He hit me in front of my kids. There was this invisible contract to never hit me in front of my kids. He broke the contract when he hit me in front of my children.

"My courage came from that because I thought, 'OK, if I can't give them the life they deserve, then there's no point in this.'

"I had done everything to keep my end of the bargain. Hitting me in front of my children was the point for me when I stood in front of the tank [referring to the famous photo of a man standing in front of a military tank in the 1989 Tiananmen Square uprising in China].

"We went to counseling and the therapist said that 'men are this way or that way,' and I should understand that.

"My husband said, 'I didn't mean anything, I just said what I needed to say and it's over, but you don't understand.'

"And group therapy wasted time because I had been brought up to keep secrets and being in a group meant telling secrets.

"I don't fool myself anymore into thinking that if I could just be this way, or do that, becoming the perfect wife—they're not going to love us for us, regardless.

"I think some women start asking questions: 'Am I unhappy, or why am I so unhappy? Is this what I want? Is this what's normal?'

297

"I always said yes, because I didn't know I had the right to say no. I remember the first time I said no. I waited for something, or him, to strike me dead. But he didn't. I thought, 'Well, why not? I can say no, and nobody's going to hit me!'

"It takes a long time. You start doing things for yourself, pay your own bills, start listening to other women and you find out you're not half as bad as you thought.

"You want to someday get off the merry-go-round and stop pretending.

"A turning point for me was when I said I wanted my own checking account. Having some financial independence made a difference.

"Our contract has to be centered around us, not around our kids. Staying married until kids graduate from college is a contract centered around our kids. We need to decide what is best for us and our kids. Staying married just for our kids might not be the best decision. It wasn't for me because he might have killed me.

"After I left him, life was very hard. But I never once thought about going back."

****

This is not an easy book to read because it is based on the concept that facing reality is far more important than languishing in a perpetual state of inaction and false hope. It faces the serious truth that women must recognize and then physically remove themselves from abuse—*every* form of abuse. There is no alternative because abuse in any form is deadly.

All women are valuable and should not be destroyed in any manner by the men they marry or with whom they are in a relationship. It requires those of us in miserable marriages and relationships to become strong enough to say 'No' to abuse.

It perhaps is shocking to some readers to realize that the end goal of the Survive and Grow Steps is to enable women to take control over their lives and ultimately, for most women in these marriages, it means eventually going it alone.

It is interesting that allowing women to plan for that eventuality

298

can be an uncomfortable concept. Perhaps because it defies the untruth with which so many of us live, or have lived—to always pretend that things are OK when, indeed, they are not.

Why should it be socially acceptable to plan for your retirement, or even plan your funeral, but not be OK for a woman to plan her escape from a man who makes her life miserable?

Fortunately, in general, today the social stigma of divorce is far less than it was only one generation ago. However, I can personally attest that when a woman divorces she is still to a very great extent a social pariah—few dinner invitations are extended by married friends. As one woman said to me, "When I divorced, I lost all of my women friends because they were wives of his co-workers. When I lost that connection, the friendships went too." Divorcing is a lonely reality.

Now, because of social media, women can reach out and feel less alone as they find each other and share their experiences and their journey. Women need support from each other as we travel through every twist and turn in life.

Courage

As mentioned throughout this book, courage is something that women intrinsically have within them, yet we are so often unaware of it. And being alone is a frightening prospect, even for women in terrible circumstances—they will endure serious trauma rather than reclaim their life and risk being alone. Hopefully, this book will serve to be a source of encouragement.

I hope that more women will speak out about the secrets hidden inside their homes. Women truly do have the power to establish standards of behavior for themselves and for their men, and accept nothing less than those standards.

If more women know they are not alone in their situation, and can lean on each other to navigate changing their lives, a huge difference in family culture can be achieved.

299

Misogyny is Alive and Flourishing

There have been enormous improvements in the past half-century in terms of women and career opportunities in the wider world. But beneath the surface, particularly in the privacy of personal relationships, misogyny is still very much alive and flourishing. This is a bold statement and may incite strong rebuttal, but it is what I have experienced myself and observed in the circumstances of other women.

While men are, of course, still attracted to women, they seem to be less attracted to attributes that often accompany being 'female.' A sort of hetero-androgynous (my term) maleness has emerged—men who want women with the sexual attributes they crave and need, but also want their women to be battle-hardened wage earners, non-emotional about their children (nannies and impersonal child-care facilities raise many children today) and uninterested in needing, wanting or expecting tenderness, compassion, comfort, or deep caring from their men.

With the economic reality that in most families two full-time paychecks are necessary to survive, women carry a heavy burden, often without emotional (or even actual hands-on) support.

Due to financial reality, women have had to go into the workforce for many decades. Yet the majority are still expected to plan for, organize, supervise, and cover all the other bases—home, children, food, clothing, shelter, transport. Men are doing more on the home front today, but there is a difference between 'participating' versus 'taking responsibility for'—this is the fine point that men consistently miss.

Put in terms men can perhaps relate to, there is a difference between being the ball carrier and being the coach that plans and oversees the entire game from start to finish.

As one woman (a psychologist with a busy practice) said about her husband and toddler son, "He [husband] is clueless about what it takes to make sure that 'Joey's' needs are met on every front."

Understanding the extent to which this drains the emotional and physical capacities of women seems to be beyond the empathy-capability of men—and in fairness to them, no one is teaching them. They do not

300

understand that women have limits they reach, emotionally and physically. We are not a bottomless pit of love, energy, drive, youthfulness, enthusiasm, and lust for them. And when a man chooses to be impossible-to-please and abusive, the weight of responsibility carried by a woman is unconscionable.

Finding a Mate

We women are greatly influenced by a desire that is so strong in us that we throw our instinct and our intelligence to the wind—the desire to mate. It's still the primary way we are validated and the world is definitely structured for couples rather than singles.

Men who are not the 'nice guys' they appear to be rarely lack for women to get in line and take the place of the woman who proceeded them in a relationship with him.

Men can emotionally abuse multiple women (the classic narcissist or passive-aggressive) and there is always another woman willing to take him on, to try and change him. It never works but it keeps the tabloids and online gossip pages busy for celebrities. The same is true for every socio-economic level of women, even without any tabloids to record it.

Buyer Beware

Maybe we women should consider conducting a more in-depth examination before we are hooked—we should even talk to the women who walked down the aisle before us. Why wouldn't or shouldn't we? And why wouldn't we be honest with a woman who might ask us about our previous man. She may still fall for his public persona but at least we could tell her about our experience with him.

Isn't it interesting that we will have a detailed inspection conducted on a home we consider purchasing, but we don't thoroughly inspect the men we decide to date or marry? Or, we think we do—we spend time with them, enjoying their public persona, i.e. falling for him, and even adjust to his peccadillos as they emerge (by then we're hooked) but how much do we really know about him?

You can't find out what he is really like by listening to him talk about himself because men are consummate liars. I know I'll get flak over this, but it's true—why else would an American football game require seven referees for twenty-two players, an official for every 3.1 players? Think about the lesson in this—one adult male must keep an eye on three other adult males lest they cheat (a form of lying). For perspective, think about an elementary school teacher who watches over thirty wiggly, noisy, small children.

We also misinterpret male behavior:

The intellectual stoic who appears to be the rock you think you can always rely on, turns out to be a giant slug you drag through life. The life-of-the-party guy turns out to be an impossible-to-please, self-absorbed egotistical prick. The always-organized, always-on-time, dependable date turns into a counts-every-penny, scowling cheapskate. The list is endless.

And then many of us discover that we are trapped.

Our Job

Are men the perpetual bad guys in this story? Yes, the narcissists, passive aggressive men, anger addicts, addicts (all forms of addiction), and batterers are definitely the bad guys.

Not merely 'bad boys' they may charmingly portray themselves as being. These are bad men and they destroy women. When a woman divorces or otherwise escapes from them, we should listen to what her 'running for her life' means. None of us should get in line to be his next target. There is a very good reason a previous woman got out.

But perhaps we women are not doing our job. By that, I mean, we give men a free pass too many times under the misdirected admonition that we are to be supportive of him regardless of what he does or fails to do. Or, we are afraid, with good reason. And in the case of harassment in our place of work, we feel as trapped as we are in our personal life.

We put up with too much.

We don't have standards for our men that we require they meet *before* we let them into our life and our underpants.

When the bad behaviors are demonstrated, a strong and self-valuing woman does not put up with it, endlessly hoping things will change. She never allows more-than-once and she doesn't make excuses for him. And she doesn't hide the truth.

But we are often legitimately and horrifically trapped.

What We Should Do First

Only when a woman knows herself thoroughly can she create a list of '*must* have' and 'will *not* tolerate' in a man.

It is this lack of knowledge about ourselves that causes us to fall for men who seem to have what we want. One of the biggest mistakes we make is assuming that one or two shared interests ('He adores camping!') reveals enough about him. It doesn't.

We don't determine first and up front, what connections *we* need in a long-term relationship. Instead, we accept the few that we think match and tolerate (or fume about) those that don't match.

We lack the self-respect, the self-value, and the in-depth knowledge about ourselves that we need in order to make better choices. And to not panic and settle.

Until we learn to enjoy our own company, we cannot determine what it is in our life we are willing to share, or give up, for a long-term relationship.

When a woman has a clear sense of inner value of herself, and solid core values, she is very careful in her selection of a man. But even then, you can be fooled. As one woman said to me when she learned I was writing this book, "Tell them you never know what you're really getting [in a man]."

Investigate him like you're a home inspector—check out the attic, the basement and talk to the previous owners. Wait to find out about the plumbing [sex] until after you've thoroughly investigated the rest.

It should be a great deal more difficult for a man to get into our life and our vaginas than we often allow.

Until women together become stronger in our convictions, and more supportive of each other, we will remain vulnerable to abuse. Men stick together and we women need to become much better at that skill. When a woman is hurting, we need to go out of our way to be there for her and with her. And we need to be honest with her.

We need to have values we do not compromise—become women with standards for our men that we require they meet before we commit ourselves to them.

The brutal truth is, if he doesn't meet our core value standards, he isn't worth our effort, no matter how good he looks or what a 'nice guy' everyone says he is.

About the Author

Kathleen Keith has spent the past few years telling women she meets, who are struggling in a difficult marriage or going through a traumatic divorce, about the Survive and Grow Steps she developed that enabled her to escape from a miserable marriage. With the encouragement and urging of these women, she is now sharing the details of her Survive and Grow Steps in this book. Ms. Keith is a former businesswoman who, as a divorced mother, raised her child and now devotes her time to writing, gardening, hiking, and her grandchildren. She lives in Los Angeles, California. Ms. Keith is available for speaking engagements. Email: SurviveAndGrowBooks@gmail.com.

Printed in the USA
CPSIA information can be obtained
at www.ICGtesting.com
LVHW021557161023
761246LV00010B/212